From
First Kicks
to First
Steps

From First Kicks to First Steps

Nurturing Your Baby's Development from Pregnancy Through the First Year of Life

ALAN GREENE, M.D.

McGraw·Hill

New York   Chicago   San Francisco   Lisbon   London   Madrid   Mexico City
Milan   New Delhi   San Juan   Seoul   Singapore   Sydney   Toronto

Library of Congress Cataloging-in-Publication Data

Greene, Alan R., 1959–
    From first kicks to first steps : nurturing your baby's development from
pregnancy through the first year of life / Alan Greene.
        p.   cm.
    Includes bibliographical references.
    ISBN 0-07-142786-4
      1. Infants—Development.   2. Infants—Care.   3. Human reproduction.
  I. Title.

RJ134.G74   2005
649'.122—dc22   2004002300

1 2 3 4 5 6 7 8 9 0   AGM/AGM   3 2 1 0 9 8 7 6 5 4

ISBN 0-07-142786-4

Photo Credits: Pages 1, 142, 164, 238, 239, and 259 Starlene Todd; pages 16 and 60 Lisa Drake; pages 12, 75, 81, 97, 109, 116, 134, 140, 175, 233, 277, and 312 Tami DeSellier; pages 18, 121, 155, 182, and 250 Kevin Kelly; pages 19, 26, 34, 42, 66, 72, 83, 100, 105, and 112 Beth Kleiner, M.D.; pages 22 and 242 Heidi Mize; page 27 Paul Cunningham; page 166 Pam Dillard; page 47 anonymous; pages 53, 56, 90, 130, and 228 Sergio Salvador; pages 118 and 219 Greg Juhn; page 148 Chaz Nichols; pages 179, 189, and 198 Matthew Millman; pages 204 and 266 Harriet Trezevant; page 205 Erik Drake; pages 262 and 288 Cheryl Greene; page 270 Glynna Fenske; page 291 Mindy Swagel; page 316 Gwen Greene.

This book is printed on acid-free paper.

I dedicate this book to The Next Generation. They are the bearers of our hopes, the masters of fun, the mirrors of self-understanding, and our best teachers. Generation Next, the leading edge of humanity, is where the future dabbles in the present.

Cheryl and I dedicate our lives to GenNext
around the world and to our own next generation.

Contents

Foreword

You're in for a real treat! *From First Kicks to First Steps* is a special book and a unique contribution for parents, providing rich information on your baby's growth, development, and changing needs. Although quite comprehensive, it is easy to read and digest.

Parents will gain much from reading the book *together*. By helping parents relish the small changes in their infant's development, Dr. Greene widens one's view of the baby's world and makes parents and babies curious and delighted detectives in this joint exploration. He takes development to a new and delightful level; making each stage, starting at conception, interesting and one in which parents and their baby are co-participants.

I (Marshall) have encouraged Alan to write this book for years and I am so happy with the result. I first met Alan when he was a resident in pediatrics, watching him care for tiny, premature babies in the neonatal intensive care unit. I was struck then by his blending of scientific expertise with a very human approach to the babies and their families. I followed his fascinating career in the years since and am not surprised that millions of parents have come to appreciate this same approach on his pioneering website.

In 1993 Alan joined A.B.C. Pediatrics in San Mateo, California. There he enjoyed a full and varied pediatric practice. However, he wanted to have a more profound and wider effect on his patients. In 1995, at the urging of his patients, he started DrGreene.com as a free public service with the hope that he could answer questions more completely than was possible during the ever-accelerating pace of private practice. Since Dr. Greene's initial website began there has been a continuously growing community of parents corresponding with him, first from his own practice, but now from all over the world. People ask questions, and like a ripple effect, Dr. Greene's thoughtful and studied answers help others who have the same question. One of the advantages of this book is that readers can reach him in the chat room at DrGreene.com for answers to questions not answered here.

In *From First Kicks to First Steps* Dr. Greene tackles complex subjects with compassion and feels himself into parents' experience, validating their concerns as well as their feelings. His own life experiences as well as working with countless families have deepened his awareness and his sensitivity.

He can speak from the heart. He has a passion about his work that does not cloud his wisdom; it just deepens it.

He describes for you how important habits start very early, such as healthy eating, and provides simple guidance to make changes that last a lifetime. By showing the wide range of normal behavior, he recognizes that a different solution or explanation might work better for one child than another. He helps parents feel confident in choosing the alternative that seems right for their child, their family, and their situation.

Each page is a jewel of information and the more one reads the more facets are uncovered and brought to light, illuminated by Dr. Greene's clear and easy-to-understand explanations.

—Marshall Klaus, M.D., and Phyllis Klaus, MFT
Coauthors of Your Amazing Newborn; Bonding: Building the
Foundation of Secure Attachment and Independence; *and*
The Doula Book: How a Trained Labor Companion Can Help
You Have a Shorter, Easier, and Healthier Birth

Preface

A hundred years ago, a naturalist and botanist named John Muir used to take people on trips to a place in the wilderness called Yosemite, to help them see the grandeur of nature in a new way. My goal is to take you on a journey to help you see your own baby with deeper wonder and awe. And to help you see yourself in the same way. I'll point out a few things to you, but it's not what I'll say, it's what you see with your own eyes and hear with your own ears that will astonish and move you.

This is a story to delight, encourage, and inform you about your baby. It begins at the amazing moment when a mother first feels the flutter of her baby's tiny, fully formed feet kicking inside and continues until that child's first, tentative independent step—a new footprint on the earth. This period is a time of dazzling transition and accomplishment for children—and a period of unparalleled joy, wonder, fear, doubt, and exhaustion for mothers and fathers.

Most books that cover the months of pregnancy are limited to the concerns of the pregnancy itself. *From First Kicks to First Steps* celebrates your developing baby and the transformative relationship between you and the baby. This is a parenting book to help pregnant couples start thinking of themselves as parents.

For many there is a huge gap, a chasm they have to leap across, between the end of pregnancy and finding themselves at home with a new baby. Rachel, on the television show "Friends," broke down in tears during labor and said, "I was so good! I read everything on pregnancy and labor, but I forgot to read the part about when the baby comes—and now the baby's coming!" This book guides you both before delivery and through the unfolding experience afterward.

The idea for *From First Kicks to First Steps* came from the convergence of requests I've received from families in my office, from couples in prenatal classes I've taught, and from the flood of requests we get online at DrGreene.com. Parents asked me for a warm, wonderful book about their baby even before the baby is born. When prospective parents' attention has turned toward their new baby, they've asked me for a book that feels relevant, affirming, and informing. Many mothers ask for a book that will also intrigue fathers.

Over and over, couples have asked me for a book that treats pregnancy and infancy as two parts of one experience, not two separate ones. Tammy, a mother of seven whom I've only met online, recently pleaded for this book: "Dr. Greene, you have to write it! You owe it to parents to tell them what they need to know, when they need to know it." *From First Kicks to First Steps* is a book you can clutch to your side from pregnancy through the first year. It uniquely bridges that hospital-to-home gap.

I've written each chapter with readers' questions in mind. Along the way, I've quoted other parents' (and pre-parents') real questions and woven the answers into the main text. I write as a pediatrician, a son, and a father of four. Each chapter is grounded in solid science, infused with practical reality, and colored with the continuing wonder one feels at bringing a new life into the world.

In the "before birth" sections (Parts I and II), the focus is on the astounding parent-child dance of development that takes place even without your being consciously aware of it. With this as a foundation, we will go on to examine the important new roles you will play as parents, even before your baby is born—exploring what it means to provide a safe, nurturing, gently stimulating environment in which your child's development can take place.

And then, one day, that nurturing environment disappears in a flood. The earth moves, and your family is born. I will help you understand the many ways in which the miracle of your child's unfolding development does not change at birth. The same deeply programmed choreography continues, without your causing it or even necessarily being aware of it. We will examine your revamped roles in providing another safe, nurturing, gently stimulating environment at each new phase of development.

Throughout this unique and unforgettable journey, we will examine and celebrate the remarkable, reciprocal interplay between you and your child, and we'll see how this helps both you and your child grow and transform in amazing ways.

As parents you will learn that "spit happens." Messes, complications, and inconveniences—some as surprises and some in the everyday routine—are an integral part of parenting. As I was writing this book, spit happened in the form of a second-floor plumbing accident that came dripping into my office. My writing haven became a torn-up mess. But in the midst of the mess and inconvenience came a surprising e-mail from Mary Morgan, the wife of Dr. Benjamin Spock.

I have a short list of personal heroes. High on the list are my own father and mother, and my wife Cheryl. Mary Morgan and Dr. Spock are also on that list, along with a very few others.

At a time when knowledge of children's health comprised either inconsistent folklore or closely guarded secrets of medical professionals, Dr. Spock threw the doors of understanding wide open, making information plain and accessible to parents. It's no wonder that his trailblazing book became an unprecedented bestseller of the twentieth century, outselling even *The Lord of the Rings*. And the latest edition is just as relevant, a towering reference for the twenty-first century.

My plumbing mess turned into a magical experience when Mary loaned us a great treasure—a classic Winnebago named Tortes, where Dr. Spock sat to write! The Spockmobile (as my kids call it) became a place of great inspiration for me. Sitting at Dr. Spock's table, my gaze was often drawn to the pictures there, especially one of Ben and Mary. I was deeply moved and grew determined to give you my very best.

Along the way and afterward, I will be available to you as a free resource. This is the first major parenting book whose author personally hosts daily, live "office hours" online—an open door unlike any other. Having read this book, you will know the larger story, from the mystery of the first kick you feel to the magic of the first step your baby takes. I look forward to meeting you online and discussing the unique story of your own new little footprint on the earth.

Note: Families come in all shapes and sizes. Each brings its special strengths and challenges. Throughout this book, I describe a variety of configurations, even though I avoid cumbersome language to mention all the possibilities. When I speak, for instance, of the value of having Dad cut the umbilical cord, I mean it deeply. I also see the value of having another partner do it or of Mom herself helping in this emblematic task. I refer to your baby often as "he" and just as often as "she," understanding that my shorthand is wrong half the time—more frequently if you have triplets. Soften your focus to see the casting that works for you. This is your story.

Acknowledgments

It may take a village to raise a child. It takes a throng to birth a book. First my deep thanks to Vicky Bijur, my patient and savvy agent, who guided this project through its many ups and downs and who found us a home at McGraw-Hill, with Judith McCarthy, an amazing editor (and insightful mother). My thanks also to Mandy Huber, Kathy Dennis, Karen Steib, Lydia Rinaldi, and to the rest of the team at McGraw-Hill, from the artists to the marketing team. And thanks to my dear friend, health pioneer Tom Ferguson, M.D., for helping me connect with Vicky and getting this whole ball rolling. And thanks to those from years past who tried to get the ball rolling. This book wouldn't have happened without your kind nudges.

Thanks to my friends and colleagues, pregnant and non-pregnant, who reviewed the manuscript and offered helpful suggestions. I especially want to thank Dana Weintraub, M.D., one of my favorite pediatricians, and skilled pediatric social worker Kate Phillippo for their astute comments while about to meet their own new babies.

Deep thanks to Mary Morgan, the wife of Dr. Benjamin Spock, whose generous gift of their writing space is one of the great thrills of my life. Mary, your spirit and Ben's inspire me every day. Ben was the one who started it all!

My wife Cheryl, the heart and soul of DrGreene.com, has also been the heart and soul of this book. Inspiring, challenging, tirelessly rereading—and taking care of our family when I would disappear into Tortes or the Scribble Den. What a joy!

My heart vibrates with thanks for the rest of the amazing DrGreene.com team: to Bev Richardson, our Community Manager (Truddlebug); to our community hosts Belsamm (Sharon), Bensmommy (Julie), HDC (Heather), Marice (Marice), Ranchmom (Lynda), Serentity (Jennifer), Shmeea (Nia), Tammy (Tammy), and Tmom (Teresa); to Dr. Khan Van le Bucklin, registered nurse Suzie Ragni, and our social worker Mindy Swagel; to our artists and engineers Marcus Howell and Garret Zuiderweg; and to our truly incomparable engineer, Garry, who died tragically during the final days of preparing this manuscript, leaving behind five wonderful kids. Garry, we will always miss you. Your wit, your wisdom, your love and appreciation of your children, and your mystical superhuman multilingual coding abilities will not be forgotten. Christopher, Jeremy, Natalie, David, and Stephanie, your father was an amazing man, who was loved, enjoyed, and respected.

Gale Wilson-Steel and the MedSeek team have given and given to make DrGreene.com available to readers everywhere. Gale, thank you most of all for believing in the mission.

I didn't learn to be a pediatrician in a vacuum. I've learned a bit from all of my teachers, colleagues, partners, and patients along the way. Thanks in particular to Marshall Klaus for being a mentor, inspiration, and friend. Thanks to Myles Abbott, my children's pediatrician and my teacher when I was a pediatric resident, for being such a fabulous role model of what it means to practice pediatrics. And thanks to Donnica Moore of DrDonnica.com, a pioneering women's health website. Women and children first!

I deeply appreciate the important and instructive work of my many colleagues, especially Drs. Fernando Mendoza, David Bergen, Lisa Chamberlain, Larry Hammer, Carrie Loutit, Tom Robinson, Ted Sectish, Paul Sharek, and Elizabeth Stuart in the Division of General Pediatrics at Stanford (along with the invaluable Peggy Simons), and Mary Lake Polan, M.D., Ph.D., Chair of GYN/OB. I've also benefited from, and learned so much from, the practical, caring wisdom of many nurses at Stanford and at Children's Hospital Oakland, Mills-Peninsula Hospital, and A.B.C. Pediatrics (including Amy, Anne, Bobbie, Fe, Frances, Gail, Gayle, Georgia, Gladys, Janice, Joan, Kathy, Linda, Margie, Marian, Mary, Michelle, Nancy, Peri, Rachel, Rosemary, Sam, Sue, Teri, Vajihe, and many, many others). My thanks to nurses, midwives, obstetricians, doulas, lactation consultants, and pediatricians everywhere!

Thanks to my partners in practice at A.B.C., the memorable staff there, and the wonderful parents who invited me into their families as their pediatrician; to the entire team at Lucile Packard Children's Hospital at Stanford, where we work together to make life better for kids and their parents; and to the team at ADAM where we work to illustrate health in words and pictures.

Before, during, and after my training, I learned from my family—parents, sisters, wife, in-laws, and a tight-knit extended family. I keep learning so much from you all. And to my incredible children, Garrett, Kevin, Claire, and Austin, thanks for learning about and experiencing life together. When I look back at your baby pictures and think of all the mistakes I made—and how wonderfully each of you turned out—it gives me deeper faith in you and in the process. From the first time I felt you kick, through the millions of steps you've now taken, my love for you continues to grow.

Photo Credits

Thanks to the many friends of DrGreene.com who shared their stunning photos for this book. Special thanks to my wife, Cheryl, for collecting and placing the photos in the book. I only wish we had room to publish them all. Thanks to Dr. Beth Kleiner of Peninsula Ultrasound for the beautiful pre-birth photos, Tracy and Jay Barnes, Michael Callahan and Dana Weintraub, Melisa Charlton, Heather and Paul Cunningham, Tami DeSellier and Pedro Cafasso, Steve and Pamela Dillard, Erik and Lisa Drake, Georgia Drake, Jeff and Cherene Fillingim-Selk, Lee and Mandi Goodall, John and Gwen Greene, Greg and Leslie Juhn, Mark and Lisa Helm, Kevin and Gia-Miin Kelly, Sarah Larsen, Heidi and Justin Mize, Chaz and Roberta Nichols, Jeff and Laura Nickel, Sergio and Julie Salvador, Mindy and Eric Swagel, Cheryl and Roger Tallman, Starlene Todd, and Warren and Harriet Trezvant for lending us your precious photos.

Paul Cunningham (page 27)
Tami DeSellier (pages 12, 75, 81, 97, 109, 116, 134, 140, 175, 233, 277, and 312)
Pam Dillard (page 166)
Erik Drake (page 205)
Lisa Drake (pages 16 and 60)
Glynna Fenske (page 270)
Cheryl Greene (pages 262 and 288)
Gwen Greene (page 316)
Greg Juhn (pages 118 and 219)
Kevin Kelly (pages 18, 121, 155, 182, and 250)
Beth Kliener, M.D. (pages 19, 26, 34, 42, 66, 72, 83, 100, 105, and 112)
Matthew Millman (pages 179, 189, and 198)
Heidi Mize (pages 22 and 242)
Chaz Nichols (page 148)
Sergio Salvador (pages 53, 56, 90, 130, and 228)
Mindy Swagel (page 291)
Starlene Todd (pages 1, 142, 164, 238, 239, and 259)
Harriet Trezevant (pages 204 and 266)

Part I

Footprints

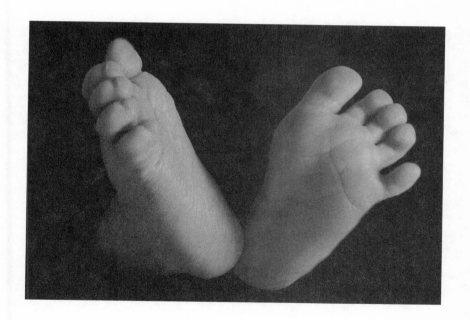

1

Beginnings

Conception

The world will never be the same! You have the journey of a lifetime ahead of you. Together. Thankfully, a map for this journey is written into the core of your being. Only time will tell how you travel, but we can unfold the map and take a look. Better, we can look at life itself.

Let's begin with the magical moment when a woman first feels her baby kick. The baby has long felt the mother, now the mother feels the baby. Perhaps the father feels the baby as well. This moment echoes the experience of the parents' parents and grandparents before them, a thread of continuity tying 21st-century parenting to our earliest roots.

The first butterfly flutter of a kick may seem too soft to leave a footprint, but it does—a lasting footprint on your hopes, your fears, your soul. With that first kick, your experience of the world changes. It's a gentle, new knock on the door of the world.

Knock Knock, Who's There?

What's happening inside? Who is it that you feel, first fluttering and then tap-dancing (and by the end, sumo wrestling!) in your tummy? And when?

For convenience and consistency, obstetricians count the 10 months (40 weeks) of pregnancy from an observable moment—the first day of the last menstrual period before the pregnancy. This is about two weeks before the new life appears, but the exact number of days varies. When obstetricians tell you how many weeks pregnant you are, this is how they are counting. The same method is used for most other pregnancy books.

Louise Brown was the first baby born who had been conceived in a laboratory. Since her birth in 1978, over a million babies have followed in her footsteps.

Here, we'll be looking at the story primarily in baby time, from the moment of conception where sperm and egg scramble their DNA. To conceive, at its root meaning, is to bring together to create something new, whether that something is a new baby or a new idea (concept). We'll be talking about the timing of events in this book in terms of days or weeks of active growth after your baby's conception. Conception may take place a couple of weeks after menstruation, perhaps hidden deep inside after a moment of joining by Mom and Dad. On the other hand, it may take place far earlier, in a modern laboratory after careful planning and great effort.

To translate the dates you hear at the OB's office or read in other places to the timeline of this book, subtract about two weeks. Because each passing week can feel like a success in pregnancy, this method may feel like it puts you behind. But the advantage is that it allows us to talk more accurately about your baby. It helps you to feel in synch with your baby. And a full-term pregnancy is over in only 38 weeks!

By Day 56 after conception, your baby already has perfectly formed tiny little feet, with five little toes and a unique footprint. In Part I, we will review the sweeping epic of how these tiny feet came to be and introduce you to who it is that has been kicking, even months before you feel it.

Someone New

I remember as a young boy hearing the story of the chess master's reward. The master had the choice of receiving as his reward $10,000 for every square on the chessboard or just one cent for the first square, two cents for the next, four cents for the next, and so on. The wise chess master chose the pennies, resulting in a staggering fortune. How much would this be? A million dollars? Ten million? A hundred million? A billion? A trillion? No— it came to more than $92 quadrillion! This simple doubling process produces a treasure that truly staggers the imagination. Something even more staggering happens within the body of every pregnant woman. One special cell, the fertilized egg, becomes two cells, then four cells, then eight cells, and so on, until someone of incredible uniqueness and complexity is created.

A Unique Beginning

The special cell that begins this magic is not as common as a penny. It is rare indeed. Where does this special cell come from? With more than six billion people on the planet, creating countless possibilities for coupling, two people come together. The woman has about two million eggs, each carrying a different genetic package. Of these, only about 400 are ovulated over a lifetime.

Following intercourse, up to 500 million sperm might race toward one month's egg in the ultimate triathlon, through treacherous terrain and killing currents. Just one inch would look like 28 miles to the tiny five-micron sperm; the upper regions of the fallopian tubes are almost a foot from the sperm's starting line. Each sperm is equipped with adenosine triphosphate (ATP)—its sports drink and energy bar equivalent—to fuel the exhausting race. Nevertheless, the challenges are formidable. Even though the vagina is less acidic during ovulation, acidity is still lethal to sperm (the reason that slices of lemon have been used as a mildly effective contraceptive). Less than 10 percent of the sperm survive the journey to the cervix.

Even though the mucus of the cervix is thinner during ovulation, it is still thick and sticky enough to ensnare most of the survivors. Less than 1 percent of the starting sperm ever make it through into the uterus. (You can begin to see why having 30 million sperm in an ejaculation might lead to infertility, even though the number sounds high.)

While the sperm are struggling through the thick sludge of the mucus, white blood cells swarm into the cervix and uterus, hostile warriors bent on murder of invading forces. Those sperm that make it safely across the uterus are faced with an irrevocable choice. The finish line, the mature egg, comes from one ovary. Half the sperm will struggle up the wrong fallopian tube to a terminal dead end.

Those that remain on course face swirling currents created by beating cilia (short, hairlike projections) and the rhythmic contractions of the tube walls. Meanwhile, white blood cells continue to hunt and destroy those that are knocked to and fro.

Lemons were the main method of contraception for Mediterranean women about 300 years ago. In his famous exploits, Casanova (1725–1798) inserted half a lemon, squeezed, which was perhaps the first diaphragm. Some scientists today recommend lemon juice as a natural, cost-effective choice, especially for developing nations, because of the partial success of lemon juice against both sperm and HIV.

A select few, about 0.0005 percent of those that started this triathlon, will finally reach the egg. And the quest continues as each of these struggles to penetrate the outer shell and be the first to cross the finish line of the inner membrane. At the instant one prevails, the electrical charge of the membrane changes, and the close finishers all drop away. When it comes to reproduction, nature does not like threesomes. Out of the many in the starting field, just one sperm fuses with the egg. The resulting combination is a rare treasure: a completely original genetic design exclusive to this conception.

Human Blueprints

That genetic legacy will have a lasting influence over everything from how tall your child will be as an adult to how well she spells in third grade. Many parents have questions about how the individual genetic packages in the sperm and the egg combine to create someone new. It's a fascinating story. Let's take a look.

Our genetic material (deoxyribonucleic acid, or DNA) has often been compared to a blueprint used to guide the building of a body. This quaint image is now out-of-date, akin to the old image of the electrons circling the nucleus of an atom the same way planets circle the sun. The ATCG alphabet of DNA is more like the 0110 machine code of a complex, self-learning computer program—complete with updates, patches, and a series of subprograms that automatically turn on and off as the situation warrants. It learns from the environment and is able to swap bits of code with other programs. Our DNA is far more dynamic than the unchanging two-dimensional image of a blueprint. It is more like cutting-edge artificial intelligence, except of course that it is natural intelligence—the wisdom of the body.

Our marvelous complement of DNA is divided into genes, which are the individual units that will determine the specific traits of your baby. They affect obvious characteristics like hair color, eye color, and skin complexion, but they also affect subtle things like food preferences and even the types of toys he and/or she will gravitate toward in play. As humans we have about 25,000 genes.

Starting Points

I like to call each gene a "Starting Point." Genes don't necessarily determine where things will end up, but they determine where things begin. Our life experiences, the food we eat, the things we choose to do, and the people and culture around us all influence our growth—even before we are born.

My sisters are identical twins with identical genes (they share the brand-new genetic makeup unique to their conception). Nevertheless, from the first day, we could tell that their personalities were different, shaped by their interactions and positioning before they were born and during the birth process.

Another way to picture the Starting Point idea is to think of a boat tied to an anchor by a long rope. The boat may be directly above the anchor (the starting point), but over time it may move to any one of a number of other positions, influenced by winds and currents and the intentions of the people on the boat. Some genes have long ropes—allowing for a lot of variability—such as the genes that determine food preference. Others have shorter ropes that almost fix the boat in place—such as the genes for eye color or footprints—but even these allow movement.

Do my twin sisters share footprints? No, their footprints and fingerprints are unique. Identical twins form when a single egg splits in two after it has been fertilized. The two individuals start with virtually identical genetic makeup. Their DNA cannot be distinguished by today's techniques (though I predict even this will change as we learn more about how our environment affects our DNA). Their genes direct how their footprints will be formed, the patterns of ridges and whorls, but the exact print is influenced by what is going on in their pregnancy environments. Nutrition, blood supply, positioning, and growth rate all affect the final prints. Each baby's footprint is one of a kind!

The same is true for triplets and quadruplets. The Dionne quintuplets, the first surviving quintuplets, were examined by experts in 1934 with great interest. Their footprints were strikingly similar, but each print was unique.

New Insights

On April 14, 2003, the incredible Human Genome Project was completed, pulling back the curtain to let us see who we are in a new way. The announcement came fifty years after James Watson and Francis Crick's revolutionary April 1953 paper announcing the discovery of DNA. They proclaimed that the blueprint of a life is made up of two strands. When these strands unbraid, each is the template to make a new copy.

The Human Genome Project created a detailed map of these strands, a code book of who we are. The team identified for the first time all of the genes in human DNA and worked out the basic sequence of the more than 3.1 billion molecule pairs that make up our DNA. Each gene is made up of an average of 3,000 of these molecule pairs. Typed out, just the initials of the genetic code for one human would fill about 200 volumes the size of the Manhattan phone book (1,000 pages each). Your baby will be born in a new era.

The Human Genome Project has already resulted in a few surprises. Our 25,000 genes are far fewer than expected (many other animals—and most flowers—have more). I recently spoke with David Stewart of the Cold Spring Harbor Laboratory. He ran the Gene Sweepstakes, a four-year international contest where top genomic scientists wagered on how many human genes there would be. Educated guesses ranged from 27,000 to more than 150,000. When the Human Genome Project was completed in 2003, the prizes went to the lowest bets, because the actual number of genes was lower than anyone had guessed.

But our genes also have more options than expected—they tend to make more types of proteins than most other animals, and each type of protein tends to be more complex. Boys are about twice as likely as girls to have a bit of new or different DNA that they did not copy exactly from their parents.

To me, the most striking finding is that all humans are more than 99.9 percent identical at the gene level, even across what we think of as races! This is out of the ordinary among animals. Two similar looking orangutans from the same jungle will generally be 10 times more genetically different from each other than will a tall, blue-eyed Texas cowboy and a short, brown-eyed Tibetan woman. We are complex creatures who share far more than we differ.

Today's DNA test would not be able to tell the difference between them, but a footprint can.

Footprints remind us that we are unique and that we are not prisoners of our genes, but that every gene is a starting point.

Of the 3,165 million pairs of molecules in human DNA, there are only about 1 million spots where individual changes occur. This allows for plenty of variability and for billions (or quintillions) of people to be unique, but it also gives us a breadth and depth of commonality that is striking. Every person on the planet is a close relative; every person is the only one of a kind.

Getting an Early Start

When a teenage boy experiences the surge of adolescent hormones, it's not all loud music, large appetites, late nights, and pimples. During puberty his body begins to create hundreds of millions of sperm every day, and each sperm has a different combination of his genes, selected from his double set.

We have two copies of most genes, one from Dad and one from Mom. You remember from the chess master story earlier in the chapter how large a number 2 to the 63rd power turns out to be. If we had just 33 genes and each gene had just two options, there would be enough possibilities (2 to the 33rd power) for every person in history to have had a different set of genes. With 25,000 genes, the number of different possible sperm an oblivious teen could create would be on the order of at least 2 to the 25,000th power—all of them varying combinations of the genes passed to him by his parents. He might spray a quarter of a million distinct possibilities each time he ejaculates, combinations unlikely ever to be repeated. Sperm will be produced continuously from the time of his puberty all the way to his death.

Little girls are very different from little boys in this regard. If you are a woman, the egg that is growing inside you now was already present in you when you were a teen driving for the first time, when you were a little girl on her first day of school, when you took your first toddling step, and when your mother smiled as she felt you moving inside. All of the eggs a woman will ever have were produced while she was still inside her mother.

If you are expecting a little girl, your daughter's eggs will already be formed between the 12th and 20th weeks of your pregnancy. You may have part of your grandchildren already inside you.

Sperm are not so durable. They are usually history within days of being created. If they are not ejaculated, they might live up to 40 days in the body before they die, and the body composts them back into the stuff of life, making room for the next new crop. There would be no way to store more than that.

A man makes thousands of new sperm every second, awake and asleep. It takes around 100 days to make each day's new crop of hundreds of millions of sperm from start to finish. It takes about 74 days from selection of the genetic package to the production of a semimotile sperm. Then they go on a 20-day road trip through the twisting turns of the epididymis while they gain their full motility. Finally, they sit and wait to mature for at least six days in the vas deferens before they are ready for duty. The whole process, from start to finish, from birth to death, is over in a few months. Within two seasons they are gone. But every now and then, the rare sperm finds a mate, and they go on to share a lifetime together.

The Chromosomal Connection

Chromosomes are the structures that hold our genes. They are far too important for us to keep just one copy in a safe spot in our bodies. We have a copy of the entire set in almost every cell in our body, to tell that cell what to do. Normally, humans have 46 chromosomes holding the 38,000 genes of our DNA. These 46 chromosomes come as 23 pairs. We have named the first 22 by number, like a street address for the genes. Chromosome 1 is the largest and chromosome 22 is the smallest, with the rest ordered politely in between. The last pair are called the sex chromosomes, named X and Y for their shapes. Girls have two X chromosomes (XX), one inherited from each of their parents. Boys have an X and a Y (XY), with the X from their moms and the Y from their dads.

Sometimes, perhaps in the great genetic shuffle, or while creating new sperm, or in the long dormant period of storing and protecting those precious eggs, some children end up with extra bits or missing bits of chromosomes. Trisomy 21, Down syndrome, is a condition in which a child has three copies of chromosome 21. My sister had a daughter with a far more severe triple-copy chromosome, a condition called Trisomy 13, or Patau syndrome. She felt, as many women do, that something she had done or not done or eaten or not eaten during pregnancy may have caused this. It did not. Chromosome problems, if they occur, are present at the moment of conception, at the moment the genes combine. If there is a chromosome problem, there is usually a miscarriage, often before women know they are pregnant. There are also wonderful children who are born with irregular chromosome patterns and who lead very happy lives. Later, in Chapter 9, we'll talk about chromosome testing, how you can learn how the chromosomes sorted themselves out, and whether you are carrying a little XX or XY.

Blue Genes and Blood Brothers

So how do the two genes given by Mom and Dad interact? Not too long after your baby's born, friends, family, and complete strangers will begin offering their opinions on whom the baby favors.

"She has her daddy's eyes."

"Your baby looks just like you."

"He has your long fingers; I bet he'll be a piano player."

When parents bring their baby to see me, after the "conehead" of delivery has had a chance to disappear, I enjoy looking at the baby's features with them. With the aid of a mirror, I help them see specific physical traits that the baby inherited from each of them and some that are a blend of the two. I explain that these visible characteristics are an outward sign of a much subtler dance of inheritance.

You may have studied some genetics in high school or college or even have a Ph.D. in genetics, but the topic feels brand-new when your genes and your partner's are combining to launch a new life. There is a new level of relevance when learning that some of your genes will dominate your partner's—and some will submit—in your own baby. Curiosity and imagination arise as you consider which genes will merge to produce a blended trait. Which genes will play hide-and-seek, only to reappear in your grandchildren or in their grandchildren? Which traits in your baby will be surprises, nothing you have seen in either of you but the hidden legacy of earlier generations?

The modern science of genetics had its start in 1866 when an Austrian monk named Gregor Mendel provided a simple yet powerful description of how traits are passed on from one generation to another. Sometimes inheritance is as simple as the Mendelian genetics they teach in high school. Some traits are dominant; some are recessive. A child needs two copies of a recessive gene, one from each parent, to express that trait. Blue eyes were the classic example I learned in high school. Two brown-eyed parents can have a blue-eyed baby if they each carry one blue and one brown gene. About a quarter of their kids will get a brown gene from each parent, have

brown eyes, and never be able to have blue-eyed children of their own. About half their kids will get one brown gene and one blue gene and will have brown eyes themselves, but they might one day have a child with blue eyes. Finally, about a quarter of their children will get two blue genes, have blue eyes, and pass a blue gene on to their children.

This simplified type of genetics holds for other traits such as nearsightedness and the ability to roll the tongue. Many diseases and conditions are inherited in this way. But the larger story is much more complex. We'll see in Chapter 4 how we've learned that even eye color is far more complicated and more interesting than this. Genes combine to produce traits in almost every way you could imagine—and then some!

Mendel's breakthrough work in genetics was unappreciated until 1900, more than fifteen years after his death, when the discovery of blood types made genetics exciting. Researchers dusted off his forgotten studies and applied them to blood.

What's Your Type?

I get a surprising number of questions from parents both online and off about blood types and how they work. Some of this is because they are curious about touchy aspects of paternity, theirs and/or their babies'. But much of it is because they are concerned about how the combining of blood types might affect the health of their baby.

> ### Blood Puzzles
> Can a mother with AB+ blood type and a father with O+ blood type have a child with B— blood?
>
> **Drtaft**
>
> I've been trying to learn more about blood types. I was told one time that there could be problems with certain blood types. . . . If I am A+ and my spouse is O—, would this be an issue to be considered?
>
> **Juliana**

We might begin the story of blood types with a 32-year-old man named Karl Landsteiner, who observed in 1900 that mixing blood from different sources sometimes produced unexpected reactions, from bursting red blood cells to unusual clumping. Not only did blood from humans have such reactions when mixed with animal blood, but it also sometimes happened with blood from other healthy people. Very quickly afterward, the ABO blood types were worked out from these experiments.

ABO blood group inheritance is different from the dominant/recessive eye color inheritance we discussed earlier, because both parents' genes are expressed in their children's blood. A child's red blood cells grow all of the antigens (immunologically distinct molecules) inherited on the genes from both parents. It's a codominant relationship.

The A and B blood types were just generic names given to the first two antigens discovered. The O type is the name for blood that makes neither antigen. Each person receives an A, a B, or an O gene from each parent. A person whose genetic type is either AA or AO will have A antigens on the surface of the blood cells and thus be blood type A. Those with genetic type BB or BO will have blood type B. If a child gets an A from one parent and a B from the other, neither will dominate, but the child will have blood type AB. Only those with genetic type OO will have blood type O. This means that if a child has type O blood, the parents might have type A, type B, or type O blood (but not type AB). Conversely, if two parents both have type O blood, all of their children will have type O blood.

Here is a list of possible and impossible situations:

Parents' Blood Types	Possible Children	Impossible Children
A and A	A, O	B, AB
A and B	A, B, AB, O	None
A and AB	A, B, AB	O
A and O	A, O	B, AB
B and B	B, O	A, AB
B and AB	A, B, AB	O
B and O	B, O	A, AB
AB and AB	A, B, AB	O
AB and O	A, B	AB, O
O and O	O	A, B, AB

Not only are blood types different, but some types of blood are incompatible with others. The white blood cells in some types will perceive other types as enemies, attacking and destroying the other (alien) blood. This is especially important when lots of blood is exchanged, as in a transfusion.

If a mother's blood type is O and the baby's is different, then the mother's blood might consider the baby's blood to be foreign and mount something of an attack. This is not a serious problem. If those helping to deliver the baby are aware of the situation and watch carefully, they can easily treat the jaundice that might result.

Mixing Blood

The mixing problem can be more significant between negative and positive blood types, a classification we call the Rh system. These genes were first discovered in the rhesus monkey, hence the designation *Rh*. The Rh incompatibility story is one of the great success stories of modern medicine.

The Rh system is actually far more complex than the ABO system in that there are thirty-five different possibilities that a child could inherit from each parent. These possibilities are roughly grouped into positive and negative types. People are called Rh negative if they do not have the rhesus (Rh) antigen on the surface of their blood cells. In this system, the positive types are dominant over the negative. Thus, if your genetic type is $++$ or $+-$, your blood type will be Rh positive. Only if your genetic type is $--$ will you be Rh negative. This means that if both parents have Rh-positive blood with the $+-$ genes, they could have children who are $++$, $+-$, or $--$. In other words, their children could be either Rh positive or Rh negative. Children who are Rh negative can have parents who are either Rh positive or Rh negative.

If Rh-positive blood cells from a baby get into the bloodstream of an Rh-negative mom, the body of the mother will interpret this as an enemy invasion. Unprepared, the mother's blood will begin to make antibodies against the foreign Rh protein. The next time a blood exchange occurs though, her body is primed to seek and destroy all Rh-positive blood cells. All-out war can occur inside the mother's body.

During the pregnancy, this war is often not noticed, but a condition in the baby called *hydrops fetalis* can be the result. Rh incompatibility produces a wide variety of outcomes. Sometimes mild anemia and a little jaundice are the only signs there has been a conflict. But sometimes the results are catastrophic. The first pregnancy is rarely a problem because blood is often not exchanged until the time of birth. But with each subsequent pregnancy, the risk for hydrops increases.

In 1963 an event occurred that began to change the story. Jorg Schneider, who was at the Freiburg University Hospital in Germany at the time, became the very first investigator to give pregnant, Rh-negative women a shot of Rh antibodies to prevent their immune systems from mounting their own response to Rh-positive cells.

The exact date of this achievement was August 9, 1963. One year later, Schneider reported that nine Rh-negative women, following delivery of Rh-positive children, did not develop Rh antibodies during subsequent Rh-positive pregnancies. Since then, prevention programs have been implemented in many countries around the world, and the risk of hydrops has plummeted. By giving anti-D globulin (the brand name is RhoGAM) to Rh-negative moms during and shortly after each pregnancy (including after any miscarriages and abortions), 99 percent of those women will not develop anti-Rh antibodies.

When I was born, hydrops fetalis was an almost hopeless situation. Today, preventing Rh-negative moms from being sensitized is extremely successful at preventing hydrops wherever the guidelines are followed. All of this with a couple of simple but ingenious shots!

Still Blazing Trails

Today there are over 600 known blood types. Blood is almost as unique as a footprint. But the combinations of blood type also provide a history of your baby, almost like the geologic layers in a fossil dig. The ABO blood group is one small example of this. Historically, different blood types have been more common among different peoples. The natives of Central and South America were almost exclusively type O. Type O was also common in northern and western Europe. Type A was especially common in the natives of Australia, where type B was nonexistent. Type A was also common in Western Europe. Type B was most common in central Asia and northern India. Today people with any blood type might be found anywhere in the world.

Because of the high-resolution map provided by the Human Genome Project in 2003, your child's detailed blood type, coupled with his or her DNA, provides a trail that could lead back through your parents, their parents, and generations of ancestors to the dawn of history.

And at this end of the trail is your new baby, a matchless combination of the two of you.

2

An Incredible Journey

Days 1 Through 13 in Baby Time

In a few short weeks, an amazing cascade of events completely transforms your baby. This transformation starts with a road trip back down the route discovered by the sperm, in the direction the egg was heading before they hooked up. After finding a likely spot to settle (location, location, location!), there will be no more journeys until a baby is ready to emerge into the world at the end of your pregnancy.

The Voyage Begins

Let's look at this momentous first journey. Foreshadowing the days when she and Dad will carry their son in a backpack or push their daughter in a stroller, a mother now gently carries this glorious dot to its next destination. In a way, she has already pushed her baby in a stroller! Even though parents don't yet know that they are pregnant, a healthy fertilized egg sends signals to Mom that trigger a stream of maternal hormones to enable her to softly push the little one along with quiet muscle contractions, a gentle current of secretions, and tender brushes of hair cells that line the fallopian tube. She is already behaving like a mother, even when she sleeps.

Unlike the sperm's frenzied, whip-propelled race to the egg, the tiny dot is leisurely carried on its victory journey over about a week. It reminds me of rafting down a lazy river instead of shooting the rapids. It's a honeymoon for the new coupling.

This is where "two really do become one." In many ways, having children is the marriage of two people.

Days 1 to 3 After Conception

On the first day of its voyage, the fertilized egg—unique in all the world—divides into two identical little balls that are squashed together. If the two new cells do not stay stuck together, identical twins are the result (fraternal twins occur when two different eggs are fertilized). If fertilization takes place in a laboratory and a pipette carries the embryo to its next destination, twins might be carried in two different pregnancies, years apart.

On the second day of the journey, these two identical cells each divide at about the same time, leaving four identical cells squashed together. Then eight. A community of cells is forming. Every day the number doubles once or twice. The little cluster of cells is called a *morula* (Latin for "mulberry"). By the end of the third day, there are 16 to 32 cells all packed into the original outer flexible shell of the egg, like a tightly filled bag of marbles. Because

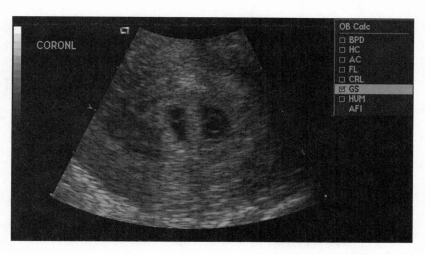

Twins!

of this shape, the cells are no longer identical. Some are on the inside and some are on the outside, which will soon trigger various cells to develop differently. The cells still have the same DNA and the same genes, but different genes are turned on and off in different cells, giving different instructions.

Days 4 to 6 After Conception

About the time the morula leaves the tributary of the fallopian tube for the open ocean of the uterus, its shape changes from a packed cluster of cells to a hollow, fluid-filled ball, one cell thick, that we call a *blastocyst*. It's like a tiny, living water balloon within the flexible shell of the original egg. But one end of this balloon becomes thicker than the other.

Most parents think that the cells descended from the fertilized egg eventually become their baby. But most of the cells formed so far will become the environment for the baby—the placenta and the membranes in which the baby will live. Only the cells at the thickened end will become your child.

This profound thought—that your baby and your baby's environment are made from the same cells—reminds me of naturalist John Muir, who taught that we and our environment are all connected, all made of the same stuff, all poured from the same fountain. In the first chapter, we learned that humans are 99.9 percent genetically identical even across what we think of as races. We also share 98 percent of our genes with chimpanzees and more than 90 percent with other mammals, even little mice. And 85 percent of our genes with fish such as the zebra fish. We share genes with birds and reptiles, insects and worms, flowers and roadside weeds. We even share 23 percent of our genes with yeast. In all of us, DNA passes down from one generation to the next. We share the same origin, the same creator or ancestor. There is continuity between your baby and the sac she grows in and among all life on earth.

Layers of Life. As the blastocyst thickens at one end, there are two layers of cells. The cells in each of the layers will have drastically different destinies. Even though they have identical potential, like the cells that become the baby and those that don't, the future of these cells will depend on having been in the right place at the right time.

We call the outer layer the *ectoderm*. From these cells will grow the brain, spinal cord, nerves, sense organs, and skin, including those unique footprints that are soon to appear.

The inner layer is the *endoderm*. This will become the inner lining of the body from the mouth through the esophagus, the stomach, and the intestines, all the way through to the baby's bottom on the other end.

For now, all that can be seen are layers of identical looking cells. The distinctions that will have huge consequences are subtle indeed. The whole package is about 0.1 mm in diameter. My favorite micropoint rollerball pens have a 0.2-mm ball at the tip. The barely visible speck of life that's being formed is half that size, and the baby is the tiniest part.

So far, the changes we have seen are growth and reorganization of matter found in the original egg and sperm. The supplies already packed in the fertilized egg fuel these changes. This won't be sufficient for the flurry of growth and change to come. Not by a long shot! The traveling morula-turned-blastocyst RV needs a hookup. The child needs its mother.

Hooking Up

About a week after conception and about three weeks after the first day of the last menstrual period, before any pregnancy test has shown positive,

What About Dads?

The intimate connection between mother and baby might cause fathers to feel left out, but as it turns out, they are central to it. Modern genetics and the science of genomic imprinting have taught us that genes inherited from the mother and the father play different roles in early development. Each cell contains genes from both, but in some cells, more of Dad's genes are turned on, and in others Mom's genes are. At this stage, maternal chromosomes are responsible for directing the growth of the budding embryo; paternal chromosomes are responsible for directing the cells that build the surrounding environment—including forging the very placenta that connects mother and child. The father is literally in the middle of this connection.

before Mom has even missed a period, a marvelous event happens. Mother and baby form an amazing connection.

Days 7 to 13 After Conception

Mom's body knows she is pregnant even though her conscious mind doesn't. Hormones turn the lining of her uterus into a soft, welcoming embrace to hold the new visitor.

While this is going on, the blastocyst finally hatches from its original transparent shell. Shedding this firm, flexible membrane allows for rapid new growth. It also allows for unprecedented connection. The blastocyst and the mother's uterus lining hold each other close in a process called *implantation*, the most intimate human snuggle. Enzymes melt away protective layers, and the two fiercely latch on to each other.

Over the course of about a week, an intense connection grows. A pipeline. But far more complex—mother and baby are being knit together. The blastocyst tunnels into the uterine lining, cutting through the walls of blood vessels and bathing in Mom's lifeblood. Meanwhile the outer rim cells become a tough membrane we call the *chorion*, which will become the bag of water that won't break until soon before you see your baby face-to-face.

Fingers from the chorion reach out and grasp the mother. The connection that forms between the two is a new organ called the *placenta*. In this meaty lump of tissue, blood vessels from Mom and baby intertwine deeply while staying separate. This organ is not part of just Mom or just baby, but of both. This shared tissue is the place of an ongoing exchange, a silent con-

versation, where hormones from the mother and the baby signal changes in each other's bodies and where nutrition is delivered and waste removed. The placenta is a tangible expression of a deep relationship—mutual, nurturing, protective, profoundly linked.

Never again will this connection be so physical, so tangible. But as the years pass and your child matures and the balance changes, parenthood invites you to enjoy a new level of deep relationship—still mutual, nurturing, protective, and profoundly linked. A key to maintaining and growing this relationship throughout the years ahead is to foster ongoing exchange, as illustrated by the placenta. And over time to build bridges where this exchange can take place.

Your child's teenage years may seem like they're too far away to imagine, but they come more quickly than you guess. Adolescence is often the period where parents and kids are most disconnected. My favorite way to stay close to my kids is to consciously build bridges (thinking back to the placenta). I find areas in which each of my children has enthusiasm, where their blood warms. I develop my interest in at least one of those areas with each of my children at all times. I learn everything I can about the topic and become

Planning Ahead

At the same time the placenta is forming, so is something called the *yolk sac*. In chicken eggs and other bird eggs, the yolk is there as food, because the babies don't connect to the mother through a placenta. In humans, the yolk sac produces blood cells for the babies until their own organs can. It also produces sex cells (under the primary direction of chromosomes inherited from the father). The mother hasn't even missed a period yet, and the new little one inside is already taking steps to give its parents grandkids!

an enthusiast myself. By having at least one area where we can really meet, really connect and be comfortably close, a parent-child exchange continues to nurture, protect, and carry away waste, even when disagreements and stress arise or the time pressures of modern life might pull us apart.

These bridges are different with each child and have changed over the years as their interests have changed. My interest is real, not feigned, and even more vivid because the interest is shared. For me, these bridges have included a student production of *Les Misérables*, video games such as *Everquest* or *Kingdom Hearts*, one very cute Chihuahua, the music of Blink 182, Warhammer tabletop gaming, middle school football, elaborate home Halloween productions, snipe hunting, chess tournaments, Magic baseball, Texas Hold'em, Harry Potter, Pokémon, Elmo on "Sesame Street," the spoon with which I fed my babies solid foods, and their very first toys.

But before all of that is the placenta.

About the time implantation begins, the placenta begins to make a hormone called *human chorionic gonadotropin*, or hCG. This trickles into Mom's blood, swirls to the ovaries, and calls to them to pump out more estrogen and progesterone to carry this adventure forward.

Traces of this same hCG spill into Mom's urine and become the life-changing yes-or-no of a pregnancy test. (A medium earthquake shook the San Francisco Bay Area and my desk as I was writing this chapter—a fitting underline to the momentous shaking and changing that come the moment a pregnancy test turns positive.) Some home pregnancy tests might advertise that they will give you the big news three days before your next period is due. But this only works for about half of pregnant women. Implantation needs to occur before hCG is produced, and because of the natural variability in the timing of ovulation and implantation, this does not necessarily occur before the first day of a missed period. Tests might be positive as early as six days after conception, but it might be much longer. About 10 percent of healthy blastocysts have not yet implanted by the day the period is expected. And some take an even more leisurely first journey. Thus, researchers estimate that the chance of detecting a true pregnancy one week after the first day of the missed period is 97 percent.

But when the test turns positive, it is hCG that you see turning the colors on the stick or disk. You are not just getting news; you are looking at a project Mom, Dad, and baby made together.

3

Setting the Stage

Days 13 Through 20 in Baby Time

The powerful connection with Mom ushers in an unequaled time of change and growth for the baby. The taps are wide open. Suddenly there is a luxurious amount of nutrition available. It's like a kid in a candy store getting everything he wants. The quiet, economic rearrangement of the blastocyst, the careful management of limited resources, gives way to over-flowing surplus (eventually up to 75 gallons of blood a day will flow into and out of the placenta). Guilt-free gorging! This superabundant surplus pro-motes startling growth. If your baby continued to grow at this pace beyond the next few weeks, he would be about a million times the size of the earth by the ninth month—which would not make for a comfortable delivery.

Even more amazing than the growth is the revolutionary change that takes place in this similar-looking ball of cells. By the end of a brief trans-formation period (within 56 days of fertilization), babies have elbows and knees, eyelids and nipples, and even hair follicles on their chin and upper lip! Babies begin to cry, to urinate, and to move about (unfelt by the mother). The external genitals are noticeable, and the internal organs have been created. Astonishingly, babies have a four-chambered heart, working fingers and toes, and their own brand-new footprint.

These days are as uncertain as adolescence and at least as powerful in development as the first three years after being born. Sometimes mothers feel that their role is not important during this stage. To the contrary, with-out the maternal connection, neither the amazing growth nor the dazzling change would be possible. But the powerful parenting role is so deeply nat-ural as to be almost unnoticed.

As a mother, this is one of the few times in life that you can pack your child's fruit in her lunch and she won't trade it with a friend. You can feed

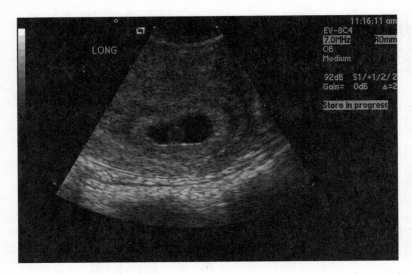

The yolk sac at only 26 days

her veggies, and she won't balk! You can ask her to wear a helmet or a seat belt, and your wish is her command. After birth, getting a baby to sleep may be a major challenge (although I will show you ways to solve this). But now you get to sleep *for* your baby rather than trying to get your baby to sleep. Your role now is parenting at its most basic—to feed your baby and to provide a safe, nurturing environment. Later, when your baby can hear you and then see you, your role will expand. Later, you won't take away your baby's waste with the placenta, but by changing diapers; you won't feed your baby by eating, but with a spoon. Now, however, these basic parenting tasks are already a natural part of your life.

Beyond the tiny pen-point dot of the early blastocyst, every ounce of the baby who will be born will have been built from food that the mother eats during pregnancy or from food that she has eaten before conceiving a child. After the baby is born, a special time for many families occurs when Dad gets a chance to feed the baby. Of course, Dad can feed the baby during pregnancy too—by preparing meals for Mom.

In Chapters 5–7, we'll look at the nuts and bolts of feeding and protecting your baby at this stage. We'll look at what to seek out and what to avoid. These are parenting choices that can have lasting impact on your child's development. But even without this knowledge, much important parenting is happening automatically.

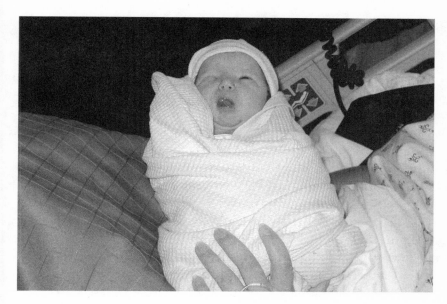

Running on Autopilot

While mothers are instinctively being parents, an explosion of changes occurs. As we tour this spectacular season of possibilities and transformation, let it sink into your heart that this quiet miracle, this intricate navigation on autopilot, is a model for the larger season of possibilities called childhood. The most precarious, the most critical season of childhood occurs during these first 56 days. It is far more important than what vegetables you feed your toddler or which college your teen goes to (if any). You couldn't control this development or direct it consciously if you tried. It unfolds even when you just relax. Understand that the miracle of unfolding development does not stop here; the choreography continues after birth—without your causing it or even being aware of it. Your crucial role as parents includes providing a safe, nurturing, gently stimulating space for this development.

Day 13 After Conception

We left the development story at the implantation, the hooking up, that is complete by around Day 13 when uteroplacental blood circulation begins. As we continue to follow these first 56 days from conception, keep in mind that even at this young age, children are individuals and do things at their own pace and in their own way. The day markers are typical, not absolute.

Typically at Day 13, the spot where the blastocyst burrowed into the wall of the uterus has healed over, but sometimes this bloody connection leaks a bit. Bleeding from the implantation site, because it happens near the 28th day of the menstrual cycle, is sometimes mistaken for a period. This could lead a couple to conclude that they are not pregnant when indeed they are; and it could throw off the estimated time of delivery, calculated from the first day of the last menstrual period. Thankfully, there will be other ways to "synchronize your watches" with the baby in the coming months.

But whether there is bleeding now or not, what there is *not* is a menstrual period. The mother-baby hookup is transforming the baby. It is also transforming the mother. The missed period is a sign of how deeply parents and children affect each other. This week I went with my parents to a reception where my father was honored with the hanging of his portrait at his university. Important academic dignitaries and friends were present. People had traveled to San Francisco from Boston and Hong Kong. But my parents' eyes were on my sisters and me (and our children). I'm a grown man and my parents are retired, but it was palpable how much my presence meant to them and how much theirs meant to me. The first missed period is a foretaste of this impact, this interconnectedness. Our lives will never be the same.

The baby is already causing other changes in the mother, both large and small—perhaps morning sickness, unusual fatigue, or "electric" nipples. Parents may suspect they are pregnant and may even have confirmed it with a pregnancy test. This is a wonderful time to begin a journal, even if you have never written one before.

Day 14 After Conception

I remember as a child hanging wallpaper with my father. We started with a plumb line. He showed me how to take a white string and tie a heavy bolt to one end as a weight. We took a chunk of soft blue chalk and rubbed it up and down the string, turning the string and our fingers powdery blue. He held the top of the string against the wall near the ceiling; the weight created a taut string and, thanks to gravity, hung straight down. Dad let me snap the string once, leaving a blue line on the wall—the guideline for the first section of wallpaper. By joining each successive section of wallpaper along the line of the preceding one, the whole room was connected and aligned.

On Day 14, a plumb line appears on the surface of the disc of cells that will become the baby. We call this line the *primitive streak*. Now the embryo has a top and a bottom, a back and a front, a left side and a right side. This living plumb line will be a critical guide for development, and for the next week will be an important source or starting line for new cells.

The plumb line also marks an ending, as each commitment does. After this, two twins cannot rejoin to become one baby (although before this, they might). And any twinning that happens after this will not be complete: it will result in conjoined, or Siamese, twins.

As you might guess, the formation of the primitive streak is an especially vulnerable time in pregnancy. With the plumb line being established and the newly opened spigots from Mom's bloodstream, this next week is a time when toxic exposures can cause big problems. Before this, the baby is relatively isolated from outside interference, but if a toxic exposure does get through at this time it is more likely to result in a miscarriage than in a birth defect. (We'll look at important toxic exposure in Chapter 7.) The period from three to eight weeks is the time of greatest sensitivity to outside disturbance. Each organ system has a period of greatest sensitivity. Scientists have created "fate maps" of which exposures on which days are most likely to damage which organs. For example, binge drinking during the third week after conception sometimes results in devastating damage to the area that will become the baby's face and brain. Many women may not yet know they are pregnant. A pregnancy test may still be negative, and the menstrual period not yet a concern.

Perhaps part of the reason for the nausea and marked fatigue that so many women feel during the vulnerable early weeks of pregnancy is both to alert them to the new life within and to make them less likely to take action that might harm the child. Also, pregnancy heightens a woman's sense of smell, alerting her to fumes in the environment she may not have noticed before.

Setting the Stage (Week 3 After Conception)

Weeks 4 through 8 after fertilization will be the time when all the major organs of the baby's body are formed. Week 3 sets the stage. It is the laying of the foundation. It is a tale of two tubes.

The Gastric Tube

We call the third week following fertilization *gastrulation*. You might guess that this word has to do with the gastric tube that forms during this week— but no. It's the process where the three foundational layers of the body are formed. We already saw the outer layer of cells called the ectoderm. From these cells will grow the brain, spinal cord, nerves, sense organs, and skin. And the inner layer of cells, the endoderm, will soon become the inner lining of the body, the gastric tube, which runs from the mouth through the esophagus, stomach, and intestines.

This week a new layer forms: the *mesoderm*. These cells will become the baby's bones and muscles and other internal organs. Once this layer is in place, sheets of endoderm cells roll into a long tube that quickly fuses, closing like a zipper. This tube is the primal gastrointestinal (GI) tract from the mouth to the anus.

During the middle of the third week, the embryo is about 1.25 mm long, which is about the distance between the two parallel lines of this capital F. Already there is a hidden space inside, where the baby will interface directly with the outside world one day. Part of the world will be swallowed by the baby; part of the baby will be excreted into the world. Already this tiny life is preparing for future independence, but it won't come too quickly. The first part of the outside world the baby is being prepared to swallow is the milk that Mom's body is preparing to make. For now, both ends of the gastric tube are sealed.

The Neural Tube

Meanwhile, the cells that will become your baby's brain and spinal cord form a groove along where the spinal cord will be. Soon this will zipper shut and be called the *neural tube*. The baby is already growing so complex that a sophisticated network, or early neural cells, will be needed to coordinate development from here.

The 1.25-mm-long embryo is teardrop shaped, though more than a hundred of them would fit in a teardrop. At its widest point, it is about 0.68 mm wide, but unlike a teardrop that falls when a child skins his knee, this teardrop is widest at the top. Adults' widest point might be at the shoulders or chest or belly or hips, but the embryo is widest by far at the head. And for now, the head makes up about one-third the length as well. Clearly, this is where the action is.

We've learned that folic acid in the mother's diet is important for developing the neural tube. Supplements are prescribed to pregnant women to reduce the chance of neural tube defects. This is a very specific example of how the benefits of the good things you eat are passed along to your growing child.

The Stalk

By Day 19 or 20 after conception, the embryo is floating, tethered to the placenta by a narrow stalk that will become the umbilical cord. The tether is shorter now than it will ever be again. Later, when you cut the physical umbilical cord (I often ask the father if he would like to do it), it is as if an invisible, ever longer and more flexible cord remains. When their child is in early infancy, parents often feel tethered to the baby by the seemingly constant need to feed and deal with diapers. Later, when the baby starts toddling, she will amble off to explore the world, but that invisible tether will draw her back again and again to check in and refuel her courage and glee. As she grows, the cord stretches further and becomes more complex. She is tethered to a broader family, to friends, to teachers—nourished by a web of connections.

For now, this single tether, narrower than a hair on her parents' heads, will facilitate a total transformation.

4

Total Transformation

Weeks 4 Through 8 in Baby Time

Week 4 After Conception

At some point during the fourth week, within 25 days of conception (what your OB will call six weeks pregnant), a brand-new human heart begins to beat. The music of the universe has added a pristine note. Later you will thrill to hear that heartbeat at a prenatal visit. Later still, you may feel it while feeding your baby on a quiet night when everyone else is asleep, as you reach out and gently place your hand on her chest. You will feel the rhythm when you hug your child close after he has been running in a soccer game or while his heart pounds with a fever.

Now it beats steadily, although no one hears it yet. It will continue to beat every minute of your child's life. Our hopes lay in the unspoken promise that it will still be beating long after you and I are gone.

Even in the absence of blood vessels, this simplified heart begins to push and pull fluids throughout the body. It is the percussion section, beating the time for the dance of organ formation that is about to come.

The Great Divide

As the fourth week after conception ends, the embryo is at the halfway point of 56 days of wonder. A scant four weeks ago, it was a single cell, a unique joining of one sperm and one egg. Four weeks from now, all of the major organs will be formed and in place; your child will look human. At this halfway moment, however, the embryo might be mistaken for a stork embryo. (Where *do* babies come from?) Or perhaps for the embryo of a

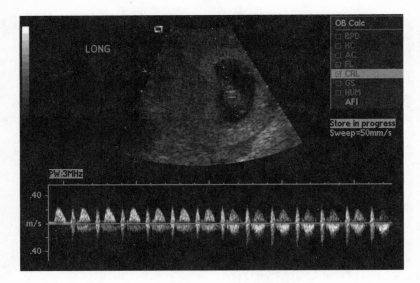

OB Calc
□ BPD
□ HC
□ AC
□ FL
☑ CRL
□ GS
□ HUM
AFI

Store in progress
Sweep=50mm/s

PW:3MHz

A beating heart

future cherished pet dog, cat, hamster, or goldfish. But outward appearances can mask hidden truths.

By this time, most women know they are pregnant. The changes a woman feels in her body and her delayed period are, more often than not, too clear to be ignored. A pregnancy test should be boldly positive. But this knowledge is personal and intimate. Others only know the truth if she has shared the news with them. She has not begun to "show."

Concealed inside is a tiny collection of millions of living cells. Unlike the first few that looked and acted like twins, these cells are a complex citizenry composed of many different cultures. Some parts (notably the tail and the gills) will soon be absorbed into the human culture and disappear.

The embryo is now about 4 mm long, about the size of a capital C. He or she curls into the fetal position and floats silently in a saltwater sea of amniotic fluid—not unlike a tiny sea of tears or a salty soup (more on that later). The embryo is literally hanging by a thread—the thread-thin umbilical cord through which the mother (and father) already feed the baby and carry away the dirty diapers (waste filtering by primitive kidneys has already begun). But this thread is strong and alive and can be the safest place to call home. Meanwhile, the embryo, hidden from sight and sound and touch, carries secrets of its own.

Hints of the Future

The fourth week after conception brings strong hints of the future. The specialized cells begin to take their places throughout the body; the colonists that will soon build a host of new organs have arrived. These colonies of cells are already starting to function before the organs take recognizable shape: a simple brain, a beating heart, a network of nerve cells, sensory cells that are starting to respond to stimuli. Clusters of cells that will become eyes are now visible as two discs. Similarly, the cells that will become the ears, stomach, liver, and lungs are in place, though not as easily identified. All of this in something the size of a grain of rice! The director has called, "Places!" The actors have found their positions and are ready for the drama to unfold.

The Second Month (Weeks 5 Through 8) After Conception

As if they were being filmed with time-lapse photography, the primitive organs rapidly begin to take shape. This is another vulnerable time for the baby. Earlier threats were more likely to have wide-ranging effects throughout the body. Threats at this time are more likely to affect the organs developing the most on that day.

During this period, the age of a baby is estimated by its *crown-rump length*. The crown, of course, is not the headwear of a little prince or princess destined to rule, but the topmost point of the head. The rump end of the measurement is on the midline of the body, between the tops of the buttocks. In the fifth week after conception, the crown-rump length is 5 to 8 millimeters.

Week 5 After Conception (Seven Weeks from the Last Menstrual Period)

Development proceeds on a need-two-now basis: the heart and the brain are vital for development, so they assemble quickly. The baby won't be eating for a while, so the gastrointestinal (GI) system can wait a bit.

This week the primitive heart transforms into a four-chambered marvel in less time than it takes me to finish building a K'Nex roller coaster with my kids (some adult assembly required). By the end of the week, the similarity to an adult human heart is conspicuous.

Meanwhile, the brain grows both larger and more complex. Within the week, it increases in size by about 40 percent and arranges itself into five different parts. Already the cells that will be the cerebral cortex, the home of conscious thought, are starting to connect.

Little nubbins of arms and legs appear, the suggestion of an ear, the hint of a nose, but this week belongs to the heart and the head—the life force and the essence, the producer and the director. Together, the heart and the brain make up about half of the body (and that includes the tail, which is at its longest this week).

Week 6 After Conception

As a general rule of thumb, development proceeds from head to tail (which, by the way, starts to shorten and disappear this week). This week the face begins to come together. The ears become visible bumps; the muscles that will turn the eyes to look at you in the delivery room start to form; the nose area hooks up to the brain via nerve cells. The gills disappear. The two halves of the jaw fuse. The beginnings of teeth appear, although you won't likely see them until your baby has learned to sit on her own and perhaps be fed with a spoon. The muscles that your baby will use to smile (and to cry) make their debut.

The upper limbs develop before the lower. First the arm buds lengthen and then divisions appear, portents of shoulders, arms, elbows, wrists, and hands. By the end of the week, the primal hand is dividing into fingers. The legs and feet follow suit in three or four days.

The simple tube of the GI tract segments itself into the esophagus, stomach, liver, and so on. And the liver begins growing your baby's own blood cells, successfully stealing this job from the yolk sac.

The yolk sac also loses its other job, preparing the sex cells. These flee the shriveling sac and take up their places on the body where the baby's sex organs will develop.

At the end of this week, the crown-rump length is 10 to 14 millimeters, about half an inch long, or the size of a blueberry. The embryo weighs less than a liter of air, a paper clip, or a five-carat diamond (which all weigh about 1 gram). But this little crown-rump featherweight is strikingly complex and changing at a pace that almost defies imagination.

Healthy Babies and Mom's Healthy Smile

While you are thinking about your baby's developing teeth and gums, it's a good time to think about your own. The right dental treatment can increase the odds of giving birth to a healthy baby. One recent study looked at hundreds of pregnant women who had previously given birth to premature babies, and who were at high risk of doing so again. All of the women in the study had gum disease. Those whose gum disease was treated had an 84 percent reduction in premature births! The study suggests that it would be wise for women who are pregnant or who are considering becoming pregnant to have their gums examined. Dental x-rays, though, are unsafe during pregnancy. The authors recommend that gum disease be treated either before pregnancy or during the second trimester to help give the best start to the new baby.

Meanwhile, the brain and heart continue to develop rapidly. The heart is pumping blood through an increasingly complex circulatory system. The brain has divided into the parts that will control emotion, thought, and movement. And it is online, connected to the spinal cord and clearly regulating bodily functions such as heartbeat and muscle contraction.

And at the end of this week, your baby develops a sense of smell.

What Is There for the Baby to Smell? The amniotic fluid is like a living bowl of salty soup. The cells in the baby's nose can detect the ingredients in that soup and send messages about them to the brain. The composition of the amniotic fluid varies from woman to woman and from time to time, partly depending on what she eats.

Smell is an important component of flavor. I remember the elementary school science experiment where I held my nose, closed my eyes, and tasted slices of apple and raw potato. Without smell, I couldn't tell the difference between the two.

Does What the Baby Smells in the Womb Make a Difference Later? Soon after babies are born, they are able to use smell alone to pick out their mother's nursing pads from those of other mothers. Perhaps one way they prepare to do this is by becoming familiar with the unique smell of their amniotic fluid before birth. After birth, babies clearly select and prefer the smell of their amniotic fluid from that of others.

We don't know everything that goes into creating the individually unique aroma of amniotic fluid, but one ingredient is Mom's diet. This was first discovered when garlic was smelled in the fluid of women who had eaten garlic.

Careful studies have since suggested that the flavors and smells of amniotic fluid teach babies much about the foods and aromas of their local culture—what they should trust and what they should not. Preferences for ethnic cuisine appear to be present by birth.

Dr. Julie Mennella carried this a step further with a fascinating study involving carrot juice. As part of the study, one group of pregnant women drank 10 ounces of carrot juice four times a week for three consecutive weeks. Another group of women in the study drank water. Months later, after the babies had been born and had grown enough to have been eating cereal for four weeks, it was time to look for a difference between the groups. An observer who did not know which group each baby belonged to studied the babies as they ate cereal mixed with carrot juice. There was a dramatic difference. Those who had sampled carrot juice in the amniotic fluid readily accepted and enjoyed the carrot juice in the cereal. Those who had missed this earlier experience protested and made unhappy faces when they tasted the carrot.

Parents ask me every week how to help their children learn to like vegetables and other healthy foods. During pregnancy may be the easiest time to influence the trajectory of your child's later diet. Eat the foods now that you will want him to eat later. Avoid the junk foods that you don't want her developing a taste for.

Week 7 After Conception

Development continues to proceed at a phenomenal pace. Each time the moon circles the earth and is again overhead, the baby hidden inside has changed appreciably. By the end of the week, the crown-rump length will be about 22 millimeters, or more than three-quarters of an inch—a 50 percent increase from the week before. You can picture the size of your baby this week if you have a pocketful of change. The crown-rump length of the image of George Washington on a quarter is about 22 millimeters (if you assume the end of his ponytail is the rump). Like your baby, his head makes up about half the image.

Unlike your baby, George's upper lip is already complete. By the time your baby is nine weeks along, his tiny upper lip will have grown all the way across, and your little one will have one more thing in common with the first U.S. president.

A Splash of Color. So far, the dramatic event unfolding inside has been a dazzling but colorless affair. This is the week the very first pigmented cells in the body appear.

For the first time, pigmented eyes now add color to the developing face. In children and adults, blue eyes are a recessive trait. At least three gene locations are involved in eye color inheritance; only two of them are well understood. At the first "green-blue" location, you get a vote (gene) for green or blue from each parent. If both votes are blue, blue wins the primary. But because green is dominant over blue, just one vote for green makes it the winner. At the second "brown-blue" location, you get a vote for brown or blue from each parent. Again, if both votes are blue, blue wins this second tally, but even one vote for brown makes brown the winner. To get eye color, combine the two totals. Brown is dominant over green, which is dominant over blue. Just one brown gene means that brown is the ultimate winner. If no brown genes are inherited, just one green gene means that green is the winner. If all four genes are blue, the eyes will be blue.

For all four genes to be blue, you must inherit two blue genes from each parent. A blue-eyed parent has only blue genes to pass on. A brown-eyed parent has at least one brown gene. The other genes may be brown or blue or green. A green-eyed parent must have at least at least two blue genes (having inherited a blue from each parent at the brown-blue location) and at least one green gene. The remaining gene may be green or blue and will determine if that parent can ever have blue-eyed children.

I have blue eyes. My youngest son has green eyes. He must have received two blue genes from me and a blue gene (in the blue-brown vote) and a green gene (in the blue-green vote) from his mother. But her eyes are hazel. Hazel, gray, and black eyes involve variations added by the less well-understood third location. And the inheritance is even more complicated in practice, because eye color is linked to skin and hair color as well.

You might enjoy trying a nifty online interactive eye color calculator for expecting parents, which helps you predict your baby's eye color based on your (and perhaps your parents') eye colors. You can find the link at www.DrGreene.com. Just type "eye colors" into the search box there.

But whatever color you will see when you look at your child's kindergarten photo, the eyes appear blue in the seventh week after conception. Often, the baby's eyes still appear blue at birth. Final eye color may not be evident until the time she is rolling over or setting off on her own across the floor.

What Difference Does Eye Color Make? Is eye color simply decorative? Something to help us attract each other, like the vibrant plumage on a bird? Something to give us family or community identity? Or is there a functional significance as well?

The brown pigment present to a greater or lesser degree in the iris of the eyes is the same melanin found in the skin to protect from ultraviolet damage. The melanin absorbs some of the light, letting less of it into the eyes. Surprisingly, the blue color in mature eyes is not blue pigment. Eyes are blue like the sky is blue, because of the way they scatter light.

As you might guess, those whose ancestors lived closer to the equator are more likely to have dark eyes. Those whose ancestors lived closer to the poles have lighter eyes that are less protective, allowing more light deeper into the eye.

Those with brown eyes are relatively more protected from melanoma (and other skin cancers), from certain eye cancers, and from macular degeneration (cumulative damage to the retina from too much sunlight). The cells of the retina are irreplaceable. Macular degeneration is a leading cause of blindness. Brown eyes (and sunglasses) tend to protect the retina.

Research also suggests, for completely unknown reasons, that children with brown eyes who get meningitis are less likely to have hearing loss as a complication. I only mention this tidbit to illustrate that all of this marvelous development is far more interconnected and complex than we could ever understand.

Blue eyes or green eyes provide relatively more protection against cataracts, a clouding of the lens. One of the great wonders of the new human body developing within is its ability to repair or replace damaged cells. The story of replenishment, replacement, and repair is repeated in almost every part of the body. The lens of the eye is a notable exception. Already at seven weeks after conception, the lens is floating free in the eye. The cells of the lens will never be replaced; once complete, the proteins of the lens are never replenished. The lens cannot repair itself; damage accumulates over a lifetime. Light-colored eyes (and sunglasses) tend to protect the lens.

People with blue or green eyes are also more likely to develop freckles or moles. Interestingly, research suggests that people with lighter eye color are less likely to be depressed or fatigued in the winter (a condition called seasonal affective disorder).

As we will discuss later, the right sunglasses can be very important for kids—and not just because it makes them look so cool. Wearing sunglasses during childhood is one of the best things you can do to protect your child's vision later in life. Why mention this so early in your pregnancy?

Every pregnant woman is a pair of designer UV400 sunglasses. Your baby's translucent skin offers almost no protection to the rapidly growing tissues that would be exquisitely vulnerable to the sun. For now, you are your child's sunglasses and sunscreen, shade and shelter. Without even thinking about it, you are totally protecting your child from dangerous ultraviolet rays all around you that would otherwise have a deadly impact.

Superman is vulnerable to Kryptonite. Its presence quickly withers him. But shield him with lead and power courses through his veins.

Your tiny superman is even more vulnerable to the rays from our sun. But his mother is a protective shield that allows his body to accomplish intricate and powerful feats that we are only beginning to understand.

Is It a Boy or a Girl? This is the week that a tiny "penis" is visible. What surprises many is that it is present in both boys and girls. In girls, this protrusion will become the clitoris; in boys, the definitive penis. For now we call this an indifferent penis (although, *indifferent* is an interesting word to pair with *penis*). Parents often think that if you don't see genitals on an ultrasound you probably have a girl and if you see a penis, it is definitely a boy. That's true—if you wait long enough to take a look. If you could see your baby perfectly right now, you still couldn't tell.

This is also the week that teeny, tiny eyelids form to cover those baby blues we were talking about earlier. How cute is that?

Week 8 After Conception

This is the week where it all comes together. This baby began as a tiny dot of cells that didn't have a crown or rump to measure. After forming an amaz-

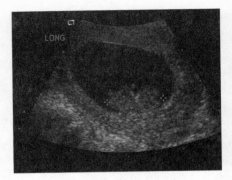 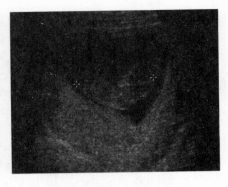

54 days after conception   60 days after conception–what a difference a few days can make!

ing connection in the placenta, dizzying change and growth have led us by Day 56 to a tiny, well-formed human who is 30 millimeters long, or about 1½ inches from stem to stern. The same crown-rump length as John F. Kennedy's image on a half dollar! But the baby weighs only ⅟₅₀₀ of a pound.

And is magnificently, wondrously complete. No longer an egg or a morula or a blastocyst, it is now ready to graduate officially from embryo to human fetus. To be sure, there is still work to be done; the baby could not yet survive outside of the mother. And there is lots of growth to come. But the creation of different organs and systems now gives way to maturation and growth, not head-spinning change.

Your little one now has elbows and knees, eyelids and nipples, and hair follicles on the chin and upper lip that would have been hard to imagine just weeks ago. A diaphragm separates the lungs in the chest from the intestines in the belly. Functioning kidneys allow the baby to contribute to its own fluid-filled world. The little gourmet even has working taste buds (don't forget the carrot juice!). And on those baby feet with teensy separate toes are brand-new footprints.

A Sigh of Relief

We have just observed one of the most complicated, massive building projects ever conceived, on a time schedule that boggles the mind. Proportionally, it outmatches the building of the Pyramids or a modern skyscraper.

Dozens of experts couldn't conceivably coordinate and manage this phenomenal cascade of events.

And yet this wonder of the world has happened successfully again and again throughout history with everyday parents. This was your own story, before memory, inside your own mother. And it was hers before you.

Your baby has already made it through life's most precarious time (more babies are miscarried before Day 56 than are carried full term—often without parents ever knowing they were pregnant). You have already ferried your baby safely across the period of greatest changes and most critical growth.

The everyday miracle of unfolding development does not stop on Day 56, but continues throughout pregnancy. And the choreography continues after birth—here is the great news—just as naturally. It continues through your baby learning to nurse, to lift her head, to say "dada," to take her first steps. And it will continue after the story of this book, when she starts to toddle, to throw tantrums, to do her homework, to drive a car, and to move away from home.

Your role as parents in all of this is crucial. Understanding your child's development can make yours easier and more rewarding. But being a parent does not call for you to be a superhero or a developmental genius. Your job is simply to do what you can to provide a safe, nurturing, gently stimulating space for life and love to unfold. And, of course, to clean up the poop!

5

Proactive Parenting

Parent Time

"Trust yourself. You know more than you think you do." These are the immortal opening words of the towering *Dr. Spock's Baby and Child Care*, which has sold over 50 million copies and influenced generations of parents since it was first published in 1946. Today I am sitting at the collapsible table in Tortes, the Winnebago that belonged to the late Dr. Benjamin Spock and his wonderful wife, Mary Morgan. Their picture smiles down at me, an inspiration.

The exquisite choreography of development we witnessed in the previous chapters also inspires parents, reminding us of the deep wisdom that is built into us and into the parenting process. This foundational truth allows us to relax. At the same time, it gives us the confidence to take an active role as parents.

Teach Your Children

As we saw in the last chapter, when mothers drank carrot juice during pregnancy, it changed the way their babies responded to carrot juice. This is interesting nutritionally. It's also interesting in what it says about the functioning of the sensory organs before birth. But I find it especially arresting because of what it tells us about how we teach our children.

Even before our babies are born, we are teaching them about the wide world around us. We communicate our choices, our values, even without thinking about it.

We'll see in future chapters how our babies learn from what they see and hear *during pregnancy*. After they are born, they will continue to learn, day and night, from what we say and do. Within a couple of years, they will learn to speak and understand our language, just from listening to us speak and trying to imitate what we say. This is quite an accomplishment. When was the last time you learned a language? Imagine tackling another and becoming fluent in the next two years. Meanwhile, babies will also be learning the figurative language of our habits, our relationships, our emotions.

This truth hit home to me one day as my toddling son finished brushing his teeth. When he was done, he tapped his toothbrush on the side of the sink to dry it—tap, tap-tap, tap-tap, tap. It was precisely my habitual toothbrush percussion rhythm! But I had never noticed before that I had this minor routine. He had.

A Fresh Start

When I meet with parents before their baby is born, I like to take a moment to reflect with them about this momentous time. I often ask them to consider what habits they now have that they wish they had avoided. What would they change in their lives if they had known earlier what they know now?

The answers I hear often mirror the topics you see on magazine covers in supermarket check-out lines. People wish they ate better, weighed less, exercised more, and managed their finances more wisely. Given a fresh start, some would go out for football or learn to play the piano or speak Spanish. Some focus on credit cards and how easy it is to get in too deep. Others' greatest wish is that they had learned how to have mutually satisfying relationships without so many painful missteps.

Having a child is one of life's great fresh starts. It can give smokers the extra oomph they need to stop smoking and spenders the extra thought for the future they need to start investing.

This is a powerful time for parents; it can also make a huge difference for children. They are masters of observation and imitation—even before they are born. They will learn about how their parents really live (not what they say they believe, but what they believe in practice). If you want to teach your baby about things you are not yet doing, this is a great time to start doing them! Even the attempt will teach her that these things matter to you.

For instance, parents often identify overspending as a problem they would like their children to avoid. How might they address this? Children have a

legitimate need for new experiences. In order for play to be fun, it has to involve some degree of novelty. Kids can satisfy this deep thirst for newness by always getting new stuff, but this can lead to costly habits down the road (financially and emotionally). It can lead to the oft-repeated refrain, "I'm bored!" However, kids can also satisfy this strong drive by learning to discover new ways to enjoy the things they already have. This can lead to growing creativity and imagination, as well as fun that satisfies more deeply, relationships that last, and credit card balances that can be paid off. We'll talk about how parents and kids can learn this fun skill together, by both curtailing overspending and enjoying the adventure of creative alternatives, in a later chapter.

Once parents have identified one or two things they would most like to change, I like to talk with them about strategies for teaching these things to their kids. I'd be happy to brainstorm ideas for your specific areas with you at www.DrGreene.com during my daily chats.

Teaching your children is a core part of parenting. This will get increasingly multidimensional as pregnancy progresses and even more so as your child grows after birth. For now, teaching starts with what you eat.

Eating for Three

I'm a fan of delicious, healthy nutrition being a family matter. Eating together is a bonding experience that goes back to the beginning of human history. Getting and preparing food for someone can be a tangible way to express love and connectedness.

Research on obese children has taught us some interesting perspectives about family dynamics. Often the obese child doesn't eat worse or exercise less than other members of the family. Instead, he doesn't have a metabolism that can get away with unhealthy patterns as easily as others can. Having the child eat better or exercise more often leads to disappointing results. The habits are too ingrained, supported by peer pressure, a sedentary culture, and a mega-advertised, supersized food industry.

However, if the whole family—those who appear to need help and those who don't—makes changes together, the results are far better. If the family makes active play a daily habit and healthy food the delicious norm, this can be stronger than the avalanche of forces conspiring against improvement.

Expecting a new baby is a great time for a couple or family to eat for that baby—together. This doesn't mean that Dad and the other kids should take prenatal vitamins, but that everyone involved can eat in ways that support health, for themselves and for the new member of the family who is depending on them for nutrition.

This new baby has never seen a TV ad or a convenience store check-out counter, but she may still be getting a day-glow orange, partially hydrogenated, artificial, high-fat, processed cheese food product for lunch.

A serving of junk food isn't a reason to feel guilty, but pregnancy is a wonderful time to be aware of what you are eating as a family and to choose whatever you will feel best about.

Cravings

Eggs, olives, and potato chips. These were the foods the BBC announced Madonna craved during her second pregnancy. Most women's cravings aren't international news, but stories of cravings do enliven family histories, child-birth groups, Internet parenting sites, TV sitcom plots, and countless magazine articles.

For the record, my wife Cheryl had a craving for tuna fish sandwiches. An intense, drop-everything, I-need-a-tuna-fish-sandwich-now craving. We knew the location of every sandwich shop in our town and the surrounding towns, as well as which sandwiches were acceptable (a judgment that was by no means consistent).

My mother reports no prominent cravings when pregnant with me or my twin sisters (and we all turned out just fine).

Who Gets Cravings?

Mothers who are teens and thirtysomethings; rich and poor; rural and urban; American, African, European, Australian, Asian, and Indian—all have reported pronounced cravings. I've even known partners of pregnant women to get sympathy cravings. Some studies put the sudden-intense-desire rate as high as 86 percent of all pregnant women; others put the number as low as 33 percent. Most studies estimate more than 50 percent. But the different studies ask the questions differently, so they are hard to compare.

One study in South Africa posed the same questions about cravings to what they called "rural black, urban black, Indian, colored (European-African-Malay), and white" populations and found pronounced cravings in most women in each of the groups (results ranged from 67 to 84 per-cent—not different enough to be significant). In a study in Saudi Arabia, researchers found no differences between education levels and pregnancy food habits. A study in Sri Lanka found that pregnancy cravings were "significantly higher in women who married after a love affair than in those who had an arranged marriage." And they were also more common in those who believed in devil dancing and gods than in those who did not. Perhaps these women were more attuned to the instincts of their bodies than to the dictates of the rational mind.

However you define the women who get them, cravings are common.

What Do Women Crave?

Pickles and ice cream are a famously craved combination and a good example of how individual and unusual craved items might be. I know women who have had cravings for salted tomatoes in milk, ice chips, cough drops in spaghetti sauce, and elementary school paste. I had one patient whose pregnant mother craved the aroma of new doorknobs. (Remember, the sense of smell intensifies during pregnancy. I have never been able to smell doorknobs, new or otherwise.)

What Do Women Reject?

Food aversions during pregnancy are about as common as food cravings, even though they don't get as much press. Why the void? After all, unanticipated repugnance for once-loved foods seems like interesting enough sitcom fodder. But because cravings tend to be more situational and specific, they also tend to be more compelling stories. Cravings are often of the immediate "I want it and I want it right now and I mean now" variety, whereas aversions are more of an ongoing, steady "I can't stand the sight of it or especially the smell of it" phenomenon. Cravings can be quite specific—"I want Snyder's of Hanover Kosher Dill Potato Chips dipped in Ben and Jerry's Organic Chocolate Fudge Brownie Ice Cream, now, please, honey." Aversions are often to general categories—"I'm a meat-lover, but now meat makes me nauseous. And the aroma of coffee in the morning? Ewwwwww!"

Just as with cravings, there are "bestseller" lists of aversions. South African pregnant women of all ethnicities were most likely to find meat, fish, coffee, or fatty foods repugnant. Saudi Arabian women were most likely to express a new distaste for milk, dates, fungreek (an ingredient in hot curry dishes), tea, coffee, colas, or meat. The early U.S. study pointed to meats, poultry, coffee, alcohol, and sauces flavored with oregano. Tennessee teens voiced a newfound loathing for meat, eggs, and pizza. Vegetarians were most likely to hate vegetables (yes, vegetables!), strong-smelling and strong-tasting combination dishes, greasy foods, coffee, tea, and alcohol. In the large Sherman and Flaxman study, meat, fish, poultry, eggs, coffee, tea, soda, and vegetables were the most-repugnant winners.

So vegetarian women may crave meat and loathe vegetables; meat lovers may find themselves hating meat. Aversions are most common toward foods

Chocoholics Anonymous

Researchers have attempted to categorize craved items and have come up with different lists of the most common groups. The South African study mentioned earlier reported that the top pregnancy foods are sour foods, savory foods, sweet foods, fruit, and milk (that about covers it!). In some populations in this study, earth and clay also made the top of the list. A study in the *Indian Journal of Public Health* listed the top-craved foods in the following order: sour foods (65 percent), unripe fruits (40 percent), meat and fish (47 percent), ripe fruits (30 percent), food from almsgiving (26 percent), and jam and bread fruit (22 percent). What do women in Saudi Arabia suddenly feel they can't live without? Salty foods, sour foods, sweets, dates, milk, eggs, and meats. Clay, ice, plaster, and paper made the list but weren't quite as popular.

One of the first scientific studies on pregnancy cravings was in the United States, where women reported pining for milk, ice cream, sweets, candy (particularly chocolate), fruits, and fish. In another study, Tennessee teens in particular longed for sweets (especially chocolate), fruits and fruit juices, fast foods, pickles, ice cream, and pizza. Another study of only vegetarian women found the most common urgently desired foods to be high-protein foods (especially milk), followed by fruits and sweets. Chocolate was not specified among the sweets, but ladies, what do *you* think?

The largest study to date, which also led to the most powerful statement of the purpose of food cravings and aversions, was conducted by Sherman and Flaxman from the Department of Neurobiology and Behavior at Cornell University. It included interviews with 6,239 women. Leading the yearned-for list (in order) were fruits and fruit juices, then sweets, desserts, and chocolates, followed by dairy and ice cream. All categories of food showed up somewhere on the list.

that spoil easily or can naturally contain toxins. Women with specific needs for individual foods are less likely to be averse to them. If a woman has anemia, for example, she may be less likely to develop an aversion to iron-containing foods such as liver. Food aversions are most likely to arise when the risks of a type of food outweigh the benefits of that food for a particular woman or group of women.

Where Do Cravings Come From?

Scientifically, cravings are harder to pin down than aversions. One school of thought is that cravings are primarily psychological. When you're pregnant, because you are eating for two and cravings are to be expected, you give yourself permission to desire (and eat) a hot fudge sundae with extra hot fudge that your willpower would ordinarily make you resist. There may be a bit of truth to this, but on the other hand, I've not met many women who wait to get pregnant to give themselves permission to gorge out on pickles, cabbage, or laundry starch.

Another school of thought suggests that the changing food desires throughout pregnancy are just a side effect of fluctuating hormone levels, with no real significance for the mother or the baby. Researchers who support this view often point to similar but less dramatic cravings preceding menstrual periods and during menopause as supporting evidence. This may be partly true, but the general trajectory of taste preferences during pregnancy seems uncannily to parallel the changing needs of the baby. And the pinpoint cravings many women experience seem too utterly specific to be only happenstance.

Yet another trend of thought has been to try, with varying success, to tie the cravings to nutritional needs of the mom or the baby. This line of thinking is supported by the work of Valerie Duffy, Ph.D., in the Yale Pregnancy Study. Her team followed changes in taste preference throughout pregnancy. Women tended to have a heightened perception of bitter tastes in the first trimester, perhaps to warn them against consuming infected meats, toxic plants, or alcohol during this critical period. Perception of bitter tastes returned to normal later in pregnancy. In contrast, the perception and preference for sour foods tended to be much higher in the second and third trimesters than before or after pregnancy (is this where the pickle thing comes from?). A taste for sour foods is known to promote a more varied diet. It also increases fruit consumption (fruits are high in nutrients and high on lists of craved foods). A preference for sweets peaked in the second trimester, which is when the need for calories increases and the fetus needs more glucose for body growth. A preference for salty foods increased steadily throughout pregnancy, as the need for retaining more fluid in the circulation increased (here are those pickles again—and Madonna's potato chips).

This line of reasoning gets even more specific. Perhaps vegetarian women who crave meat do so because their bodies know that they need extra protein, iron, zinc, or vitamin B_{12}. Perhaps women who crave fish are actually hungering for fish oils that contain DHA and ARA, which are important omega-3 and -6 fatty acids that aid their baby's brain growth. And perhaps those who crave dirt are experiencing a yearning for iron that they need in their diet.

The problem with this line of thought is that when looked at scientifically, beyond a few clear examples, the needed nutrients are often not present in the foods craved. At best, the cravings line up haphazardly with deficiencies, which has led researchers to shake their heads in frustration. The evidence just doesn't add up. I have a theory about why this is and what cravings mean.

Referred Pining

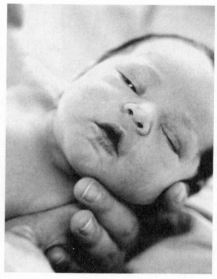

When I was in medical school, I was fascinated to learn about a phenomenon that we call *referred pain*. This is pain felt at a distance from the true source. A classic example is pain from a heart attack felt along the left arm. This happens because the same nerve is supposed to detect problems in the heart and the arm. When the nerve is irritated, the brain has to guess where the problem is—and the guess often includes the arm, even when the arm is uninjured and the heart is in jeopardy. Because of the powerful, observable fact of referred pain, physicians view pain as a signal that something is wrong—but we don't assume that the problem is in the same spot that hurts. Irritation of the diaphragm muscle often hurts a specific place in the shoulder. Lung problems may show up as back pain. Or pain behind the belly button may result from a hidden problem in the lower right belly at the appendix.

I propose that cravings are a type of "referred pining." The cravings are a true signal that the body is yearning for specific nutrients, but these nutrients may or may not be present in the specific foods craved. The craved foods just happen to be on the same desire pathway as the mother's real needs. Cravings for calcium-rich foods may indeed suggest a need for more calcium and desires for salty foods, for more salt. Cravings for clay, earth, and ice chips may suggest a need for iron or other minerals, even if the minerals are not found in the objects desired. Other cravings may be less straightforward.

Devil Dancing and Gods

I suggest that women neither blindly follow cravings as if they are godlike insights nor reject them as devilish phantasms in the face of a modern scientific understanding of prenatal nutrition. Rather, I recommend paying attention to cravings and responding to them in light of what you know about what your body needs.

If the craving is for something healthy, you may just want to go for it, although I still like considering what the cravings may be saying to you. It might be time to pull out a list of the nutrients needed in pregnancy (see the discussion in the next chapter) and see if anything rings a bell. If a craving is for something potentially unhealthy (raw fish or too much tuna), find another way to get the nutrients your body may be yearning for (such as salmon, walnuts, or flaxseed). Be aware that if your craving is for supersized chocolate volcano sundaes and you eat whatever you desire, you may end up with more hip souvenirs from the pregnancy than you want.

Thankfully, just a little bit of the craved food is often enough to satisfy.

6

Food for Thought

Eating for the Future

I've stuffed this chapter with information you can marry with your intuition to help you make wise choices. It will help you appreciate and remember to take your prenatal vitamins and will sharpen your instincts about how to eat well. And this is the chapter that discusses chocolate during pregnancy (chocolate while nursing comes later). But be warned—we also talk about liver.

⭐ **A Wise Question**
How does what I eat feed my baby? Does it all come through like in breast milk? Or does the placenta protect them from junk food in my diet?

Burlingame

Eat—It's Good for You

The basic structure of a fetus at 56 days is largely complete, but over the months remaining until birth, it will increase in size by a staggering 1,000 times! Nutrients that Mom eats during pregnancy or that she has eaten beforehand will be the exclusive fuel and the raw material building blocks of this fantastic growth. There is nothing else.

This is a special time. A mother and baby together have different nutritional requirements than either of them will ever have alone. Because the mother is the one doing the eating, we'll look at these needs from the perspective of changes that may be needed in the mother's diet.

Sadly, nutrition has not been an adequate priority in mainline medicine. The current 2002 edition of my favorite obstetrics textbook still contains nutritional advice based on the 1989 Recommended Dietary Allowances (RDAs). We've learned a lot about nutrition since then, but much of it hasn't filtered into physicians' texts, much less popular parenting books. The data in this book are current as of the most recent Dietary Reference Intakes for each nutrient at the time of publication. Prenatal vitamins are designed with these recommendations in mind.

But throughout this chapter, keep in mind that the handful of vitamins and minerals in the tablets are just the Hollywood stars of nutrition. Each whole food contains a cast of thousands of micronutrients that we are just beginning to understand. Some of these important "extras" don't even have names yet. A diet rich in a variety of foods in which the "leading actor" nutrients occur naturally is probably the best diet for pregnancy.

The prenatal vitamin is a spectacular safety net. Getting extra of these same nutrients from food is generally great, but taking more vitamins as additional supplements is unnecessary, unwise, and potentially unsafe.

Folate and Iron

Out of all the vitamins, minerals, and other nutrients in our diets, we only know of two whose requirements increase by 50 percent or more during pregnancy: one is a vitamin—folate (also known as folic acid)—and one is a mineral—iron. A deficiency of either folate or iron can lead to anemia in the mother and in the baby.

The baby uses folate when forming its neural tube, the ancestor to the brain and spinal cord. To do this, adequate supplies of folate are most important at about 21 to 28 days after conception. This is the reason that getting plenty of folate around the time of conception can help prevent birth abnormalities called *neural tube defects*. Women who eat plenty of folate-rich foods can store folate supplies for two or three months.

Folate occurs naturally in a variety of foods, including green (especially leafy) vegetables, dry beans, peas, and fruits. In addition, it enriches organ meats such as liver and kidney, although cooking can destroy folate. Much of it is lost when boiling food or cooking it at a high temperature.

Prevention of neural tube defects is the poster child for folate supplementation. But folate is also critically important whenever a new copy of DNA is made. Each new cell in the baby's rapidly growing body requires a new copy of his DNA. In addition, folate is critical for the process of cell division. It's a necessary ingredient as the one-celled fertilized egg divides and divides, again and again, into the trillions of cells present at birth. About six weeks after conception, the baby's nervous system alone is adding about 100,000 new nerve cells an hour!

Clearly, women are meant to eat more of at least some folate-rich foods during pregnancy. Folate is one important reason, but there may also be other nutrients in these foods whose requirements we have yet to understand. Perhaps folate is a reason that fruits, fruit juices, and sour foods are so often the foods of dreams at this time.

Women who could possibly get pregnant should get at least 400 micrograms of folate per day. During pregnancy, the recommendation increases to at least 600 micrograms per day. A survey of typical American women from 1988 to 1994 estimated an average woman got about 250 micrograms per day. Those who ate lots of fruits and veggies got more. In 1998, a federal law mandated that enriched cereal grains include folate. Now the typical American adult probably gets about 340 micrograms a day from food.

Prenatal vitamins usually have 1,000 micrograms (equal to 1 milligram) of folate. This is equivalent to getting about 500 micrograms of folate from foods, which should be plenty with just a little extra help from the diet.

Iron requirements also soar during pregnancy. Both the mother and the baby need iron to build red blood cells. A pregnant woman's blood supply increases by one-third over the course of the pregnancy. Babies must grow their entire blood supply from scratch—and scratch includes iron. Iron is also a foundational building block of muscles and of a number of enzymes that carry out vital processes throughout the body.

Iron occurs naturally in a number of foods. These include fruits and vegetables such as raisins, apricots, prunes (and prune juice), spinach, kale, and other greens. We get iron when we eat legumes such as dried beans, soybeans, peas, and lentils, as well as grains such as oatmeal. Especially rich sources of iron include meat, fish, poultry, and eggs. Liver tops the list. As with folate, there may be nutrients other than iron that promote eating these foods during pregnancy. Perhaps iron is one reason why women lay awake dreaming of some of these foods (I can almost smell the juicy cheeseburger with sliced apricots).

A savvy meal planner and smart cookware can turn up the heat on iron intake. Eating or drinking foods high in vitamin C (such as orange juice) at the same time as foods high in iron helps the body to absorb and use the iron. Cooking in cast-iron pans can also add iron to foods.

Many foods, especially cereal grains, are now iron-fortified. The iron here is poorly absorbed, but manufacturers have dumped in enough iron to make up for this. In addition, prenatal vitamins contain plenty of iron.

Pregnant women need about 27 milligrams of iron per day to supply themselves and their babies adequately. A healthy baby born at term should have a store of about 500 milligrams of iron in her body, all of it a gift from her parents.

Vitamin B_6 and Iodine

The requirements for two other nutrients increase by more than 40 percent during pregnancy. Again, we have one vitamin and one mineral: vitamin B_6 and iodine.

Vitamin B_6, also called pyridoxine, is actually a group of six closely related compounds. This gang of six functions as coenzymes in over 100 different important metabolic processes, including the creation of serotonin and other neurotransmitters that help you feel good and think fast. B_6 is vital for normal brain and muscle function, and it is used by the body to help remove unwanted excess metals. Most B_6 is stored in muscles, where it can remain for quite a long time.

What Dad Eats Counts Too

Dad's diet, like Mom's, may help babies before they are even born. Researchers have found that men who take in enough folate may make their offspring less susceptible to cancer later in life, according to a study published in the February 2001 *Fertility and Sterility*. For years, women have been encouraged to get enough folate to help prevent birth defects. Now, folate appears to encourage strong, healthy sperm that produce healthier kids. This breakthrough suggests that other choices in Dad's life not yet studied may also play a role in the strength and vitality of his sperm and the subsequent health of his children.

Pregnant women need 1.9 milligrams per day of vitamin B_6. As with folate, B_6 is often destroyed by cooking. Most charts I've seen list B_6 as occurring primarily in milk, muscle meat, and organ meats (liver), but you don't have to eat meat to get enough. Thankfully, B_6 is also present in large amounts in a great many fruits, vegetables, grains, nuts, seeds, legumes, fish, and poultry. A baked potato has about 0.7 milligrams—the same as a raw banana. A half cup of cooked beans has a bit less, but the same amount as half a cooked chicken breast. A 3-ounce serving of pork loin has 0.42 milligrams, about the same amount as an avocado, a 12-ounce glass of tomato juice, or 2 ounces of sunflower seeds. A 3-ounce serving of roast beef has about 0.32 milligrams, about the same as 2 ounces of walnuts or 1 cup of spinach.

Typical American women get about 1.4 milligrams per day from their diets, enough for their nonpregnant needs. Increasing your variety of whole foods should do the trick during pregnancy. Moreover, prenatal vitamins contain plenty of B_6.

Iodine is a mineral essential for the normal functioning of the thyroid gland. This is especially important for developing babies because thyroid hormone regulates the developing brain, heart, kidneys, muscles, and pituitary gland. Mothers also need more for themselves during pregnancy.

Iodine occurs abundantly in foods and plants grown in the sea. Even where the sea is now gone, if the soil is rich in iodine, this iodine makes it into plants grown in that soil and into the milk of cows that eat those plants. Today, iodized salt shows up in so many foods that iodine deficiency in pregnancy is unusual.

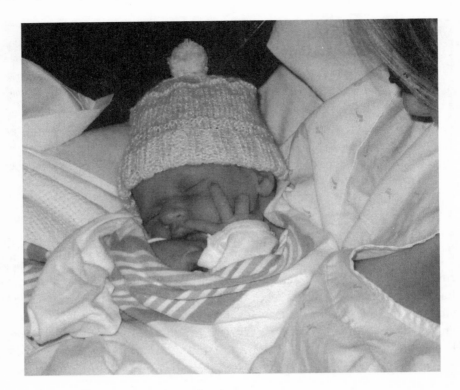

Zinc

The requirement for zinc, which is found in almost every cell in the mother's and baby's bodies, increases by more than 30 percent. The baby needs zinc to support its burgeoning growth and to make each new copy of DNA. Zinc is vital for the newly awakened sense of taste and smell. It supports a healthy immune system and facilitates the body's repair and remodeling work. Like vitamin B_6, it is an active player in over 100 different critical biochemical processes in the body. Low zinc levels can lead to slowed fetal growth and premature delivery. Pregnancy outcomes in general are measurably better when mothers have a healthy amount of zinc.

Most Americans get their zinc from red meat and poultry. Other rich sources of zinc include beans (baked beans); nuts (cashews, pecans, walnuts, and almonds); seafood (oysters and flounder); whole grains (bran or oatmeal); and dairy products (yogurt and cheese). At least some of the naturally zinc-rich foods belong in a pregnancy diet. Zinc is also a common ingredient in fortified cereals.

Pregnant women need at least 11 milligrams per day. Prenatal vitamins typically contain 15 milligrams.

Niacin, Riboflavin, Thiamine, Pantothenic Acid

There are only a few remaining nutrients of which we know women need to increase their proportional intake during pregnancy. Like all of the nutrients we have covered so far in this chapter, niacin, riboflavin, thiamine, pantothenic acid, chromium, and omega-3 fatty acids all need to become bigger parts of the pregnancy diet. Total amounts of other nutrients, such as fiber, selenium, vitamin A, and vitamin C also need to increase slightly during pregnancy, but not as much as overall calories do.

The words *niacin*, *riboflavin*, *thiamine*, and *pantothenic acid* may make your eyes glaze, or they may sound familiar from the side panel of a cereal box or a package of bread. Because they are so widely used as supplements, deficiency is unlikely. They are all coenzymes active in a variety of metabolic processes in both moms and babies.

Niacin occurs naturally in whole grains, legumes, and nuts, as well as in meat, fish, and poultry. Riboflavin shows up in whole grains, as well as in milk, meats, and (again) liver. Thiamine, is found predominantly in whole grains but also in great quantities in pork. Pantothenic acid is widely dispersed in whole grains, yeast, potatoes, tomatoes, eggs, broccoli, chicken, beef, and (care to guess?) liver.

These vitamins are all contained in prenatal supplements—unlike the following two nutrients.

Not Found in Most Prenatal Vitamins: Chromium and Omega-3 Fatty Acids

Chromium. Chromium is a mineral that works with insulin to maintain normal blood glucose levels. This can be especially important during pregnancy. Only 30 micrograms a day are needed, but many people don't get enough. Food sources include brewer's yeast, onions, broccoli, turkey, tomatoes, Romaine lettuce, grape juice, ham, potatoes, green beans, (yes) liver, beef, chicken, oysters, eggs, wheat germ, green peppers, apples, bananas, and spinach. It's also in butter, molasses, and black pepper. I won't mention that it's present in beer, because that's definitely a no-no right now! (Except, per-

Nuts! Allergies, Omega-3s, and Yogurt

We're just beginning to learn about how diet in pregnancy affects asthma, eczema, and allergies in children. We know that over 90 percent of food allergies in young children are to one of five foods: milk, eggs, peanuts, soy, or wheat. Some speculated that mothers' avoiding these foods during pregnancy might reduce allergies. But studies have not shown any preventive effect from avoiding these foods, except perhaps for peanuts and maybe even other nuts. This may be worthwhile in families where allergies are a particular problem. However, the most important thing we know to avoid for allergy prevention is not a food, but tobacco smoke. On the positive side of the diet, several studies show a significant benefit in preventing allergic disease by eating omega-3 fatty acids and eating the beneficial bacteria found in active culture yogurt.

haps, for alcohol-free beer. This can still have a small amount of alcohol in it—Muslims and liver transplant recipients are urged not to drink it—but this is similar to the amount in orange juice. It seems fine to me, in moderation, if it doesn't whet your appetite for the alcoholic variety.)

Chromium is not available in most prenatal vitamins or in most enriched or fortified breads and cereals. A diet rich in whole grains and cereals, however, will probably provide enough chromium.

Omega-3 Fatty Acids. Omega-3 fatty acids are polyunsaturated fats that are literally building blocks of the baby's developing retinas and brain. It surprises most people, but the brain is about 60 percent fat. Mothers can turn some omega-3s into DHA, which crosses the placenta in preference to other similar fatty acids and becomes the primary structural long-chain polyunsaturated fat in the brain—as long as plenty is available. The available amount depends on Mom's diet. When the supply is lacking, babies assemble their brains from substitute ingredients. DHA is a premium ingredient now added to a growing number of formulas for babies.

Omega-3s also have many proven benefits in adults, including improved heart health, reduced inflammation, and decreased autoimmune diseases.

Mothers can get it in fish, flaxseed, walnuts, some vegetable oils (such as canola oil or soybean oil, but not most other oils), and to a lesser extent in eggs and meat. Pregnant women need 1.4 grams per day. Ten ounces of salmon and two ounces of walnuts would provide enough omega-3 fatty acids for a pregnant woman for a week. These fatty acids are not present in most prenatal vitamins. I suspect they were the main source of my wife's insistent craving for tuna fish sandwiches.

Calcium

My favorite obstetrics textbook says that vitamin D requirements double during pregnancy and that calcium and phosphorous requirements each go up by 50 percent. The latest scientific evidence, however, suggests that requirements for vitamin D, phosphorus, and calcium don't go up at all during pregnancy.

It is true that a woman delivers about 25,000 to 30,000 milligrams of calcium to her baby over the course of her pregnancy. If she needs 1,000 milligrams per day for her own needs, it would seem that she would need more to provide for the extra needs of her baby. But the current recommended amount for pregnant adult women is still 1,000 milligrams per day. Research has shown that a woman's body recognizes the need for the extra calcium and gears up the intestines to absorb a higher proportion of the calcium in her diet. More is absorbed, and more is stored. If women are getting just the routine amount of recommended calcium, pregnancy is a time of calcium feast, not famine.

The problem is that many, if not most, women do not tend to get the amount they need from what they eat and drink. A glass of skim milk has about 300 milligrams; a cup of yogurt about 400 milligrams, a cup of cooked broccoli about 180 milligrams. Perhaps this is why dairy products appear on so many lists of strongly desired foods during pregnancy. Calcium-fortified juices and other foods are good alternatives if you need some extra calcium. Prenatal vitamins vary in their calcium content. Most have at least 200 milligrams—but that still may leave a huge calcium gap.

Calories

"Eating for two" is an oft-repeated phrase during pregnancy. But when it comes to the additional amount that women need to eat, it is more like eating for 1.1. OK, for some women, perhaps a bit more—but generally not as much as eating for 1.2. If you would normally have a 10-ounce glass of orange juice, now you'll want an 11- or maybe a 12-ounce glass—not two glasses!

You need an extra 300 calories per day, more or less, to support all of the growth and changes in both your body and the baby's. This isn't much! (An apple has about 120 calories.) And you want these extra calories to be packed with nutrients.

Pulling It All Together

A prenatal vitamin is a wonderful safety net, containing most of the vitamins and minerals that we have learned mother and baby need. It can let you relax and enjoy eating, but I wouldn't let it steer you away from the general type of diet pregnant women are designed to eat.

You can achieve optimum nutrition for yourself and your baby with a delicious and balanced diet of different kinds of whole foods. Be sure to enjoy a variety that includes plenty of fruits and vegetables, grains, and legumes, as well as lean protein sources.

This will also leave room for some yummy desserts and for following some of those intense cravings. If the cravings persist, rescan the list of nutrients we've discussed here to see if any insight "pops" as to what your baby and your body might be trying to say.

The Future Is Now

The doctor of the future . . . will interest his patients in the care of the human frame, diet, and in the cause and prevention of disease.

Thomas A. Edison

You'll notice some of the things *not* found on the list of foods needed in pregnancy include partially hydrogenated oils, high fructose corn syrup, modified food starch, processed white flour, artificial flavors, artificial colors, and chemical preservatives. These are all common in highly processed food products and have become staples of the modern diet.

Some of these may be fine for the baby. But by choosing meals of whole foods or food products with short ingredient lists that don't sound like chemistry sets, you will avoid experimenting on your child to find out.

Liver

We're getting close to the part on chocolate, but first a word about liver. You'll have noticed that many of the vitamins and elements needed in larger proportions during pregnancy are present in liver. Liver is loaded with iron and folate, the two nutrients at the top of the increased-need list. Does this make liver a great food choice for you? The glory of the gestational gourmet? I think not.

Here's one good reason. Liver is also loaded with vitamin A. While vitamins are necessary for life, too much of a good thing can be toxic. This is especially true of the fat soluble vitamins E, A, D, and K. The requirements for E, D, and K do not go up at all during pregnancy. Slightly more vitamin A is needed, but not as much as the increase in calories. Your diet can be proportionally lower in vitamin A at this time.

The recommended daily amount of vitamin A is 770 micrograms (compared to 700 micrograms before pregnancy). This is 2,567 international units. Prenatal vitamins usually contain about 2,700 international units, covering your current needs.

One study found that babies of women given more than 10,000 international units of vitamin A per day during pregnancy had double the risk of birth defects. Other studies suggest that up to 25,000 international units a day may be safe. But everyone agrees that too much vitamin A is toxic. The official upper limit recommended during pregnancy is 10,000 international units per day, including that obtained in food and supplements combined. You are unlikely to get too much from a prenatal vitamin coupled with a normal balanced diet—with one exception.

A single 3-ounce serving of liver can contain up to 30,000 international units of vitamin A! There is no proof that eating liver causes birth defects, but I can't recommend eating liver regularly during pregnancy. (Nor can I recommend taking extra supplements of the vitamins or minerals found in your prenatal vitamins.) Of course, many pregnant women can't stomach the sight or smell of liver anyway, no matter how it is prepared.

Chocolate, though, is another story.

Chocolate

One of the most commonly used pregnancy handouts suggests that women reduce or eliminate chocolate from their diets while pregnant. But choco-

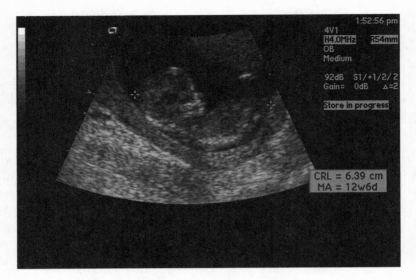

Your baby is growing every day.

late is high on the list of the most desired foods by many pregnant American women. Interestingly, chocolate love during pregnancy seems to be less strong in Europe and many other countries. What's the story here?

Recent research into dark chocolate has uncovered a variety of health benefits, including lowering blood pressure and raising levels of antioxidants that seem to protect against heart disease, aging, and some cancers. Some research suggests that it can lower "bad" cholesterol, reduce weight, and improve the mood.

Many of these benefits may be erased, though, if you eat milk chocolate or consume the chocolate with milk or other dairy products (there goes that triple hot fudge sundae!). Great taste, of course, is a benefit not erased by pairing chocolate and milk.

Perhaps pregnant European women don't desire chocolate as much because their diets are already higher in beneficial flavenoids and other polyphenols. These compounds are also present in many fruits, vegetables, teas, and red wine (but no wine now!).

Apart from the health benefits of chocolate, what are the concerns?

- **Caffeine.** We know that too much caffeine is not healthy for Mom or baby and can lead to increased risk for miscarriage and preterm labor. Some studies have detected a possible increase in the risk of sudden infant death syndrome (SIDS) with as little as four cups of coffee a day during pregnancy. Research suggests, though, that low-to-moderate caffeine intake is probably fine. What is a moderate amount of caffeine? The March of Dimes has set its safe level at less than 300 milligrams per day. A cup of coffee might have 120 milligrams or so (depending on how it is brewed). A 12-ounce can of Diet Pepsi has 36 milligrams, Pepsi One has 55.5 milligrams. A cup of green tea has about 15 milligrams; hot cocoa has 14 milligrams; and an ounce of milk chocolate has only about 6 milligrams. A regular size Hershey bar is 1.55 ounces. Chocolate lovers, do the math.

- **Heartburn.** We know that chocolate contains theobromines, substances that relax the stomach "lid" sphincter which, when tight, helps stop acid from sloshing up to cause heartburn. Later in pregnancy, heartburn is common. Mothers plagued by this may want to do everything they can to tighten that sphincter, even eliminating chocolate. But from my perspective as a physician, they can decide how to balance their own pleasure and pain.
- **Fetal growth.** One study from Poland, published in the *Polish Journal of Veterinary Science* in 2003, looked at the effects of feeding large amounts of chocolate to pregnant mice. These happy mice each ate the mouse-equivalent of four and a half Hershey-sized, 1.55-ounce chocolate bars every day. The leg lengths of the baby mice of the chocolate-gorged mothers were shorter than those of their peers.

But wait. Perhaps you have heard that chocolate, though healthy for humans, can be toxic to dogs and some other pets. This is true. Dogs cannot deal well with the theobromines in chocolate. Cats do a much better job but still can't take chocolate as well as humans. How do mice compare to humans when it comes to chocolate tolerance? Current evidence is scant and somewhat contradictory. Some websites even suggest leaving M&M's as mouse poison (where the dog can't reach them). But to be safe, let's assume chocolate is healthy for mice. I think it probably is.

This would suggest that too much of a good thing is no longer good. Consider: four and a half of these chocolate bars daily (200 grams of milk chocolate) would also be more than 1,000 calories from chocolate daily—not contributing much to a balanced and varied diet.

Dark chocolate is richer in beneficial nutrients but also richer in the bioactive compounds that raise concerns. Our family's practice is to have a large bar of Endangered Species Organic Dark Chocolate in the house and to break off two or three squares a day to satisfy chocolate cravings, sample the health benefits, but stay within an amount that is safe and sane.

Three satisfying squares add up to less than 18 grams of fine dark chocolate—about 78 calories and a luscious treat.

Chocolate during nursing is another chapter in this tale.

Eating for the Future

With all that we know about tobacco, how can people still smoke? It's easy. They're enticed by big business; they enjoy it; it's cool; and it's very, very habit forming.

Now for the sobering truth: poor nutritional choices cause every bit as much cancer, death, disability, and chronic disease as cigarettes do. The modern American diet is public health threat number one to our children. With all that we know about junk food, how can people still eat it? It's easy. They're enticed by big business; they enjoy it; it's cool; and it's very, very habit forming.

What an opportunity you have! For generations, many parents had no idea that they could start their children on the road to good nutrition before they were even born.

Just for perspective, you may want to watch an hour of children's cartoons on television or watch a group of kids in a fast-food joint. You'll be struck by the amount of unhealthy food powerfully, enticingly, and seductively marketed to our kids with songs, toys, commercials, and cartoon characters.

How much better to have a tradition of good nutrition before they meet that onslaught. How much better to support their enjoyment of delicious, healthy foods when solid foods are first introduced!

And now is an even more special opportunity. In the womb, your baby's eyes are shielded from the seduction of commercials, from the kid's meal toys, and from the "group-think" of peer pressure. All she knows is what you feed her and what her dad feeds you. She loves what she eats, grows from it now, and develops tastes for the future.

The prenatal vitamin is an important way to fill in the nutrient gaps, but it won't train your baby's taste buds. Babies were designed to thrive from what mothers ate long before these and other supplements were invented. When I was growing up, my father grew tomatoes in our backyard. These vine-ripened tomatoes were absolutely delicious—far better than any others I can remember having. As plants grow, the new growth is built from materials taken from the soil. Nothing can be incorporated into plants unless it is present in the soil. Plants grown in depleted soil are just not as healthy. But plants do the best they can with whatever materials are available. They can do a lot with a little.

You are your baby's soil. When you first meet your baby face-to-face, you'll be looking at cheeks and toes built from the food you have eaten.

What an opportunity!

7

To Protect and To Serve

Avoiding Harmful Toxins
That Can Cross the Placenta

The placenta is a barrier that will protect the baby from some things, but it is best to assume that any substance that makes it into the mother's body may make it into the baby's as well—and sometimes at higher concentrations. The placenta is a tangle of Mom's and the baby's circulation, but the two don't connect directly. They are separated at all points by a fatty, semipermeable membrane (like the ones some of you may remember playing with in high school biology). Oxygen and important nutrients cross from the mother to the baby. Waste is carried away by the mother.

The membranes in the placenta can be an effective filter to stop large items, such as bacteria, from entering the baby's domain. But many small molecules, especially ones that dissolve in oil or fat, can cross easily. It simply wasn't designed to protect from modern chemicals.

Parents can make conscious choices to help provide a safer environment for their children. Now is always a good time to start.

Organic—a Choice for Our Kids

Pesticides are one example of chemicals that can cross the placenta easily. The good news is that this exposure is easy to control.

DDT is perhaps the most famous pesticide. DDT used in the United States decades ago appears to have caused an epidemic of premature births that has only recently been detected. According to a fascinating study published in the July 14, 2001, issue of *Lancet*, scientists who studied stored umbilical cord blood samples from mothers who had delivered before 1966

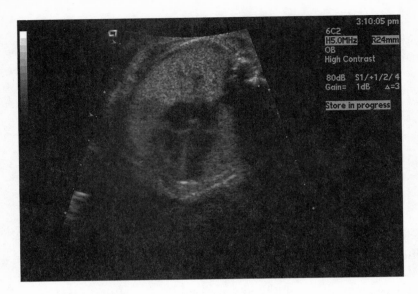

A four-chamber heart

found elevated levels of DDT breakdown products among the group who had premature deliveries or low-birth-weight infants. This means DDT was responsible for a host of medical problems and the deaths of many babies—but the link wasn't proven until more than 30 years later! DDT use in the United States was stopped in 1972 because it caused reproductive damage to birds (the bald eagle and brown pelican were nearly extinct), but DDT is still widely used in 25 other countries for insect control.

We know that, at high enough levels, pesticides and other chemicals found in today's food cause a variety of significant health problems in children, including cancer, attention deficit disorder, learning disabilities, genital abnormalities, and reproductive problems. We don't know yet what levels of these chemicals are safe.

We also know that the common pesticides used in foods are fat-soluble and are present in measurable levels in amniotic fluid. In 2003, the Centers for Disease Control and Prevention released the results of a sweeping Body Burden study. It showed that the same chemicals that can pollute our water, air, and food are also polluting our bodies—at higher levels than expected. But the amount of pesticides found in the body varies wildly among people.

Organic foods are grown without the use of chemical pesticides or other toxic, persistent chemicals that contaminate our soil, water, or food—or our children. Does eating organic products make a difference? Children tell us the answer when they pee, according to a compelling study of urban and suburban preschool kids from the Seattle area in the fall of 2002.

Organic Kids

In this study, researchers divided children into two groups: those who ate mostly conventional foods and those who ate mostly organic foods. They collected all urine produced by each child over 24 hours and did a CSI-type analysis of the urine. Children who ate conventional diets had mean pesticide concentrations in their urine nine times higher than that found in the children who ate organic! These levels indicated that the conventional foods kids had exceeded safe exposure levels set by the Environmental Protection Agency (EPA) and had increased health risks. By contrast, those children who ate organic foods were well within the EPA levels deemed to cause negligible risk.

Organic is a great choice for fruits and vegetables. To me, it is an even more important choice for meats and dairy products. Many chemicals accumulate to a greater degree as you go up the food chain. This is why large fish are often more dangerous than smaller fish. Animals may eat large amounts of contaminated food over their lifetimes and store the chemicals, and in the case of female mammals, pass them on in their breast milk. Feeding children organic foods is something simple and practical parents can do to protect their children and help them build healthy bodies.

But now, before the baby is born, is an even more critical time of development. And what you eat is what your child eats. When you eat organic, your baby does.

Scrub-a-Dub-Dub

Washing fruits and vegetables carefully before eating them can remove some of the chemicals and contaminants from their surfaces. This is a wise habit to get into, whether or not you choose organic foods. I agree with the Food and Drug Administration's (FDA's) recommendation: "Wash all fresh fruits and vegetables with cool tap water immediately before eating. Don't use soap or detergents. Scrub firm produce, such as melons and cucumbers, with a clean produce brush." A drop or two of liquid soap in a large amount of water is probably fine if you think the situation warrants it.

Garden Safely Inside and Out

Besides what we get from our food and water supplies, we can absorb pesticides into our bodies from our lawns, our gardens, and our attempts to rid our homes of pests. Choosing organic techniques at home is another great way to reduce pesticide exposure. When this is not practical, I recommend that pregnant women avoid recently sprayed areas and wear gloves when working in the garden.

But What About Other Foods?

Avoiding toxins in fruits and veggies is relatively simple, but avoiding them in other foods is essential, too. Watch out for hidden toxins in some fish, soft cheese, cold cuts, raw eggs, and even pork chops.

Something Fishy

Mercury is another dangerous molecule that zooms across the placenta. As I said earlier, my wife craved tuna during her pregnancy with my youngest son. Should such fish be restricted? Although most fish contain trace amounts of mercury, the benefits of small amounts of some seafood may outweigh the risks. But large fish that feed on other fish can accumulate enough mercury to irreversibly damage a baby's nervous system.

Mercury damages children's immune systems and kidneys, but its toxicity to the developing brain is worse. The Environmental Protection Agency, in 2004, estimated that 630,000 American children—one in every six—are born each year with levels of mercury in their blood that can cause lasting neurologic problems.

The American Academy of Pediatrics (AAP) warns that minimizing mercury exposure is "essential to optimal child health." The most important sources of mercury exposure are fish eaten by pregnant or breastfeeding mothers and fish eaten directly by children.

I agree with restricting fish intake, though this saddens me. In March 2004, the FDA and the EPA issued joint federal guidelines for eating seafood aimed at women who are pregnant, who might become pregnant, or who are nursing, as well as young children, in order to avoid harm to these populations:

To protect your baby follow these three rules:

1. Do not eat shark, swordfish, king mackerel, or tilefish because they contain high levels of mercury
2. Eat up to 12 ounces (two average meals) a week of a variety of fish and shellfish that are lower in mercury.
   - Five of the most commonly eaten fish that are low in mercury are shrimp, canned light tuna, salmon, pollock, and catfish.

- Another commonly eaten fish, albacore ("white") tuna has more mercury than canned light tuna. So when choosing your two meals of fish and shellfish, you may eat up to six ounces (one average meal) of albacore tuna per week.

3. Check local advisories about the safety of fish caught by family and friends in your local lakes, rivers, and coastal areas. If no advice is available, eat up to six ounces (one average meal) per week of fish you catch from local waters, but don't consume any other fish during that week.

If you follow the advice given by the FDA and EPA, you will gain the positive benefits of eating fish and might also decrease developmental problems from mercury in fish. Note, however, that this advice only pertains to mercury and ignores PCBs and other pollutants. Also, by FDA calculations about 6.7 percent of women following this advice will exceed safe blood levels for mercury. The FDA has stated that these blood levels are a guideline, not a bright line, and knowingly chose a fish advisory that does not keep all women below it. Their reasoning is logical and defensible, but many of us do not agree.

What About Tuna?

Tuna is one of the most frequently consumed fish in the United States. The tuna question is tricky, because mercury levels in tuna vary substantially. Tuna steaks and canned albacore (white) tuna generally contain far higher levels of mercury than canned light tuna. In fact, canned albacore tuna is one of several fish (white tuna, orange roughy, bluefish, sea trout, and grouper) in which average levels of mercury measured by the FDA in 2003 exceed the average level of mercury in tilefish—one of the "forbidden" fish. Eating 12 ounces of canned light tuna each week would, on average, put a 140-pound woman right at the FDA's upper limit of safety if that were all the fish she ate. Just eating the six ounces a week of canned albacore tuna allwed by FDA guidelines could put the same 140-pound woman 50 percent over that level! I agree with the Environmental Working Group in recommending that pregnant women not risk eating albacore tuna.

Given a choice, I would select wild salmon for a seafood meal before light tuna. Skinning and broiling the salmon can help minimize PCB contamination. Whatever else you choose, I recommend not eating fish caught by friends or family without checking with the local health department to be sure which local waters and fish are safe.

Fish can be an excellent source of nutrients, especially for developing brains. I would prefer stricter guidelines on industrial emissions (the source of the mercury, polychlorinated biphenyls [PCBs], and other contaminants in the fish), rather than depriving women and children of foods ideally suited to stimulate brain growth.

On another seafood note, it's wise to avoid sushi or other raw fish during pregnancy, especially raw shellfish such as oysters and clams, because they are at risk for carrying dangerous infections.

That's Bologna (and Cheese)!

Most people can safely eat food containing a type of bacteria called *Listeria*. During pregnancy, however, women are well over 1,000 percent more likely to get sick when exposed. Infection usually results in mild food poisoning, but it can cause severe illness in the mother and devastating illness in the baby.

Listeria commonly grows in soft cheeses such as brie, Camembert, feta, blue cheese, and Mexican-style cheese. Hard cheeses are considered safe. Cream cheese and cottage cheese are soft but safe, because they are pasteurized. Unpasteurized milk is risky during pregnancy.

Unlike many bacteria, *Listeria* flourishes in refrigerated temperatures. Hot dogs, packaged cold cuts, sliced deli meats, meat spreads, and smoked seafood have all caused listeriosis in pregnant women. If you want such foods, serve them steaming hot. Canned meats and fish or those that don't require refrigeration should be safe from infection.

Also, *Listeria* is another good reason to postpone sushi-fests until a later (postbirth) date in your social calendar.

Eggnog and Hollandaise

Raw and partially cooked eggs, meat, and poultry can pose special health risks to pregnant women and their babies. In addition to listeriosis, these foods can carry *Escherichia coli* (*E. coli*), salmonella, and *Toxoplasma*. If you eat ground beef, cook it until no pink is visible, and make sure pork and lamb are well done. Cook poultry to 180°F (with a thermometer) and eggs until both the whites and the yolks are firm. Soft scrambled eggs are a treat for later in life. And watch out for hidden partially cooked eggs, perhaps in a favorite classic hollandaise sauce over asparagus or fresh artichokes or eggs Benedict. Cookie dough is perhaps my favorite delicacy that can harbor uncooked eggs. And beware raw eggs in a certain cherished holiday beverage with a sprinkle of nutmeg. Rum and brandy aren't the only concerns with eggnog and pregnancy! Choose the pasteurized variety. Or have you ever tried vegan eggnog? This might be the time to try it. I'm enjoying a mug of soynog as I type. Not bad!

Handling and preparing possibly contaminated foods is another time to be careful. An alcohol-based instant hand sanitizer or a soapy hand scrub is in order before and after handling raw foods. Cutting boards, kitchen surfaces, and cooking utensils also get scrubbed after contact with raw meat, poultry, or fish to avoid spreading any infections. If possible, place cutting surfaces in the dishwasher where the cleaning water is much hotter than most people can tolerate. Keep raw animal foods separate from cooked ones.

Check to be sure your fridge temp is less than 40°F and your freezer is at 0° or below. If cooked food has been out of the fridge for more than two hours, you may want to find some other creative use for it, but don't serve it to your developing baby.

Pork Chops and Cat Poop

Once a baby arrives, changing diapers is a practical way to express love. In the meantime, *not* changing the kitty litter is another way you can express love to your baby.

Toxoplasma is a one-celled parasite whose primary host is the cat family. Infected cats usually have no symptoms but may shed as many as 10 million egg cysts in their feces each day for the three weeks that their acute infection lasts. After excretion, it can take from 1 to 21 days for the egg cysts to ripen and become infectious (usually 2 to 8 days). The egg cysts can survive for more than a year in moist soil. They are 0.0005 inches long, invisible to the naked eye.

If you get the microscopic egg cysts on your hands, you can become infected by rubbing your eyes, rubbing your nose, or eating food you have handled. Flies have been shown to aid the transmission of toxoplasmosis. Egg cysts get on their feet and are deposited when they land on food.

Directly changing the kitty litter accounts for many cases of human toxoplasmosis. There is a tiny risk from petting cats.

> ⭐ **Tabby Toxo**
>
> I am nine weeks pregnant. I found out I was pregnant four weeks ago. We have two cats that have been in our home since September. When I told my ob-gyn, they suggested I stop cleaning the kitty litter due to an infectious disease called toxoplasmosis that is transmitted through their stool. My question is: What are the chances that I contracted it before I was pregnant (then I know there would be little risk of it hurting the baby)? And, how do I know if and when I contracted it? I know there is a test, but will it tell me how long I have been infected/immune? We've talked to our ob-gyn, vet, and looked in some books. I don't feel any of these sources put my mind at rest. Also, is there a danger by petting them or being around them?
> Thanks.
>
> **Stephanie, San Mateo, California**

Statistically, though, your kitchen is a much higher risk area today than your cat's litter box! This doesn't mean that I suggest frolicking in the kitty litter or *not* frolicking in the kitchen—in fact, I'm a fan of kitchen frolicking—but it does mean taking care in the kitchen, because other animals besides cats also get toxoplasmosis, including cows, pigs, chickens, and goats. And you may eat these animals or drink their milk. Even though they appear well to farmers, ranchers, and butchers, infectious tissue cysts will get in their muscles and milk. Thanks to pregnancy-related cat-poop education, you are now more likely to get toxoplasmosis from undercooked meat or raw goat's milk than from your pet. One study in Palo Alto, California, showed that cysts were present in up to one-third of the pork chops tested. The cysts can survive for months at refrigerated temperatures, but cooking food to 150°F destroys them. Some parent education brochures reassure parents that freezing also kills the cysts. While freezing for more than a day does substantially decrease the risks, it should not be relied on as your only line of defense.

The danger to your baby comes from a first-time infection during pregnancy, particularly in the first or second trimesters. About 85 percent of pregnant women have no evidence of prior infection. About 1 in 200 women will get toxoplasmosis during pregnancy. They may or may not have flulike symptoms, muscle aches, and swollen lymph nodes. Prompt treatment reduces the risk of passing it on to the baby.

Congenital toxoplasmosis occurs in less than 0.1 percent of babies in the United States. There is a wide spectrum of severity in these cases. Thankfully, over half of them have no symptoms. Another third have only a mild form of the disease. About 10 percent have the severe form that can include blindness, mental retardation, or even death (that's about 1 in 10,000 babies).

Make sure that meat is cooked to at least 150°F and that fruits and vegetables are well washed. Wash your hands and kitchen surfaces after handling uncooked meat or unwashed vegetables, and avoid touching your mouth or eyes in the meantime. Or have your partner cook for you!

Prevent your cat from eating undercooked meats and wild rodents to reduce your cat's risk of becoming infected. That means keeping your cat inside.

Women should avoid kitty litter boxes when pregnant, and wear gloves if they garden. Perhaps someone else could disinfect the litter box with boiling water every week during the first two trimesters. Having another person change the litter box daily can also help remove egg-cysts before they can mature and become infectious. This is a great way for dads or other partners to get involved in caring for your baby, even before birth.

Holding Your Breath

Beware of smelly chemicals. Solvents also travel across the placenta with ease. These volatile chemicals are found in many cleaning products, paints, paint thinners, and hobby materials.

You can reduce the baby's exposure by having dry cleaning done at an environmentally friendly laundry. If you use a laundry that cleans with perc (perchloroethylene) or other dangerous solvents, have someone else make the trip to the cleaners and air out the clothes from any plastic bags before Mom gets too close.

You also may want to have someone else paint the baby's room!

Other hazardous substances to consider and avoid if possible include lead, mercury vapor, anesthetic gas, PCBs, carbon monoxide, benzene, and formaldehyde. One or more of these might be found in glues, paints, furniture wax, household cleaners, new carpets, gas stations, gas cookers, hazardous waste sites, seafood, incinerators, smog, and cigarette smoke. You should also stay away from unnecessary x-ray radiation—even dental x-rays can stunt a baby's growth. Thankfully, the radiation from computer screens and microwaves in good repair do not appear to pose any pregnancy risk.

Working as the lacquer taster in a toxic chemical plant in Springfield would create an obvious occupational exposure. Sniffing airplane glue or home pewter smelting might be recognized as a risky hobby. Usually, though, the risk is much more subtle and everyday, as from a cleaner or solvent used at work or home without thought. Or soldering a stained glass lamp (I did that).

If living or working around substances on the preceding list can't be avoided, wear protective gear, get the best ventilation possible, and shower when you can. Your partner should follow the same recommendations, being careful to shower and change clothes before being close to you and the baby.

It's a great idea for partners to have clothes to wear just for occasions of possible exposure and to store them in a plastic bag. If you're remodeling, consider sealing off the involved rooms from the rest of the house and leaving all windows open when practical to get lots of fresh air.

Drug Free and Happy

Minimize unnecessary medications of all kinds. Some strong prescription drugs (such as Accutane, thalidomide, or diethylstilbestrol) are famous for their devastating effects on unborn children. A couple of psoriasis drugs can cause trouble if taken up to three years before becoming pregnant! But even apparently gentle, common, over-the-counter medicines may not be safe for the baby, especially for the first eight weeks after conception.

Women who take aspirin, ibuprofen (Motrin, Advil, etc.), or naproxen (Alleve) during or just before pregnancy may have an 80 percent increased risk of miscarriage, according to a study in the August 16, 2003, issue of the *British Medical Journal*. Researchers at Kaiser Permanente conducted this study in the San Francisco Bay Area. When women first had a positive pregnancy test, they were asked to list any and all medicines they had been taking since their last menstrual period. Use of the three medicines mentioned was associated with more miscarriages even after adjusting for fever or other symptoms, the mothers' age, hot tub use, smoking, or previous miscarriages. Those who took the medicines in the days right around conception had a markedly higher chance of problems (a 560 percent increased risk, or 35 percent miscarriages). Most women who took these medicines for longer than a week lost their babies (an 810 percent increased risk, or 52 percent miscarriages). Acetaminophen (Tylenol) use did not appear to affect the miscarriage risk. The study compared users of all these medicines to nonusers during the early weeks of pregnancy but did not look at dosages.

Before my oldest son was born, my mother cautioned us against using any medications during pregnancy unless clearly necessary, even avoiding something as common as aspirin. Although more research is needed before we know with certainty what effects these medicines actually have on pregnancy, the latest scientific research supports my mother's gentle wisdom. Women everywhere should know about the potential risk.

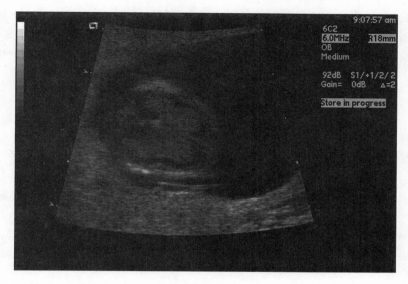

Baby's brain at 73 days after conception

Marijuana

Whatever the advantages and disadvantages of marijuana at other times in life, pot and pregnancy are a bad combination. Yes, cannabis crosses the placenta, and yes, it affects the developing baby's brain. I'm less concerned about the associated poor growth, low birth weight, excessive crying, and withdrawal tremors than I am about the impact on learning and attention.

Alcohol and the Surgeon General

Many people are aware of the strongly worded federal warnings about tobacco use. However, the Surgeon General's Advisory on Alcohol and Pregnancy warns against alcohol in perhaps even stronger terms. Not just that it's dangerous but that alcohol should be avoided in drinks, foods, and medicines:

> The Surgeon General advises women who are pregnant (or considering pregnancy) not to drink alcoholic beverages and to be aware of the alcoholic content of foods and drugs.

Fortunately, cooking removes the alcohol from most foods, even when wine, for example, is an ingredient. Since most alcohol is consumed in drink form, many states and the District of Columbia, in addition to federal warnings, have laws that require signs to be plastered in restaurants, inns, stores, and amusement parks—making them so common as to be almost invisible. Here is the one from California:

> Warning: Drinking distilled spirits, beers, coolers, wines, and other alcoholic beverages during pregnancy is known by the State of California to cause birth defects and other reproductive harm.

Similar signs are now required to warn about mercury-containing fish.

★ Alcohol's Long Shadow

One of my brothers was born at only three pounds and was diagnosed as hyperkinetic and put on Ritalin. . . . I am curious if my mother's drinking is linked to his hyperactivity? My 30-year-old brother is no longer on Ritalin, but he is somewhat slow. Can you please advise me? Thanks!

Grafton, Massachusetts

Alcoholic beverages have been a part of human civilization from the very beginning. Only in the last few years has it become clear that drinking alcohol has many negative effects on the developing baby within. The first scientific paper suggesting these harmful effects of alcohol came out of France in 1968. At first, this new idea was not widely accepted. Then, in 1973, an independent group published a study detailing the patterns of malformation found in the offspring of alcoholic mothers. The mounting evidence was persuasive, and the newly recognized entity was named *fetal alcohol syndrome*.

Alcohol is now recognized as the most common major destructive environmental agent to which a fetus is likely to be exposed. It is directly responsible for 10 to 20 percent of mental deficiency in babies with IQs in the 50-to-80 range, and it causes one in six cases of cerebral palsy. Infants with fetal alcohol syndrome tend to exhibit poor growth and have small heads. The average IQ for those with full-blown fetal alcohol syndrome is 63.

A study in the August 2001 issue of *Pediatrics* demonstrates the association between relatively low prenatal alcohol exposure and later childhood behavioral problems. Attention problems, aggression, and delinquent behavior were three times as likely among six- and seven-year-olds if their mothers had taken as little as one drink per week during pregnancy. A glass of wine can be a relaxing and healthful choice at many times of life. Nevertheless, during the magical months of pregnancy, it's worth protecting the child growing within you from even small amounts of alcohol.

We've seen that the first trimester of pregnancy can be a vulnerable time. The third trimester is generally safer. However, evidence published in the February 11, 2000, issue of *Science* suggests that drinking alcohol even once during the third trimester can permanently damage the brain of your baby. Alcohol has its biggest effects when the synapses (connections) of the brain are forming—during the last trimester of pregnancy and the early childhood years. When the developing baby is exposed to alcohol for even a few hours, a number of brain cells and synapses are permanently deleted.

You've Come a Long Way, Baby

Tobacco, whether used by the mother or someone near her, is directly damaging to the placenta and to the developing baby. The list of proven problems is long, but none is more devastating than sudden infant death syndrome (SIDS).

On average, smoking during pregnancy doubles the chances of SIDS, and the odds increase with each cigarette. Other drugs of abuse such as cocaine or heroin increase the risk by as many as 30 times. But as of 1998, smoking still occurred in 25 percent of pregnancies in the United States. Smokeless tobacco (spit tobacco) can be just as bad for unborn babies.

Tobacco use during pregnancy or baby's first year causes more preventable SIDS deaths than any other single factor.

We also know that tobacco exposure during pregnancy causes a variety of increased health and behavior problems in infancy and early childhood. Recent evidence suggests that when mothers smoke during pregnancy, their choice may affect their children for the rest of their lives. The January 5, 2002, issue of the *British Medical Journal* reports an analysis of 17,000 births during one week in March 1958. Medical records were reviewed when those babies were 33 years old. The study showed that those whose mothers smoked had almost a 40 percent increased chance of being obese, and more than a 300 percent increased chance of having developed type 2 diabetes at an early age. Because both obesity and diabetes contribute to increased mortality, maternal smoking during pregnancy may shorten the adult life span of these children. We also know that the risk is high if the mother is continually subjected to secondhand smoke at home or at work.

You *have* come a long way! You're expecting to bring a new child into the world. Tobacco can be a very tough habit to break without help. If you or someone in your life wants to quit, for your sake *and* your baby's, talk with your doctor or call the American Cancer Society quit line at 800/227-2345.

Big Brother

State governments know something that many pregnant women do not: pumping gasoline is a risk to a developing baby. Most states require warnings like the following to be posted on gasoline pumps:

> Warning: Chemicals known to the state to cause cancer, birth defects, or other reproductive harm are found in gasoline, crude oil, and many other petroleum products and their vapors.

If you normally fill your own tank, this is the time to enjoy the opportunity to get full service at the pump. An attendant might even lend a hand at the self-serve island for someone who is pregnant. Give friends, family, and (why not?) total strangers a chance to pump for your baby. And keep your windows up while you wait. It's very easy for those fumes to cross the placenta.

Agitate and Advocate

Fire-retardant chemicals that easily cross the placenta are almost impossible for women in some countries to avoid. Perhaps our best option is to be spokespeople and advocates for our children.

Researchers have found levels of flame retardants in the bodies of U.S. women to be 75 times higher than the average levels found in European women. These chemicals, called polybrominated diphenyl ethers (PBDEs), save hundreds of lives each year by preventing or slowing fires. However, animal studies suggest that some of the PBDEs used as flame retardants can damage memory, learning, sperm counts, and pubertal development in children. The good news is that the levels proven to cause these problems in animals are 10 to 20 times higher than those found in American women. The bad news is that levels in American women appear to have doubled between 2001 and 2003.

We do not know how the PBDEs get into women's bodies. We *do* know that these are persistent chemicals that bioaccumulate: each time an animal eats another animal that's lower on the food chain, the pollutant is stored in the bigger animal's fat, reaching higher and higher levels as it moves up the food chain. Perhaps women are getting their PBDEs from the animal fat in meat and dairy products. The chemicals then cross the placenta and also later appear in the breast milk where they pass on to the nursing baby, one step higher on the food chain.

Perhaps woman are inhaling PBDEs directly from the environment. Not surprisingly, PBDEs are in house dust. They are widely used in the United States in carpets, furniture, mattresses, and plastics. The polyurethane foam used as padding in so many products may be the worst source.

Looking Before We Leap

Europe made the choice to ban PBDEs. Some international manufacturers, such as Ikea, have begun using thicker foam to avoid PBDEs and still meet safety standards for fire resistance. In August 2003, California became the first U.S. state to ban two of these chemicals now accumulating in pregnant and nursing moms and their babies.

This makes sense to me. We don't know what levels are safe in animals. And, shockingly, all of the studies to date are animal studies; there have been no studies on the effect of the chemicals in humans. Yet we have chosen to commercialize them and scatter them all around us. They are now found in our bedrooms, our kitchens, our offices, our cars, our food, and even in mother's milk. I believe we should learn about chemicals such as this *before* giving the green light to make new persistent chemicals virtually unavoidable in our environment.

Parent Power

Our babies don't have a voice in the political process, but we do! Let's speak up on behalf of our children. I'd love it if every pregnant couple would write one letter or e-mail to a decision maker on behalf of their baby.

I recently had the opportunity to visit a couple of Organic Valley farms and dairies with my family. The farms of John and Denise Boere and of Frank and Bernadette Coelho were inspirations—and examples of what is happening on organic farms all around the world. What a joy to see farmers who didn't need to be afraid to hug their kids when they came in from a day's work!

My wife grew up on a conventional farm in the same part of California. Both of us were startled by the abundance of life and health on the organic farms. When I scooped up a handful of soil, I also scooped up a handful of worms. In the absence of toxic pesticides, the soil was rich and teeming with life. The creeks were filled with healthy fish and frogs, and the farms were havens for wildlife on the ground, in the ground, and soaring over our heads.

I paid particular attention to the frogs in the creek. They live in water, just like your baby does throughout pregnancy. Like your baby, the frogs have permeable skin. Atrazine, one of the most commonly used pesticides in modern agriculture, is known to cause developmental and reproductive problems in frogs, even at very low levels. It can cause infertility in frogs (and in farm workers). But the choices organic farmers make can reduce toxic exposure. And our own choices can go a long way toward reducing babies' exposures to this and similar chemicals.

And vote! None of my four kids can vote yet—but my wife and I can.

I often think of something I learned from Gary Hirshberg, the CEO of Stonyfield Farm Yogurt (one of my heroes of responsible business). Gary teaches that the cash register is one of our most important voting booths. What we vote for at the checkout counter changes the world. You can now see the results of this in the windows of many fast-food restaurants, which feature new premium salads and veggie burgers in response to many people "voting against" traditional fast food (and bland, wilted salads). Will healthy options spread? Will they continue at all? It all depends on how we vote. Every time you check out, what you choose influences not only today, but what choices will be available tomorrow.

8

Take a Deep Breath

Weeks 9 to 12 in Baby Time

As the 56-day period of fantastic metamorphosis winds down, parents are about 10 weeks pregnant, with at least one eye on the end of the first trimester, two weeks away. After the swirling, dazzling flurry of change, the pace in the womb *appears* slower.

The baby's huge liver, like a wartime factory converted to peacetime work, quietly creates generation after generation of red and white blood cells because the bones don't yet have marrow to do the job.

And in the quiet, for the first time, the baby begins to stir. This movement isn't the submissive strolling down the fallopian tube propelled by Mom's body. Nor is it a gentle, passive swaying in the salty amniotic sea. It is a tiny, tentative, quiet movement *in the active voice.*

An urge sparks in the baby's brain. The signal speeds silently along a nerve. And the baby stretches, flexing and extending her spine. Within two weeks, these stretches may be accompanied by cute little yawns. But first, another twinkle in the brain and—hold your breath—tiny muscles bend an arm at the elbow. Another "thought" and the fingers curl. Your baby has made a fist.

Mirror Worlds

As the baby is beginning to move is a good time to talk about parents beginning to move. Regular physical activity can have profound benefits for mothers and babies. I'm also convinced that developing a habit of activity now is another way to begin teaching your child. Kids observe and learn.

Early in pregnancy, many women experience fatigue. For some, the desire to rest is almost overwhelming. I suspect there may be a quiet message here

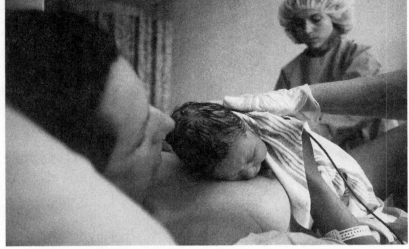

for women: *rest!* The peak of the fatigue tends to overlap the height of the baby's first 56 days of intense activity. Sleep is important during this period—I'm a fan of going to bed early, intimate pillow talk, and afternoon naps. This doesn't mean you shouldn't get active or go for walks at some point during the day. As the fatigue begins to decrease, regular physical activity becomes even more important.

Walk for Your Baby and Yourself

Regular physical activity, at least during the first half of pregnancy, has been associated with both healthier babies and healthier moms. According to a study published in the June 2003 issue of *Hypertension*, walking and other moderate physical activity begun during pregnancy was associated with a lower risk of preeclampsia, a pregnancy complication where the mother's blood pressure rises and blood flow to the baby decreases. The only effective treatment for preeclampsia is delivering the baby, so it results in many premature babies. In this study, the risk of developing preeclampsia was further reduced if the exercise was begun before pregnancy. Researchers found that the pace of walking or other activity was more important than the distance covered. Those who walked at least three miles per hour enjoyed the best results. Among those who didn't intentionally exercise, those who climbed one to four flights of stairs each day still had a lower risk than those who didn't. Taking the time to exercise may seem difficult in today's busy world. Nevertheless, our bodies and our babies will demand our time one way or the other. It is far more enjoyable to spend this time on pleasant walks now than on visits to the doctor later.

A Shot of Insulin

The hormonal shifts of pregnancy are a challenge for maintaining healthy blood glucose levels. Up to one in eight women will develop gestational diabetes during their pregnancies, increasing health risks for themselves and their babies.

Researchers at the University of Southern California School of Medicine found something amazing. They looked at women who had already developed gestational diabetes. The fasting blood glucose levels of these women were high enough to require insulin. Half of the women got the recommended insulin. The other half got personal trainers. Which would you rather have?

Trainers supervised women in a simple exercise bike program. The result? Aerobic exercise was *equally effective* to insulin. Blood glucose measurements were statistically the same in both groups. Simple exercise is a prescription-strength way to decrease blood sugar peaks and swings. And fetal heart rate tracings suggested that the babies in the studies liked the exercise as well.

Three 20-minute sessions of aerobic exercise weekly have a surprisingly powerful impact. And the blood sugar benefit is still detectable five to seven days after the last session. Of course, exercise during pregnancy has many other benefits, including stronger muscles, bones, and joints; less chance of urinary incontinence; easier labor and delivery; and enhanced ability to enjoy your new baby by helping to ward off the baby blues of postpartum depression.

Meet Norm

OK, exercise is a proven, effective medicine for treating medical problems. It's far more effective for *preventing* medical problems. But I believe the truth is even more profound: exercise is normal.

Ancient Wisdom

If we could give every individual the right amount of nourishment and exercise, not too little and not too much, we would have found the safest way to health.

Hippocrates, ca. 460–377 B.C.

The scandalously high rates of gestational diabetes are not the norm. A sedentary pregnancy is not the norm—even though this statement might shock your own mother, who probably saw pregnancy as a time to take it easy. Daily, healthy activity is the way that woman are designed to grow healthy babies. Brisk walks are one great way to do this.

For most pregnant women I recommend 30 minutes of moderate physical activity every day or at least on most days. This jells with the January 2002 position statement of the American College of Obstetricians and Gynecologists.

I'm a big fan of brisk walks (alone or together); dancing (find a line dancing club if you don't have a partner who likes to dance, but avoid the margaritas—or any alcohol for that matter); swimming (I'm seeing more and more pregnant women stylin' in two-piece suits); low-impact aerobics (if you like the music); hiking (you deserve to get to someplace beautiful during this unrepeatable time); and yoga (you can also get to someplace beautiful without leaving home). Not long before my oldest son was born, his triumphant pregnant mother had a glorious hike in Yosemite, and we have a smiling photo to prove it. Swimming is especially nice while pregnant because the water supports your growing body, but be sure the water isn't too hot or too cold—no polar bear swimming. I've seen wonderful yoga and aerobics classes designed especially for pregnant women.

I am decidedly not a fan of scuba diving for pregnant women. Ever. Nor of ice hockey, motorcycle racing, skydiving, snowboarding, ski jumping, or kickboxing. Not even of soccer. Moderate activity is good; collisions are not. Nor is lying flat on your back to exercise when pregnant—it can constrict blood supply to your baby. Fortunately, many exercise classes for pregnant women make accommodations to include helpful reclining positions.

Talk with your pregnancy health care team before embarking on your activity plan. Some exercise is wonderful. Too much or the wrong kind is not. Pay attention to your body's signals. Bleeding, dizziness, headaches, chest pain, cramps, or contractions are all good reasons to stop and check in with those caring for you.

And some pregnant women should not exercise or should exercise in an even gentler way than most. This is especially true for those with heart disease, lung disease, or who are at high risk of preterm labor, as with an incompetent cervix.

Rehearsals

Another glimmer sparks in your baby's brain, another silent message courses through her body, and your baby kicks—but it's still too small for you to feel.

As your feet move on the outside, your baby's feet move within. His tiny hand movements don't yet pick up objects or point out the sights to a twin (their eyes are closed anyway). The movements of his feet don't allow him to walk across the inner wall of the placenta or even swim across the salty soup.

These movements are rehearsals. A rehearsal is a private performance or a practice session that's intended to help get ready for a public appearance.

Right now, all four of my children are involved in theater. Within the last 14 months, all of them have been on stage in productions of *Les Misérables* and *Phantom*. Watching the plays coalesce was quite instructive. The scripts were outstanding and the directors inspiring, but the implementation of this greatness was the challenge. Early rehearsals were tentative and unspectacular. Mistakes were fine, because no one was watching yet but the team. They could grow because it didn't "count." As they progressed, some problems became even more evident. In the days before the show opened, it looked as if they might never get there—even though the rehearsal season seemed at that point to have been interminable. But the shows opened, and they were stars!

Then the rehearsal season seemed as if it had been over in a blink.

From one perspective, all of childhood is a grand dress rehearsal for the great drama of life. And adolescence is a protracted "tech week" when developing characters interact with the props and sets of the big show. What are borrowing the car keys or going out on dates? Tech rehearsals. Tech week is better known as "hell week" in theater circles. Although it may seem interminable, it is over in a blink.

More specifically, the individual developmental tasks of childhood involve extensive rehearsal periods. Toppling gives way to toddling and then to track and field. Babbling gives way to cute-speak and then to the debate team.

Among other things, my wife is a director. I asked her what she thought were the keys to great rehearsals. Her responses?

- The director has to be prepared.
- The rehearsals have to be the right length—too long and they become counterproductive; too short and you don't get enough done.
- The rehearsal space has to be big enough to simulate the actual stage that will be used for performance.
- The actors need to be given direction but not too much direction.
- The actors need to be inspired. They need to catch the director's vision of where the play is going, where their characters come into the big picture.
- The actors need feedback on how they are doing. They need to be told when they are doing well and when they need to make changes: "Something wonderful is beginning to happen," "Keep going," "Pull back," "Take that entrance sooner," "That's right, now you've got it."
- The actors need to be provided for—costumes, props, sets—or participate in the tech end outside of rehearsal time.
- The actors need to be protected from too much tech responsibility.
- The actors need time off to rest, to take care of their other life responsibilities, and to "be with" their roles outside of group rehearsals.
- Sometimes actors need one-on-one time with the director outside of scheduled rehearsal time to "catch up."

Each of these insights from the theater has important similarities for how you help stage the grand production of your new little star.

But let's start simply. What is your baby rehearsing right now?

Breathing

Weeks 9 through 12 after conception witness a symphony of new movements. The baby more than doubles in length. She grows to a length of more than 3 inches from crown to rump and would look precious in the palm of your hand if that were possible. Depending on the size of your hands, she might be about as big as one of your or your partner's fingers. She also puts on weight, the hollows of her cheeks filling in, up to about 45 grams—about as much as a Hershey's chocolate bar. Her skin thickens so that you can no longer see through it. Fingernails, toenails, and even permanent teeth start to form.

But what catches my eye are the movements. The hiccups you will probably see in your newborn may start as early as Week 9. (And you'll probably feel them later too, even before you see them or hear them.) Head movements follow quickly, usually nodding up and down before shaking side to side—gotta love that positive attitude. Soon her head, arms, and legs will all be moving slowly, as if she were doing baby tai chi in an underwater park. Mother acts as dojo to a micromartial artist!

The baby may bring her own hand to her face as early as 10 weeks after conception to caress her own cheek long before you will stroke it or she will reach out to touch yours.

At 10 or 11 weeks, she will start to breathe.

Breathe?! She's underwater. The gills and tail are long gone; she is clearly a human baby. Her nostrils are corked with plugs of extra skin cells. Breathe?

Breathing Babies Before Birth

I thought babies got oxygen through the umbilical cord. Why do babies breathe before they are born if they are in water?

Palo Alto

Babies begin to breathe long before air enters their lungs. They inhale and exhale the same amniotic fluids they've been peeing. The diaphragm muscle contracts and the belly bulges out. The diaphragm relaxes and the chest expands. In and out. Breathe.

This is more than a prenatal meditation exercise or a childbirth class for a little someone who's got as much to be concerned about during labor as you do. This quiet, subtle movement is critical for life, even though doctors didn't know about it until the time I was in medical school.

This is a rehearsal. It grows and strengthens the breathing muscles—the diaphragm, the muscles between the ribs, those above the collarbones, and those in the neck—so they will be able to do the job when the umbilical cord, the current lifeline, is abruptly severed. Like a diver who suddenly loses his air supply, the baby will be ready. He's been practicing with a backup tank.

And this rehearsal does even more. It guides the growth of the lungs themselves, the almost magical exchange organs that spin life out of thin air. They are a work in progress that takes shape during rehearsal.

If the rehearsal period is cut short, if the baby is born too soon, breathing may not be possible without a ventilator. In fact, getting enough rehearsal to even try to open is the main factor in determining whether a baby can make it at all on the outside.

We know that breathing practice is not an all-day affair. Most babies breathe more in the evenings. They breathe for a while and take a break for a while. A 10-minute breathing workout is a good session at this stage.

Some have breathing that is slow and regular and appears unconscious. Other breathing is fast and uneven and appears intentional. They practice breathing on autopilot; they practice taking over the controls.

All the while, what Mom is doing makes a big difference, though we still have a lot to learn about how. We do know that what and how she eats influences breathing. Baby's breathing accelerates after a glass of sugar water, but it is uneven. It's also faster after whole foods and more regular. A cigarette rapidly shuts down fetal breathing. It changes the drive to breathe, and lung development suffers measurably. The effect lasts a long time after the mother or her partner (or the guy at the next table) has finished enjoying the cigarette.

Eating

Shortly after she has integrated the breathing thing into her repertoire, the baby starts to practice swallowing. She's still getting ready for her big debut. When the curtain rises in front of a live audience, her gastrointestinal (GI) tract will have to take over full responsibility for swallowing and digesting all of the nutrition she's going to get. By 12 weeks after conception, the entire length of the GI tract has the nerves and muscles needed to keep things moving along.

Like the practice breathing, the practice swallowing is necessary for development. During rehearsals, the length of the GI tract comes together as a coordinated disassembly line, with the acids in the stomach, the enzymes in the pancreas, and the villi (tiny fingers of lining membrane) in the small intestines all learning their roles.

The pace of swallowing varies with the changing flavor of the amniotic fluid. When there's a little extra glucose in amniotic soup, swallowing proceeds with visibly more gusto. Perhaps your baby has cravings too!

Most people think that babies get all of their nutrition through the umbilical cord. But they actually practice digesting the amniotic juice that they swallow. This juice is high in glucose, lactate, and amino acids, like a protein energy drink at a juice bar. Babies get 10 to 20 percent of their protein requirements from the high-protein drink they swallow, absorb, and use. By term, they are drinking the equivalent of a 12-ounce can or two of this every day. Even though this is practice drinking and they have an umbilical safety net, to some degree they already depend on this brew they make with Mom in order to grow. They're getting ready to nurse.

Making Faces

Sometimes little children like to practice making faces while looking in a mirror. I've watched my kids try out different smiles to get ready for a camera.

In the womb, there are no mirrors. But babies are already displaying different temperaments. This is visible in their differing activity levels, their types of movements, their rhythms, and their balance between acting and reacting. It's also visible in their faces.

An impulse arises in the brain. Facial muscles move. Different babies make different facial expressions. Rehearsing. Gaining control of that marvelous little mug. Getting ready to meet you and to enchant you with their faces.

9

How Touching

Weeks 13 to 16 in Baby Time

During the next four weeks (13 through 16 after conception), your baby makes great strides in growing into the appearance she'll have at birth. She again doubles in length. Before she was about the length of a finger; now she is about the length of a hand. Meanwhile, during this month, she more than quadruples her weight. The little slow-motion boxer would weigh in at between a quarter and a half pound. One of the most striking changes taking place in her growth is the slowed growth of her head (thankfully, because delivery is enough of a challenge as it is). The brain is still growing, in some ways even more quickly, but the new increase in brain complexity and surface area comes more from wrinkles and pleats than from size. What can be seen this month from the outside is that she is becoming long-limbed.

By now, if you took a peek, you could see whether your baby is a boy or a girl. We'll talk about taking a peek later in this chapter. A little boy's penis has made its appearance, so that an inadvertent glimpse might give away the gender secret. A little girl's vagina has already formed as well. In addition, she has grown fallopian tubes to transport the tiny eggs she is already guarding for the future.

And the rest of her life's supply of hair follicles has subtly grown in. The stage is set for pubic hair and underarm hair in her teen years. For now, she is covered by soft, almost invisible lanugo (cottony) hair. A rehearsal costume. Most of this will disappear by birth. Her eyebrows, though, are already visible. They will stay. So too might the little mop of hair on her head.

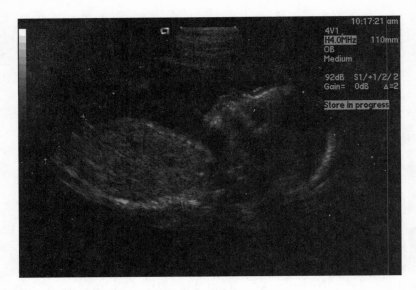

Beautiful baby at 130 days after conception

The Exploratorium

Having recently achieved the ability to move, your baby begins to explore his watery world. In the dark. With his eyelids fused closed. My kids love to play hide-and-seek in the dark. Another fun adventure is a visit to places like the Tactile Dome at the Exploratorium, the hands-on museum of science, art, and human perception in San Francisco. Inside the Exploratorium sits a large geodesic dome with a long line of kids and adults waiting their turn to enter. There's a pile of their shoes nearby. When you crawl into the dome, you leave the world of light behind. In the pitch darkness, you navigate a multifloor labyrinth lined with a tactile kaleidoscope of textures. When you successfully reach the end of the maze, you tumble down a chute into a huge, welcoming tub of birdseed and emerge into the light. You'll still find birdseed in your clothes months later.

Exploratorium literature states, "Visitors have compared the experience to being born again, turning yourself inside out head first, being swallowed by a whale, and inevitably, being enfolded in a giant womb."

When I've gone through the dome, I've been struck by the fact that even though it is an impressive sculpture exhibit that I have explored intimately by touch alone, I left feeling more aware of myself than of the dome. I felt a heightened awareness of my own body, my muscles, my posture, even the hairs on my arm, which I rarely notice. I was inadvertently exploring me.

This makes sense. We know that blind people tend to have an enhanced sense of touch. Their brains rewire to give more priority to senses other than sight. New research published in the June 24, 2003, issue of *Neurology* documents that just 90 minutes in the dark physically improves the senses of touch and spatial acuity in adults. The brain temporarily reallocates processing resources. This improvement disappears within two hours of regaining vision. What does this imply about developing babies? I have a suggestion.

The Tactile Home

Nerve cells start making their way into your baby's skin as early as six weeks after conception. They first appear just around the mouth. Soon they are present in a wider area of the face and in the palms of the hands as well. Then in the upper chest. From these areas, the regions of sensitive skin spread like a wave. By 13 weeks from conception, except for an area on the top and back of the scalp that might prefer to remain numb for delivery, the baby's whole body has come alive to the sense of touch!

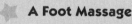

A Foot Massage

When I rub my belly can my baby feel it?

Newmom2b

Now when your baby moves her hand to brush her cheek, she feels her cheek; she feels her hand; she feels where they are in space. With her tiny opposable thumb, she is capable of grasping an intruding medical instrument. (Under normal medical circumstances, she would never get that chance.) She explores her watery world with her eyes closed, learning who she is. Her skin is sensitive to pressure, pain, temperature, and position. She may be aware of the hairs that cover her body. And of pressure on your belly. So yes, she might be able to feel it if you rub. Don't play *too* rough, but you can vary the pressure or cadence and see how your baby responds.

Most parents believe, if they think about it, that babies develop with their eyes fused closed until a certain point in time, when the eyes open. Not so! Babies develop with their eyes *open*. They remain open until the baby starts to move and explore with the sense of touch. Then the eyelids shut and fuse for a while to keep him in darkness. I propose that one of the reasons for this is to make the sense of touch as exquisitely sensitive as possible. Babies close their eyes and enter their own exploratorium, their own tactile dome, to learn about themselves.

Exploration 102

Exploration is a major theme of childhood. At various times kids will explore primarily with their eyes, their ears, their hands, their mouths, their humor, their TV remote, their keyboard, and their mouse. The vehicles for exploration will change and combine over time (hands are very important at four months and at 16 years, as well as at several times in between). But exploration is a deep and persistent drive. One of the joys of parenting is to accompany our children on this voyage of exploration, seeing the world through their hands.

One of our ongoing tasks is to create safe environments for them to explore. And often they must explore alone. These safe environments might include a hosted cast party for teenage drama enthusiasts, a monitored computer, a backyard jungle gym, a childproofed family room, a bassinet, and that first world—the womb.

Throughout all of these journeys, touch is a primal way to communicate with our children. Touch is also the sense we most restrict. The first "no" your baby hears from you is likely to be a "Don't touch." We don't often tell our children not to see, not to hear, or not to smell. Not touching is a refrain kids hear from the crib to college. Why the focus on touch? Because when we touch, we both sense and handle—we interact. This two-way power can cause trouble—including burns, cuts, and shocks. But it can also be a profound way to connect. I like creating a safe, touch-rich world for kids.

Adult Discoveries

Meanwhile, some parents explore their children, even before they feel the baby's first kick. In the 21st century, parents can have a variety of new types of "quickening" experiences in which they learn a little or a lot about their babies.

A Blood Test

Proteins and amino acids pass back and forth between the mother's blood and the baby's. A beautiful example of this is thyroid hormone. The baby's thyroid gland has only recently begun functioning, at 10 to 12 weeks after conception. Before this, thyroid hormone from the gland in the mother's neck drizzled into her bloodstream, crossed the placenta, and helped direct the growth of her baby's brain. By 12 weeks, the baby's homegrown thyroid hormone has taken over the job and moved the brain in new directions of wrinkling and complexity.

Meanwhile, the main protein in the baby's blood is called α-fetoprotein (AFP). It seems to be the workhorse of the early bloodstream. It keeps liquid in the vessels and carries molecules from place to place. The closest thing adults usually have in their blood is called albumin. Much of the embryo's production capacity is devoted to manufacturing AFP. It's made by the liver, by the yolk sac, and by the primal gastrointestinal (GI) tract. Babies pee it out into the amniotic fluid, practice swallowing and digesting it, and then manufacture it again. Some of the AFP drifts into Mom's bloodstream.

It's said that AFP serves no purpose in the mother's body, but I disagree. I suspect it provides a hidden signal to her body, communicating information about the growth and well-being of the baby—or babies. The normal levels in Mom's blood change rapidly and predictably with the embryo's growth and with the number of babies she is carrying.

If the baby has unexpectedly exposed membranes, as from a neural tube that has not closed properly, the amount of AFP that spills into the amniotic fluid may be much higher. Alternatively, with certain chromosome abnormalities, such as Down syndrome or trisomy 18, the mixed signals from the baby's DNA may lead to less AFP being manufactured. Observations of these variations led to a screening of mothers' blood called maternal serum α-fetoprotein.

The test is performed when a woman is 15 to 20 weeks pregnant (the baby is 13 to 18 weeks after conception). Eighty or maybe ninety percent of moms whose babies have a neural tube problem will have high AFP levels, but there is a lot of overlap with mothers of healthy babies. Sometimes we can explain high levels of AFP—perhaps we underestimated the gestational age of the baby or perhaps there are twins. Even when there is no good explanation for the high AFP, about 14 out of 15 women with an abnormal test end up having normal babies.

This test is not intended to diagnose problems. It's a screening net to identify some pregnancies we may need to follow more closely to look for problems. Most identified by the test are fine. It's also wise to pay attention to low AFP levels, but they are even less predictive of trouble than are high levels. A triple test, measuring AFP, hCG (the "pregnancy-indicating" hormone), and a form of free estrogen, makes the test results more precise.

A major study published in the *New England Journal of Medicine* in October 2003 followed more than 8,000 women at more than a dozen different medical centers. It found that by adding ultrasounds to certain blood tests, screening can be accomplished much earlier—as early as 12 weeks pregnant (10 weeks after conception). The ultrasound at this point measures nuchal translucency (the fluid in the back of the neck). This combination of tests is able to identify about 85 percent of children with Down syndrome. But 9 percent of the time the combined tests suggest a child has Down syndrome when he does not.

The inherent mistakes in these tests underline how important it is that it remains the parent's choice whether to have one or more of these tests. If the parents know they don't want an amniocentesis (discussed in the next section) because of the slight risk of miscarriage, they may not want to have even the noninvasive screening tests, knowing that an abnormal result may cause needless anxiety. Some parents can't relax *without* the tests. The choice should clearly be yours, not your doctor's.

A Mixed-Drink Test

Amniocentesis is a test that can accurately diagnose problems. It gives lots more information than any blood test and analyzes the chromosomes of the baby. Amniocentesis is an analysis of the amniotic fluid, that mixed drink made by mother and baby. But to get this special liquor, a sharp needle must be slipped into the womb, into the baby's world.

Traditionally, the woman is 15 or 16 weeks pregnant, though it is sometimes done earlier. This would put the baby at 13 or 14 weeks after conception, with his eyes closed, intent on exploring the smooth, soft world.

Amniocentesis is an invasive test that carries some risk. How much risk? Different studies give different answers. A large, well-designed Danish study

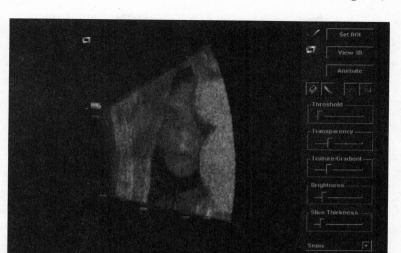

A 3D "peekaboo"

from 1986 found a miscarriage rate of 1.7 percent in those who had amnios compared with 0.7 percent in matched women who didn't get the test. Some studies have found no risk at all. Since the 1986 study, amnio techniques have improved significantly, especially by routinely using a high-quality ultrasound picture to guide the needle.

It's common for experts to say that the risk is 0.5 percent—1 baby in 200 will die because of the procedure—but many experts privately believe that the true risk is lower, probably about 0.2 percent, or 1 baby in 500. That number is very small or very large, depending on how you look at it.

If about 5 million babies are born in the United States each year and all of their mothers had amniocenteses, then perhaps 10,000 or more babies would miscarry because of the test. What a tragedy! Instead, amniocentesis is recommended in situations where the information gained is likely to counterbalance the risk. Women over age 35 are the classic example given. At age 35, the chance of finding a chromosomal problem is about 0.5 percent and the risk of the test is about 0.5 percent. With each year, the equation tilts a bit more. Women with a positive AFP are another example. About 14 out of 15 of the babies are healthy, but there is about a 7 percent chance of a problem that could be diagnosed on amniocentesis. The difficulty, of course, is trying to balance the value of important information against even a very small risk of losing a healthy baby.

If you are given the relevant facts to your specific situation (for instance, there is a 5 percent risk of Rh sensitization from the amnio in a mother with a negative blood type) in an unrushed manner, then I support whichever choice you make on the matter and your doctor should too. Parents know what they need.

Chorionic Villous Sampling

For some situations, the time to amniocentesis seems like a long time to wait. Chorionic villous sampling (CVS) is another technique for obtaining fetal cells for chromosomal and other analysis. The cells may be obtained with a needle through Mom's abdominal wall or with a catheter inserted through the vagina and cervix. Either way, ultrasound guidance is recommended. This test can be performed as early as when a woman is 10 weeks pregnant (Day 56 in baby time).

Many studies have compared the risks of amniocentesis to the risks of CVS. Putting these studies together, CVS appears to be about one and a half times as risky as regular amniocentesis but safer than early amniocentesis. You are also more likely to get ambiguous results with CVS.

A Magic Window

In an earlier chapter we talked about how addictive tobacco can be and how difficult it can be to stop. Listen to this: women who have a prenatal ultrasound tend to stop smoking. And drinking. Something magical happens when a woman and her partner look at a screen and see their baby moving. I'm fascinated more by the change in parents' behavior than I am with the technical measurements made by the ultrasonographer. The parents and the baby are exploring this amazing new life at the same time—together.

★ **Playing the Odds**
★ How accurate are ultrasounds in determining the sex of the baby?
★ The nurse told me she was 80 percent sure that my baby is a girl.
★ Should I start buying pink?

Tuere

A typical time for a routine prenatal ultrasound is when the mother is 18 weeks pregnant (the baby has reached 16 weeks after conception, is 6 inches long, is clearly a boy or a girl, and is breathing, moving, touching, experiencing, and learning). How accurate an ultrasound is at determining the gender depends on the age of the baby, the quality of the equipment, and the skill of the ultrasonographer. Today's ultrasounds tend to be very accurate, but I wouldn't assume it to be *more* accurate than your health care staff suggest at the time.

There is general agreement that ultrasound is a great tool for a number of pregnancy complications. However, whether or not all pregnant women should have a routine ultrasound remains controversial.

The arguments in favor of routine ultrasound are that it provides much more accurate dating of your pregnancy than does a menstrual period; it alerts you early on if you are having more than one baby; it locates the placenta to warn your doctor if it may be in the way at the time of delivery; it can detect many abnormalities in babies; and adding it to other screening tests makes them more accurate.

The Magic Window
Are ultrasounds really safe?

BigBelly

The main downside is the cost. If 5 million pregnant women in the United States had an ultrasound each year, the health care bill would be more than $1 billion annually. Even though the ultrasound provides lots of information, several large studies suggest that doing it for all presumed healthy babies and mothers doesn't make much of a difference in the pregnancy results—at least no difference that couldn't be accounted for by the parents stopping dangerous habits such as smoking.

Safety does not seem to be an issue. Although intense sound waves can cause damage to living tissue, the amount used in a diagnostic ultrasound is quite low. These machines have been in use since the late 1950s, and no confirmed problem from them has been found in the babies, the moms, the dads, or the ultrasonographers. Whether looking at obvious possible problems such as leukemia or subtle effects such as school performance, ultrasound has passed the test whenever it's been looked at carefully.

Do I think we should pay for ultrasounds for healthy pregnancies? I would pay for one for my own child. And I believe we should offer to pay for one for all pregnant women. But as with all of these tests, I believe the choice should be the woman's. One can certainly bond powerfully and grow a healthy child without this experience, as families have done for almost all of history. But for me, I would choose yes.

To me, the main advantage is not the information, but the connection offered to parents. When Jacques Cousteau first took cameras underwater, he opened up an enchanted new world for us to see. When ultrasounds were first turned toward the wombs of pregnant women, an even more marvelous world appeared. Sights that had been hidden for ages were now open to our view, and one of the first things we saw was our babies sucking their tiny thumbs even before they were born.

Each time a woman has a prenatal ultrasound, it provides a view of a unique new member of a changing family and starts a positive addiction to each other that is stronger than nicotine, heroin, or cocaine. I would rather spend a billion dollars on this than on many other public projects.

PART II

Dancing Feet

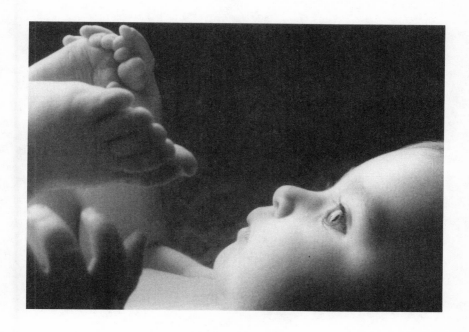

10

"Stomp!"

Weeks 16 to 20 in Baby Time

Is that the baby? Sometimes the early kicks aren't identifiable at all. Is it just a bit of gas, a tummy rumble—or might it be our child? Soon mothers and fathers will both be able to recognize the budding cardiokickboxer within.

On average, the magical moment of first awareness, when a first-time mother first knows she is feeling the fluttering of her baby's feet pressing out to touch her, happens during the 17th week after conception (at 16.1 weeks to be precise). For some, it comes earlier than expected, for others later. About two-thirds of women have this experience within 18 days of the mark, one way or the other. The next time around, the special moment usually happens a little over a week earlier. What a thrilling moment!

We call this moment *quickening*. Today, to be quick usually means to be speedy—like good pizza delivery. Or the word *quicken* might remind some of a popular accounting software program. But the root meaning of *quick* is "alive." And to quicken means to come alive.

In the Beginning

In the Supreme Court case *Roe v. Wade*, quickening was selected as critical for abortion decisions because of "a confluence of earlier philosophical, theological, and civil and canon law concepts of when life begins." In early English theology, a human soul entered the baby at the moment of the first kick. The first kick was the last act of the animal or instinctive soul and the first act of the human soul, hence the moment of quickening.

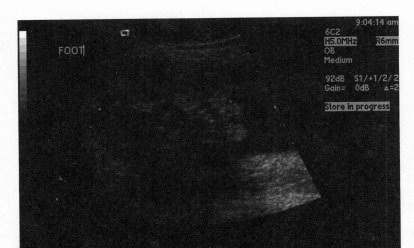

Belly dancing

We know today that the first kick a mother feels follows many unwitnessed kicks. The baby has long been dancing to the drumbeat of Mom's heart. Kicks make themselves known when the baby is large enough to brace a shoulder against one side of the uterus while pressing against the other side with a foot. Having spent months floating freely, it is a moment of being held in place by the mother's muscular embrace.

Truly, this is a quickening, a coming to life—but not of a soul. It is Mom's awareness of her baby that comes to life. This new tangible awareness leaves a footprint on Mom's heart. You will never be the same once you've been touched from within.

You have heard the baby's heartbeat; perhaps you've seen the baby on an ultrasound, but there is something profound about feeling the baby's greeting kick. Soon you might be able to make out your baby's elbow or head.

And I suspect there is also a quickening of the baby's awareness of *you* as she explores inside your body with eager hands and feet.

Not too long after Mom actually feels her baby, she is able to share this magical touch from within with others. In some ways, a father's quickening is even more profound. He doesn't feel changes transforming his own body, so these kicks are a dramatic physical confirmation of what is happening beyond his reach.

Leaps and Bounds

The baby dancing inside is now about the size of a squirrel. Pregnancy lasts about 266 days after conception. Now there are only about 152.8 days to go. The baby's length is growing rapidly at this stage. He's already at half his newborn length! The weight is growing more slowly—still about half a pound. Long and skinny.

There are eyebrows, eyelashes, and a tuft of hair on his head, as well as hair on his body (lanugo hair) that will soon disappear. This extra hair increases the sensitivity of his skin when rubbing against your body from within.

The baby also has more taste buds now than will be used at birth—taste buds on the tongue, the roof of the mouth, the sides of the mouth, even in the throat. With each swallow of amniotic fluid, the baby is learning about your habits, your tastes, your culture, your world.

In the fascinating film *Frequency*, Dennis Quaid is able to communicate through a wormhole in time with his adult son in the future. He realizes that his son will one day be sitting at his father's desk. He etches a message in the desk, and at the same moment, his son sees the message in the future. In real life, you can communicate with your soon-to-be-born son or daughter by eating your favorite fruit or savoring vegetables that you like.

Your baby stores away the secrets you share somewhere in 10 trillion neural connections amid 10 million nerve cells—a far cry from the single cell of just weeks ago. The brain is growing very rapidly these days, not in size but in connections and complexity as your baby learns at an astonishing rate about his body and yours.

His internal organs are mostly complete (though there are still no sweat glands). The bones of his skeletal system are largely in place, but they are just now beginning to harden as your baby uses your uterus as a strength-training machine for daily workouts. Much is accomplished with each kick.

Paying Attention

When those little feet make themselves known, this physical awareness transforms your relationship with your child. As you will continue to learn, *awareness* and *attention* are key parenting skills. Children grow toward attention the way sunflowers grow toward the sun. You will learn that babies are experts at doing what it takes to engage your attention, and perhaps kicking is one of their first ways to do this.

Throughout the journey of being parents, learning to be aware of the world from your little one's perspective will make the journey more reward-ing for all of you. Let's fast-forward for a moment to when you will have a four-year-old (sooner than you can imagine) and this principle will be eas-ier to grasp. Then we will come back to the present and apply it to your cur-rent choices. Here is a common scene as described by a concerned mother:

> Dr. Greene,
> My son, four years old, doesn't listen. At home, there are times when I have to ask him to do something (or not do something) several times. His preschool teacher says the same thing. She will call him two or three times from the play yard and will finally have to walk over and get him. This concerns me since there may be situations where I will need his immediate attention (e.g., crossing the street or an earthquake), and I'm afraid that he will not listen at a critical time. We have tried time-out, yelling, whispering—you name it, we've done it. This is also starting to rub off on his three-year-old sister. What do you suggest?
>
> *Covina, California*

Sometimes when we talk to our children, it feels like a surrealistic play, where we repeat ourselves over and over, and no one seems to hear. This is frustrating for us and unhealthy for our children.

Imagine that your four-year-old son is jumping on your lovely new living room sofa with sheer delight and dirty feet.

Scenario 1:
You: "Stop jumping on the sofa!"
Child: (no response)
You: "I said, stop jumping on the sofa!!!"
Child: (no response)
You: "How many times do I have to tell you? If you don't stop right now, . . ." (You think to yourself that you sound like one of your parents)
Child: (no response)
You: "Why can't you be more like your sister?"
Child: (no response)
You: "STOP THAT!!!!"
He shrugs and walks away.

Sound familiar? If you haven't been around kids much, it soon will. Occasionally, the unresponsiveness results from a physical problem. If you are ever concerned that your child is unable to hear, understand, or attend well, take her to the pediatrician for evaluation. Otherwise, this is a communication trial faced in varying degrees by most parents.

Why do children who can hear perfectly well tune parents out? Kids are passionate about a great many things. It is all too easy for our voices to come to represent nothing more than an unwanted intrusion into their world: "Stop that. . . . Stay in your seat. . . . Keep quiet. . . . It's time to stop playing. . . . Don't climb on the chair. . . . Get in bed."

Children are full of energy, wanting to play, to move, to explore—drunk with freedom. As adults, we are anchored by responsibilities, wanting peace, courtesy, safety, order—haunted by the way things should be. These agendas collide. We feel frustrated; they feel nagged; we all grumble. Neither giving in nor relentlessly pressing your own point of view will bring the results you most want.

The grand adventure of parenting is learning to bring these two marvelous worlds together in a creative union, to see the world through your child's eyes, without letting go of your own needs and desires. You can even start now.

Bi-empathy

Practice seeing events from two perspectives, yours and the person with whom you are interacting. As you become skilled at "bi-empathic vision" (a phrase I coined to describe seeing and feeling both worlds simultaneously), new ways of speaking to your four-year-old (and new ways of interacting with your unborn baby) will suggest themselves to you. New ideas will also occur to you as we discover in Chapter 12 what your baby is seeing and hearing and in Chapter 13 what sleep is like for your baby.

Have you seen the recent three-dimensional posters and books that don't require those special glasses for viewing? They can take a little practice, but if you let your focus soften so that your two eyes see the page independently, a previously invisible three-dimensional image will pop into view. With practice, you can let your focus soften with your child. Let one "eye" continue to see what you as a wise parent see, while with the other you try to see what he as a child sees. A hidden reality will emerge—for both of you!

Bi-empathic vision is the best way to teach your child what he needs to know to succeed in this world.

Let's look at how you both might feel after Sofa Scenario 1. You are frustrated, angry, concerned that you're losing control, and worried that he won't respond in an emergency. He feels hurt, squelched, misunderstood, and angry. He thinks the sofa is more important to you than he is, he resents his sister, and he wants you to leave him alone. Worst of all, he learns nothing positive.

Another Path

Now let's try the sofa scenario again, using bi-empathic vision. You might say, "Jumping on the sofa is sooo fun! I love to jump, but jumping hurts the sofa and it might hurt you. Let's go jump on an old pillow!" (You scoop him up or take him by the hand, put an old pillow on the floor, and jump together, giggling.) How do you both feel this time?

You enjoy your son, and you spend less time and energy than in Scenario 1. He is giggling, feels understood, and realizes you think he's important. He wants to listen to you. This time he learns that jumping hurts the sofa, there are better places to jump, and "Mom loves me."

This is a long process. There will be many moments of exasperation. Still, nothing compares to the thrill of bringing your two worlds together in a burst of creativity. Not only will you raise your child well, but he will raise you—to new levels of empathy, compassion, and wisdom. Your life will never be the same.

When perspectives collide unpleasantly, consider calling on your sense of humor. Humor is fun; kids love fun. Laughing and playing are part of the wonder of childhood. When you can use a light touch and inject humor and respect into a situation, bi-empathy happens naturally. You bring your perspective about what needs to happen, and your child brings his (which usually includes fun!). As you combine both perspectives, a richer view of the situation and a richer relationship emerges for both of you.

Kids also develop a strong sense of what is or is not fair. They view the world through "fairness glasses." Demonstrate respect for your child, his time, his belongings, and his desires. Expect the same back from him. He will come to understand this.

Issues for Today

Now that the baby feels more real, it is a good time to begin using bi-empathic vision to consider issues such as breastfeeding and circumcision (or not).

Breastfeeding

As your baby starts to make her kicks known, her nipples are appearing, and under them milk ducts are taking shape, preparing her to be able to feed her own babies if she chooses. It's time to start choosing what you will do with yours. We'll discuss *how* to nurse later, for those who choose breastfeeding. We'll also discuss how to select the best formula for your baby for those who choose bottle-feeding. When parents have access to the information and support they need, I trust that the decision they make for their family is the right one and should not be questioned. We'll start with a little background information on breastfeeding.

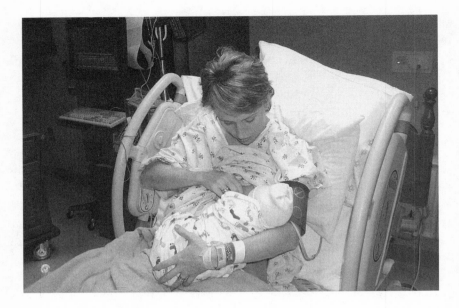

The Scientific Wonders of Breastfeeding. Many studies comparing the frequency of illness between breast- and formula-fed infants have demonstrated fewer illnesses and less severe illnesses in breast-fed infants. Breastfeeding helps protect against diarrhea, lower respiratory infections, ear infections, bacterial meningitis, and urinary tract infections. Some studies have suggested a decrease in noninfectious diseases such as eczema and asthma. How might breastfeeding do this?

- **Psychological factors.** Over the last two decades, the developing field of psychoneuroimmunology has demonstrated repeatedly that an individual's psychological state has a direct effect on his or her immune function. Perhaps the nursing experience by itself directly improves the immune status of infants.
- **Antibodies.** All types of antibodies are found in human breast milk. The highest concentration is found in colostrum, the premilk that is only available from the breast the first three to five days of the baby's life. Secretory immunoglobulin A (IgA)—a type of antibody that protects the ears, nose, throat, and gastrointestinal (GI) tract—is found in high amounts in breast milk throughout the first year. The IgA attaches to the lining of the nose, mouth, and throat and fights the attachment of specific infecting agents. Breast milk levels of IgA

against specific viruses and bacteria increase in response to Mom's exposure to these organisms. Human milk is environmentally specific milk; the mother protects her baby against the organisms most likely to be an immediate problem.

- **Lactoferrin.** Human lactoferrin is an iron-binding protein found in breast milk but not available in formulas. It limits the availability of iron to bacteria in the intestines and alters which healthy bacteria will thrive in the gut. Again, its highest concentrations are in colostrum, but it appears throughout the entire first year. It has a direct antibiotic effect on bacteria such as *Escherichia coli* (*E. coli*).

- **Lysozyme.** Human breast milk contains lysozyme (a potent digestive ingredient) at a level 30 times higher than that in any formula. Interestingly, while other contents of breast milk vary widely between well-nourished and poorly nourished mothers, the amount of lysozyme stays about the same, suggesting that it is very important. It has a strong influence on the type of bacteria that inhabit the intestinal tract.

- **Growth factors.** Human breast milk specifically encourages the growth of *Lactobacillaceae*, which are helpful bacteria that can inhibit many of the disease-causing bacteria and parasites. In fact, there is a striking difference between the bacteria found in the guts of breast- and formula-fed infants. Breast-fed infants have a level of lactobacilli that is typically 10 times greater than that of formula-fed infants. Both the presence of the lactobacilli and the action of the lactoferrin and lysozyme help protect the infant.

- **Allergic factors.** The cows' milk protein used in most formulas is a foreign protein. When babies drink most nonhuman milks, they actually develop antibodies to the foreign protein. Research has shown that without exception the important food allergens found in milk and soybean formulas resist destruction in the acid of the stomach for as long as 60 minutes (as compared to human milk protein which is digested in the stomach within 15 minutes). The foreign proteins pass through the stomach and reach the intestines intact, where they gain access and can produce sensitization. While research in this area is still relatively new, this early exposure to foreign proteins may be a predisposing factor in such illnesses as eczema and asthma.

- **Carnitine.** While carnitine is present in both breast milk and formula, the carnitine in breast milk has a higher bioavailability. Breast-fed babies have significantly higher carnitine levels than their formula-fed counterparts. Carnitine is necessary to make use of fatty acids as an energy source. Other functions of carnitine have been hypothesized but have not yet been proven.

- **DHA and ARA.** The main long-chain fatty acids found in human milk are still not present in some formulas in the United States. These lipids are important building blocks, particularly in the brain and the retina. Some studies suggest that in their absence, babies' mental and visual development is hampered.
- **Change.** Breast milk provides the specific nutrients that babies need at each age and in each situation. The early data about breast milk came from the pooled breast milk of many mothers. At that time, it was not understood how unique human breast milk is for each individual infant.

Each year it becomes clearer that human breast milk is precisely designed for human babies. The mysteries of this dynamic fluid have not been fully deciphered. Why so much choline in breast milk? Are there other important micronutrients or factors that we don't even have instruments to measure yet? While today's formulas are an excellent alternative, human breast milk is the superior food for human babies for many reasons.

Your Perspective. Different women (and their mates) come to nursing with different expectations. Some foresee it as a joyful, perhaps even glorious, experience. Others imagine it to be distasteful or embarrassing. Words that I've heard women use to describe the idea of breastfeeding include *convenient, inconvenient, healthy, natural, intimate, exhausting, fulfilling, bonding, painful, awkward, cowlike, magical, scary, soothing, economical, weight losing, body image changing,* and *invaluable treasure.* Talking about the images and emotions you have on the topic, wherever they come from, may help you to clarify your perspective.

Your Baby's Perspective. After about 266 days spent in 24/7 contact with you and being nourished from your body, she is born with instincts to seek out and feed from your breast. She might suckle a soft, warm, living nipple overlying your soothing heartbeat. Or she might feed from a nipple expertly constructed from latex rubber or a synthetic polymer called silicone while being held in your loving arms. Does this feel like the difference between kissing a person and kissing a plastic doll?

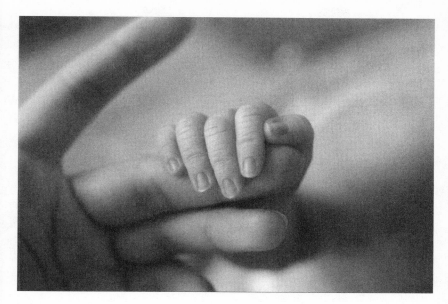

She might drink living milk designed just for her, which tastes and smells uniquely like you and changes from moment to moment, from feeding to feeding, and from month to month. In this way, she might continue sampling and tasting the foods you eat. And the medicines you take. And the chemicals you're exposed to. Or she might drink a sterilized formula made from a plant or from the milk of another species. This milk is scientifically fortified to contain the best of what we know that children need to grow. It tastes the same day after day after day.

She might drink an active milk that helps protect her from illnesses such as ear infections or diarrhea. It supports brain growth and could give her a slight (five to seven point) IQ edge. As we'll see, much brain growth happens during the first two or three years after leaving the protective environment of the uterus, and breast milk is designed to carry on this development previously fueled through the umbilical cord. Or she might drink a formula with few if any immune properties, and wake up crying from more frequent ear infections or have an irritated bum from runny diarrhea.

Manufacturers do supplement some formulas with DHA and ARA, two of the fatty acids in breast milk that support brain and vision growth. If you choose a formula, I suggest one with the levels of DHA and ARA recommended by the World Health Organization.

Bi-empathy. Choose feeding/nurturing solutions that honor both you and your child. And I believe no one should second-guess your decision, whatever it is. Breast milk allows you to continue to feed your baby after birth, to stay physically connected. It is the perfect food for babies. But today's infant formulas are the best substitutes that have ever been available. Millions of formula-fed babies have grown up healthy, smart, bright-eyed, and strong.

Circumcision

If you know that you are having a girl, you might think that the circumcision discussion is irrelevant. Likewise, if you know you are going to have your son circumcised to follow your religious heritage, it may seem like there is nothing to discuss. I've found, however, that considering circumcision can provoke strong opinions that can give you insight into yourself as a parent, whether or not you have anything to decide. When I meet with expectant parents before their baby is born, this discussion is often the most interesting.

⭐ **A Loaded Question**

I am an expecting first-time mom. I am six weeks away from my estimated due date and am eagerly awaiting a baby boy. I have some concerns about circumcision. I have heard from other moms that the procedure is routine in the United States. What are the advantages and disadvantages of performing a circumcision on a newborn?

Austin, Texas

Your Perspective. Circumcision is a surgical procedure to permanently remove the foreskin, a sensitive part of a boy's penis. The inner lining of the foreskin is a mucous membrane that helps keep the head of the penis (also a mucous membrane) soft, moist, and highly sensitized.

In thinking about this issue, consider not just how you feel about circumcision, but why you feel it. If it seems like an obvious choice because of your culture or faith, then perhaps you'll understand that passing your religious and cultural heritage on to your son is important to you. Look for ways to pass that richness along, and look for ways to connect more deeply to it yourself, now that you are a parent. Or perhaps you'll come to understand that what your parents or others in your community think is decisive in your choices as a parent.

If you want your son to be circumcised or uncircumcised to look like Daddy, then perhaps building and deepening the father-son bond is especially important to you. You'll find many ways to do this throughout this book. You may want to invite Dad to put his palm on your belly and feel his son move as you discuss circumcision.

If you want your son to be circumcised because you think the penis is easier to clean, then this might mean that convenience is very important to you as a parent. Or it may be that you are squeamish about your boy's genitals. Or that you don't know how to clean an uncircumcised penis, and learning seems difficult (see Chapter 16 on caring for an uncircumcised penis).

For some, the circumcision decision hinges on a question of beauty, somewhat like pierced ears or noses, or shaved legs or underarms. Like a tatoo, circumcision is more permanent (although foreskin reattachment has been accomplished). Appearances are important in our society. If you recognize this and want the penis to be circumcised or uncircumcised because of the way it looks, understand that appearances are very important to you as a parent and may underlie many decisions as your children grow, even without your being conscious of it.

Sometimes it is a question of fitting in with peers during the growing-up years. If your chief concern either way is that your son will be similar to other boys in the locker room, understand that social bonding is very important to you as a parent and look for ways to start helping him connect with others early.

If you want your son to remain uncircumcised because that's the way little boys are designed, you might find this same philosophy underlying your approach to issues from ear infections to attention deficit hyperactivity disorder (ADHD).

There are dozens of other reasons one might feel strongly for or against circumcision. Use your reasons as a mirror to learn more about yourself as a parent.

If you want your son to be circumcised to promote good health, honor your desires for your son's well-being. And consider what we have learned about the medical advantages and disadvantages of circumcision.

Medical Risks and Benefits of Circumcision. The American Academy of Pediatrics Task Force on Circumcision concluded in 1999 that there are specific potential medical advantages to circumcision, as well as disadvantages and risks. The following are the most scientifically established:

- **Urinary tract infections.** Boys who are not circumcised tend to get more urinary tract infections (UTIs) than their peers do, especially in the first year of life. Combining the data from several major studies, somewhere between 7 and 14 per 1,000 uncircumcised baby boys are expected to develop a UTI, compared with 1 to 2 per 1,000 boys who have been circumcised. Even though the infections might be up to 10 times more common in uncircumcised boys, about 99 percent will not have a problem either way. Urinary tract infections in the first year can lead to hospitalization. An uncircumcised baby boy has about a 1 in 140 chance of being hospitalized for a UTI during the first year of life; a circumcised baby boy has about a 1 in 530 chance. There may be an effect on later scarring of the kidney or kidney failure, but this has not been proven. By the way, evidence suggests that breastfeeding has a three-fold protective effect against UTIs in uncircumcised boys.

- **Cancer of the penis.** Newborn circumcision (as opposed to later circumcision) does seem to help protect against this devastating cancer. Men who were not circumcised as babies have at least 3 times (perhaps as much as 40 times) the risk of cancer of the penis that their peers do. But this cancer is rare either way. In the United States, it affects about 9 or 10 men out of a million. There are two ways to prevent cancer of the penis: by removing the foreskin and by keeping it clean and healthy. The biggest risk for penile cancer comes from *phimosis*, a condition in some uncircumcised males where the foreskin is too tight to retract properly. Good hygiene may be able to prevent most cases of both phimosis and penile cancer. Other important risk factors for developing cancer include genital warts, having more than 30 sexual partners, and cigarette smoking.

- **HIV.** A growing number of studies link noncircumcision in men with increased risk for human immunodeficiency virus (HIV) infection. This makes sense because the mucous membrane of the uncircumcised penis allows for closer connection and exchange of fluids. Various studies put the increased risk of infection for uncircumcised men at 1.5 to 8.4 times that of circumcised men in the same setting. But sexual practices are far more important than circumcision status in the risk of acquiring HIV.

- **Other sexually transmitted diseases.** In the same way, it makes sense that uncircumcised men would be at higher risk for other sexually transmitted diseases. Scientific data on this are inconsistent, but there does appear to be a true increased risk for syphilis. The data also suggest higher rates of genital herpes and warts. Cancer of the cervix (transmitted by the genital warts virus) is less common among Jewish and Muslim women. Perhaps this is related to the circumcision status of their mates. Practicing safe sex is important for all of us, but especially for those who have vulnerable mucous membranes because they are not circumcised.
- **Procedural complications.** Somewhere between 0.2 and 0.6 percent of boys having a circumcision also have a complication from the procedure. Bleeding is the most common of these, and infection is the second. Most of the time such complications are minor, but they can be severe. Structural problems of the penis are even less common, and again most are minor. Severe or life-threatening complications of circumcision are very rare, but they do occur.

There is no medical reason to recommend the routine surgical circumcision of baby boys. Good hygiene and safe sex practices can solve many of the possible problems, either way, but this is sometimes easier said than done.

Your Son's Perspective. In the short term, it's not hard to guess your son's perspective. If you were a baby, would you rather spend time in your parents' arms, gazing into their faces, listening to their coos, or be taken away by a stranger, strapped into a plastic restraining board, stuck in the genitals with needles containing local anesthetic—or worse, not stuck—and have a nerve-rich part of your genitals severed, leaving you inflamed, tender, and uncomfortable for hours or days?

Suzanne Dixon, M.D., in a 1984 article, demonstrated that circumcision is a stressful event that predictably alters a boy's behavior both during and after the procedure. Following the circumcision, he usually has a prolonged period of sleep and then is largely unavailable for bonding or social interaction for up to an additional 24 hours. The problem seems to be self-limited, and after 24 hours, his behavior is indistinguishable from that of his uncircumcised counterparts.

Sometimes we need to go through unpleasant experiences to get what we really want (childbirth can be that way). What is your son's long-term perspective? That is harder to guess.

What About Sex? We know that when the foreskin is cut off, the head of the penis dries out and its skin thickens measurably. Men who have been circumcised as adults sometimes describe the change as similar to applying a topical anesthetic to the penis. Some men mourn this loss of sensation. However, some men voluntarily use anesthetics to prolong erections.

The human body is designed for the mucous membrane of the head of the penis to glide back and forth across the mucous membrane of the vagina during intercourse—membrane-to-membrane contact. (Sometimes people think that a woman's lack of lubrication makes intercourse uncomfortable, but perhaps it is the man's!) Some women report greater pleasure with an uncircumcised penis, many strongly prefer circumcised.

Even though uncircumcised men may have more intense pleasure, men with an intact foreskin, on average, have a longer period of time between erection and ejaculation than their counterparts (but men without foreskins can learn to delay ejaculation).

It's difficult for anyone to guess someone else's sexual sensation, but my way of guessing what the two options might feel like is to touch the inside and outside parts of your own lips. The inside is like the sensitive, slippery, moist mucous membrane of the uncircumcised penis; the outside like the drier, less sensitive but still wonderful circumcised penis. And the difference in sensations in connecting might be like the difference between closed-mouth and open-mouth kissing—again, both wonderful.

But these are just guesses. A number of studies suggest such a difference. However, sex researchers Masters and Johnson found no difference in light touch sensation on the head of the penis between circumcised and uncircumcised men.

What About the Locker Room? The National Center for Health Statistics keeps records of trends in circumcision. Most recently, about 65 percent of boys born in U.S. hospitals are circumcised. The numbers have varied between 60 and 70 percent over the last two decades. The numbers are highest in the Midwest (81 percent) and lowest in the West (37 percent). Circumcision rates are rising in the Midwest and South, while they continue to fall in the West. Circumcision is uncommon in Asia,

South America, Central America, and most of Europe. Indeed, outside of the United States, circumcision for any reason other than religion is uncommon.

The Decision. Your own perspective will be easy to identify: pro, con, or ambivalent. You can learn much from each of these positions. Your son's perspective is harder to predict. Perhaps he will want circumcision to continue a family, cultural, or religious tradition. Perhaps his thoughts will be different from yours. Some boys who were not circumcised as babies, long for the procedure as they grow up. Some who were circumcised long to have the foreskin reattached or reconstructed. Most are happy with who they are and how they were raised. I can't tell you into which group your son will fall. I can tell you that it is far easier to get a circumcision later, if desired, than to successfully attach a working foreskin. And I can also tell you that anytime a boy is circumcised he deserves a proper anesthetic, even if someone tries to tell you this is unnecessary or inconvenient.

A Quickening

History records that Marie Antoinette once said to King Louis XVI of the House of Bourbon, "I have come, Sire, to complain of one of your subjects who has been so audacious as to kick me in the belly." In this way, she informed her husband that she was pregnant with their first child.

Parents respond when they feel their babies move or kick. Babies respond when they feel their parents rub or press on Mom's belly. It reminds me of two people in adjoining rooms learning to communicate through the wall in between.

On average, there are about 152.8 days to go in your pregnancy after you feel the first kick. During these treasure days, your baby will have active periods and quiet periods (we'll talk about sleep before birth soon). On average, you will feel your baby move or kick at least 8 to 10 times every two hours. This physical awareness, even when you sleep, is helping you to come alive as parents and helping your relationship with your baby to enter a new dimension. As the birth of my last child approached, I remember his mother not wanting the pregnancy to end because she felt so close to him. His kicks from within reminded her that he was always with her. After birth, they would be separated for the first time. But this is just the beginning.

11

I'm Not Ready!

Weeks 21 to 24 in Baby Time

You and your baby have reached another milestone! It's hard to believe, but most babies born at 26 weeks of pregnancy (24 weeks after conception) are mature enough to grow in the outside world (with the help of a lengthy, state-of-the-art hospital stay costing upward of $100,000, trying to replicate all that the mother would ordinarily do for the baby inside her). It's time to learn the location of the nearest children's medical center.

One episode of the television show *ER* dramatized the coordinated efforts and concentrated resources that were able to save the life of a tiny baby just over the hospital's lower limit of babies weighing at least 1.1 pounds (500 grams) and at least 24 weeks of pregnancy (22 weeks after conception). Today, even babies born at 23 weeks (21 weeks after conception) are often mature enough to survive. Each week beyond this makes a big difference in maturity and is a reason to celebrate.

The sophisticated teamwork required in a neonatal intensive care unit (NICU) is a powerful testimonial to how profound parents' care of their unborn child is, even if it appears simple. Mom's body monitors the baby more effectively than any electronic monitor or blood test could. When Dad feeds Mom, he feeds the baby better than any plastic tube feeding that baby could receive. The NICU is a spectacular affirmation of all that parents quietly do for their babies.

At 21 to 24 weeks after conception, babies weigh about 1 to 1.5 pounds. Their skin appears reddish because blood vessels are so close to the surface. They have little body fat or other connective tissue under the skin. The skin is covered with a substance called *vernix*, which looks rather like cold cream. This nourishes and protects the skin better than any cosmetic and functions like knee and elbow pads to provide protection during increasingly athletic

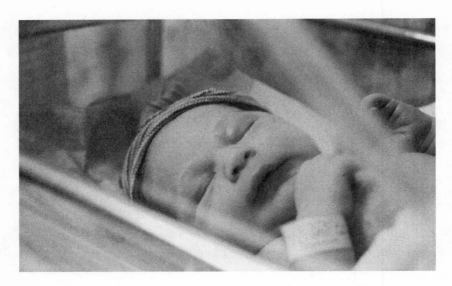

movements. Meanwhile, to rest up from all of this activity and learning, babies have already picked out their favorite sleep positions in the uterus, and they stretch when they wake up. (How cute is that?)

They are remarkably mature, but development is not complete. Nor will it be at birth, even if they are born at their due dates. Development, both physical and mental, continues. Babies already have lacrimal glands to produce tears to bathe the eyes, but these glands won't mature enough to make extra tears for crying until about six weeks after the baby's due date.

Babies at this stage have about 300 bones—an adult has 206. There's still a lot of work to do! Bones are present but not yet connected, much like the wires in some of the poseable action figures my children have played with. It will be another year before the ball-and-socket joints of the hips, the hinge joints of the knees, and the sliding joints of the ankles have matured enough for your baby to be able to learn to walk.

The modular assembly of the skull bones usually won't interlock and fuse until after babies learn to walk. And development of the skeleton doesn't stop there. Most of the bone mass is built during the teen years. In late adolescence, there is a final growth spurt of the jawbone, changing the shape of the face so your son or daughter no longer looks like a child.

Your baby develops in amazing ways within you as you simply nourish, protect, love, and communicate with her through what you eat, say, and do.

This remarkable process continues throughout childhood. Nourishing, among other things, will mean providing plenty of calcium and vitamin D. Protecting will include choosing bicycle helmets that fit properly. And she will still learn from what you eat, say, and do. But right now, the development unfolds within. Relax, it's easier than you think.

We want to do what we can to avoid babies being born too early. Prematurity is the number one medical problem among babies in the United States today. Babies are premature if they are born between 21 and 35 weeks after conception. These babies are at increased risk for a variety of other medical problems. About 1 in 8 (almost half a million) babies are born before their time in this country each year—at a cost of $13.6 billion. (Talk about a way to change both health and health care spending! Just getting more babies to term would make a real difference!)

Born Early

Within the next 24 hours, more than 1,300 babies in the United States will be born more than three weeks ahead of their due dates, although the great majority of babies will wait inside the uterus until their scheduled time has arrived. How can you tell who is likely to give birth early?

The women who have the highest chance of preterm labor and birth are those carrying more than one baby, those with structural problems of the cervix or uterus, and those who have already had a premature baby. Being younger than 17 or older than 35 also increases your chances. A long list of medical problems and lifestyle choices can affect the odds as well. But even with complete information, we don't know who will have a premature baby. It can happen to anyone.

Early labor is usually triggered by an infection, bleeding, stretching of the uterus or cervix, or a surge of stress hormones from the mother or baby—as from a decreased blood supply caused by maternal smoking or exposure to secondhand smoke or from pesticides in the amniotic fluid.

Tilting the Odds

Although you are already pregnant, there are still a number of steps you can take to help prevent early delivery. Here are some:

Eating Licorice and Premature Babies

Pregnant women who eat lots of black licorice may be at increased risk for preterm labor, according to a study in the June 2001 issue of the *American Journal of Epidemiology*. Licorice is very popular among pregnant women in some areas of the country. Women who consumed at least two and a half packages in a week were more than twice as likely to deliver prematurely compared to women who ate little or no licorice. This would make sense, because black licorice contains bioactive compounds that could boost the mother's prostaglandin production and hasten labor.

- Go to all of your prenatal health care appointments, so that any problems (such as high blood pressure or gestational diabetes) will be caught and addressed early.
- Go for relaxing walks. This can help prevent and treat problems such as high blood pressure and gestational diabetes.
- Report burning experienced during urination right away in case you have an infection.
- Take care of your teeth—brushing flossing, teeth cleaning (see Chapter 4).
- Eat organic (see Chapter 7).
- Avoid tobacco, which decreases the blood supply to your baby. This includes secondhand smoke.
- Avoid herbs, supplements, or drugs you haven't discussed with your health care provider.
- Avoid alcohol.
- Avoid long hours on your feet.
- Learn the signs of preterm labor. Labor can often be stopped if identified.

Knowing the Signs

If you start having contractions every 10 minutes or more frequently, contact your health provider, even if the contractions seem mild. The same is true if you are having cramping or bleeding or are leaking fluid from your vagina. A new lower backache, or the sensation that your baby is trying to move down and out, should also be investigated. These signs do not mean that you are in labor but that you should be sure you are not. If you are in

Teenage Premies

There has been a lot in the news about the results of a recent important study. The largest long-term outcome study ever of the tiniest of premature babies was published in the January 17, 2002, *New England Journal of Medicine*. What happened when these babies grew up? As expected, they were slightly less intelligent than their peers, with IQs that averaged about five points lower. The number of "premie teens" who completed high school was nearly as high as their nonpremie counterparts, but fewer completed college. Surprisingly, though, the tiniest of premies got into less teenage (and young adult) trouble than their peers; they had fewer problems with alcohol, drugs, crime, and unwanted pregnancies. Usually these problems are *worse* with a slightly lower IQ. Perhaps extra attention from their parents made the difference. Another consideration is that the children in this study were born between 1977 and 1979 and were followed for 20 years. Medical care has improved greatly, and I expect it to improve even more rapidly in the next 20 years. While the current study contains many valuable lessons, surprises may await us as today's tiniest premies grow up.

labor, it does not mean you will have your baby now, but it does mean it's time to take action.

If You've Already Had a Preterm Birth

If you've been through the birth of an early premature baby, you know the emotional roller coaster of life in the NICU. A landmark study published in the June 12, 2003, issue of the *New England Journal of Medicine* found that weekly injections of a derivative of progesterone substantially reduced the chances of having another preterm delivery. This major breakthrough swiftly led to new 2003 American College of Obstetricians and Gynecologists guidelines to prevent preterm birth.

Nesting

Many parents start feeling "nesting" urges as the second trimester gives way to the third and babies approach the time when they are old enough to live in the outside world. Even at full term, it will take a lot of clothes and sup-

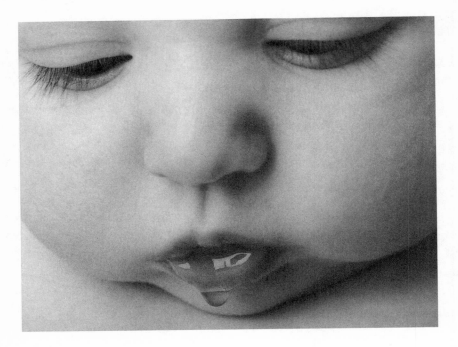

plies to match what you've been doing all along. These practical preparations are a great time to practice bi-empathy, to be ready for getting to know
your baby face-to-face. Diaper decisions are one good example of this.

Paper or Plastic?

When it comes to selecting between disposable diapers and cloth diapers
(or some combination of the two), you will have definite opinions as a parent. You might be most concerned about the convenience, the mess factor,
the smell, the cost, or the impact on the environment (even with the newer
brands designed to be "greener"). Your perspective is important. What might
your baby's perspective be?

I had never really thought about this until a hospital I worked at switched
from cloth scrubs for the doctors to disposable scrubs, to save money on
laundry bills and "lost" outfits (almost every doctor I know has kept a pair
for use around the house). The disposable scrubs were scratchy and uncomfortable in comparison to the cloth. So I wondered about diapers. I bought

some disposable adult diapers for the incontinent and tried them on. I found them less comfortable than cloth—until they got wet. The disposable diapers did a great job at pulling the moisture away from my body. They were bulky and unpleasant to walk in, but my skin stayed dry. When cloth got wet, my skin got wet.

I've known babies who had fewer diaper rashes in cloth diapers and others who had fewer rashes in disposable. But I suspect for most that cloth is more comfortable during prebusiness diaper time and disposable is more comfortable for postbusiness diaper time. This shouldn't be the basis for a decision, but practice at seeing your baby's perspective while holding on to your own. The best choice in diapers is different for different families at different times. I like using cloth when it is reasonably practical and convenient but also having environmentally lower impact disposables for other times. If I had to spend a long night in a pee-filled diaper, I would rather it was an absorbent disposable one.

While your baby isn't ready yet to use a diaper or a crib, he *is* old enough to have a pediatrician.

Selecting a Physician for Your Baby

Your baby is already mature enough to have a doctor of her own! Your baby's doctor won't actually meet your baby at least until you do, but it's not too early for a prenatal visit to begin to get acquainted. The doctor can learn about your baby's combined family history, how your pregnancy has been progressing, and any health concerns. You can learn about the doctor's personality and medical style to determine if this is the right physician for your family, and how arrangements will work with this doctor's office. Everything can be set up so that whenever your baby makes her debut, you will all be ready.

My favorite way to find great baby doctors is to talk with labor and delivery nurses at the most popular nearby hospital. If you just ask friends about which are the best pediatricians, they may recommend someone who is very nice and has a well-organized office, but who is not sharp medically in ways that are invisible to them. If you just ask other physicians, you may find someone who is brilliant, but with whom it is hard for parents or kids to communicate or whose office feels like a zoo. Nurses are usually in touch with both the scientific and the human side of physicians and their practices. And nurses are in a position to see and hear a lot of the scuttlebutt. Or you could just ask us online at DrGreen.com. We care about both sides of physicians, and we know many great doctors in many areas.

When you have a couple of candidates in mind, it is ideal to meet with each one for a few minutes to see how well you "fit." Breastfeeding and circumcision are two excellent topics for discussion to see how well you'll get along. Notice the quality of your interaction with the physician. This can be more significant than the specific information imparted. You need to feel comfortable with this person, confident that she or he is genuinely interested, and encouraged that communication will flow smoothly in both directions.

An August 2003 Reuters headline declared, "Man With Ear Ache Gets Vasectomy." A man in a clinic waiting room misheard whose name had been called as the next patient to be seen. According to the article, "the strangest thing is that he asked no questions when the doctor started preparations in the area which had so little to do with his ear." This is an extreme example of the old-style doctor-patient relationship. The now-snipped man didn't understand his own illness. He didn't expect his doctor to explain how the treatment would help his problem. He was a passive patient.

Hippocrates set the pattern when his famous oath asked medical doctors to swear to keep the knowledge of the medical arts a well-guarded secret. When our parents were growing up, this passive approach to health was considered the norm.

But we are living in one of the most exciting times in the history of health care. Our understanding of wellness and disease is unprecedented. Technical advances continue at a staggering pace. But perhaps most important, people in the 21st century can (and should) expect a new kind of relationship with their doctors.

The Millennium Health Oath reflects this new perspective. It turns the Hippocratic oath upside down, urging physicians to commit themselves to teaching people to understand health and illness. Most of our important health care choices take place between, not during, doctor visits. Less than a generation ago, access to medical libraries was restricted to health care professionals. Today, the world's medical knowledge is readily available in books and online. Physicians are expert consultants who are available to help you understand your own and your baby's health.

Practical Matters

When you find a pediatrician you love, the practical aspects of his or her office are also very important in determining whether that doctor will be able to serve the needs of your family:

- Is the office within a reasonable distance from your home?
- What hours is the practice open? Any Saturdays or evenings?
- How long in advance do you need to schedule an appointment for a physical? (This is tricky. If you have to schedule too far in advance, you are likely to become frustrated. On the other hand, if there is no waiting, you might want to ask why—perhaps the practice has just added another doctor.)
- Does the practice make same-day appointments for sick patients? Do they accept drop-ins for sick patients? If so, how long is the average wait?
- Does the doctor accept phone calls during office hours? (This often saves you a trip to the office.)
- Can you communicate by e-mail for refills, appointments, and/or health questions?
- How many doctors share after-hours on-call duties? If you have an after-hours need, will you be able to talk to one of the doctors in the same practice? A doctor from another practice? A nurse? An answering machine?
- How does the practice handle after-hours, nonemergency needs? Is it associated with an after-hours clinic? Do the doctors meet you in the emergency room? Or are you on your own?
- How do they handle billing? Do they require payment at the time of the visit, or do they bill your insurance company first and then bill you after receiving payment from your insurance?

The Beginning of Self-Care

While you are selecting someone to take care of your baby, your baby is already learning ways to take care of herself. By 12 weeks after conception, a baby's hands are most often seen up close to her face—two very sensitive areas used for exploring each other. By 22 weeks after conception, it's not unusual for babies to begin sucking their thumbs. Their hands are strong, with a grip fierce enough to be able to support their own weight. But most of the time they choose instead to wrap their lips and tongues around their thumbs and suckle.

I remember standing in a darkened room with two eager parents-to-be during a prenatal ultrasound. I watched their screen-lit faces at the moment they glimpsed their new baby for the very first time. The mother grasped the father's hand tightly as they both gazed at the flickering screen. When their tiny daughter moved her thumb to her mouth, tears of joy streamed down both parents' faces.

Some parents laugh, some cry, some don't feel strong emotions until long after the baby is born. But already the baby is sucking on a thumb or finger, comforting herself and practicing for the big day.

12

They're Playing Our Song

Weeks 25 to 28 in Baby Time

It had been a full year since the babies in the study had last heard the songs. Before that, they had listened to the songs time and time again during the final three months they were inside their mothers. Each woman had chosen a particular piece of music to play for her baby, ranging from classical to reggae to pop. But the babies didn't hear the song even once after they were born until they were tested at their first birthdays. This study was first reported in July 2001. All the babies in the study recognized their special songs and preferred them to similar sounding songs in the same style. Many turned toward their mothers when the special songs came on. Perhaps they thought of it as "their song."

Questions of Disbelief

Does my unborn baby really hear me when I talk to her?

Yeni

Is it true that I should talk to my baby before she is born?

Silkie

Can playing loud music hurt my baby?

Carie2

Early shared experiences are part of the emotional bond. We've known for some time that babies hear the world around them before they are born. We've known that they carry this memory beyond the portal of the birth experience. The 2001 study is exciting because it is the first time that these memories have been demonstrated to last longer than about two months. The special tastes, sounds, smells, sights, and moments of being rocked or cuddled from the very earliest days seem to linger on and on.

Keeping Those Eyes and Ears Open

A period of very rapid brain growth began at about 24 weeks after conception. It will speed along throughout the rest of pregnancy and the first two or three years of your baby's life, as your baby learns to crawl across the floor, walk across the room, and speak and understand a complex language. New neural connections form constantly, and the brain wrinkles as it grows in size, creating more surface area.

Myelin is the name of the white matter of the brain that insulates the nerve cells and allows for rapid conduction of thoughts. Interestingly, myelin first appears in the sensory parts of the brain and spreads from there. Why?

I once had the experience of relaxing in a sensory deprivation flotation tank. With no sight and no sound, nothing to taste or smell, floating weightlessly, only water to touch, my tension drained away. Many people picture life in the womb as something like that tank. In reality, the womb is an active learning center, with lessons constantly arriving to educate all of the senses. It reminds me of the cocoonlike spaceship in which the boy from Krypton travels to Earth in the first Superman movie with Christopher Reeve.

In early fetal life, babies float freely, but now the room is getting smaller. The legs fold into a fetal position. And the baby explores with fingertips and toes, learning the contours of this small world. Tastes and aromas that you encounter color his world. Light and sound from your world illuminate and narrate his. If you smell smoke, your baby smells smoke.

By 24 weeks after conception, babies turn to face a light shining on Mom's belly, even though their eyelids are still closed. They will also turn to face an interesting sound in the room, even though there are little natural earplugs in their ear canals to protect their ears. The early sights and sounds are muted so as not to overwhelm the developing senses with first sensations.

Around 26 weeks after conception, your baby opens his eyes and begins studying the world around him. Those natural earplugs fall from his ears, and he is listening intently to what you say and hear. Listening, learning, and remembering.

The Lights Are On and Somebody's Home

Dr. T. Berry Brazelton, one of the great pioneers in learning to understand babies, relates an interesting story that happened when he and his colleagues were studying how babies react to light before they are born. The study used an ultrasound to watch the unborn babies as they reacted to lights. First, the researchers determined which way each baby was facing. Then they shone a bright light at Mom's belly, at an angle that would have been directly in the baby's eyes if there weren't a belly and a uterus in between. The first few times this happened, each baby was clearly startled. After a few tries, however, the babies were no longer surprised. They would calmly bring their hands to their faces as if to shield their eyes from the bright light and quietly turn their heads away. They had learned about this light and figured out what to do. They were no longer concerned.

Next, the team took a pinpoint light and shone it elsewhere on the mother's belly. When the light was shining, the baby would turn slowly toward wherever the light was entering the uterus, to see what had been illuminated. Most of the babies appeared captivated by what the light revealed.

During this fascinating interchange, one of the babies became visibly upset. One of the doctors present, Dr. Barry Lester, put both hands on the mother's belly, cradling it, and began to gently rock the baby. This had a profoundly calming effect.

Dr. Brazelton quotes the mother as expressing the thoughts of all in the room, "I didn't know babies were so smart so early!"

Pump Up the Volume

Across the Atlantic, in the Laboratoire Cognition et Développement at the Université de Paris V, a pioneering psychologist named Jean-Pierre Lecanuet uncovered many secrets about what babies hear and learn before birth, before his tragic death in 2002.

Tiny microphones slipped into the uterus revealed that the noise level inside the womb is not that different from the noise level on a busy street corner. The predominant sounds were the enchanting rhythms of Mom's heartbeat, the swishing brush-cymbal flow of blood through her large blood vessels, and the echoing bass rumblings in her tummy. But along with this musical accompaniment, there was a clear melody line: the voices in the room, especially Mom's voice. These same sounds will later soothe crying newborns.

Most of the sounds that the parents heard in the room, the baby could hear inside. And music playing in the room was clearly and recognizably transmitted to the baby within.

Could the baby make any sense of this music? In one study, Lecanuet played a simple two-note sequence on a piano. First he played a low C or D and recorded changes in babies' heart rates as they noticed the pure tone. After the heart rates had returned to baseline, he played another note, and the same heart rate changes were observed. It didn't matter which note came first. The babies heard the two sounds as two interesting, new events. With another set of babies, he again played a C or a D. After the heart rates had returned to normal, he played the same note a second time. Amazingly, these babies had significantly less change in their heart rates when hearing the familiar note. They recognized what they had already heard!

Babies also recognize the pitch of voices. Babies can tell the difference between individual voices even before they are born. They can tell the difference between men and women and tend to prefer women's voices to men's. They recognize their mother's voice and prefer it to all other women's. Unborn babies can also learn to recognize their father's voice and prefer it to other men's and even women's. The more they hear a voice, the more they become attached to it—especially if it is not too loud and is sometimes in the adjusted higher pitch we instinctively use to talk with babies.

Can they make out syllables? Lecanuet did a similar study to the one with piano keys, but this time with human voices. Babies heard a pair of spoken syllables, either *ba-bi* or *bi-ba*. They listened and reacted with changes in their heart rates. Once they had returned to baseline, if the same syllable pair was spoken again in the same order, they relaxed. But if the order of these two similar syllables was reversed, the babies recognized that this was new information, and they reacted strongly again. They could distinguish between such similar syllables and notice the order in which they appeared.

The Cat in the Hat

At the University of North Carolina, Dr. Anthony DeCasper has been a groundbreaking pioneer of exploring what babies hear, learn, and remember before and after birth. In one fascinating study, he and his colleagues asked 16 expectant mothers to read aloud two selections into a tape recorder—Dr. Seuss's *The Cat in the Hat* and *The King, the Mice, and the Cheese*, a wonderful and often overlooked children's book by Nancy Gurney.

Then each mother was asked to read just one of these stories through twice a day for six and a half weeks in the third trimester. Each baby heard the story for about five hours total reading time spread out over more than a month and a half.

Three days after each baby was born, he or she was fitted with a pair of padded headphones. A special pacifier was placed in the mouth. The babies' sucking speed determined what they heard in the headphones. They heard one story if they sucked rapidly and the other if they sucked slowly. Stunningly, 15 out of 16 of these newborns figured out the mechanism and sucked at the correct speed to listen to the story that their mother had read to them before birth.

It reminds me of all the times that my toddler children have asked me to read the same story to them over and over again. I suspect they wanted the same thing even before they were born, but we didn't have a way to understand them. Dr. DeCasper's research suggests that these babies can both hear and enjoy a good book. I believe that babies like to listen to some things that are familiar and some that are new. Rhymes seem especially fun for them, because they can start to predict what sounds are coming next.

I would love for families to start taking the time to enjoy reading aloud to each other before their baby is even born. Reach Out and Read is a wonderful new program that takes family reading seriously. The organization promotes reading by giving new books to children at each well-child physical from six months to five years of age and encourages parents to read aloud with their children. Founded by Robert Needleman, M.D., at Boston University, it has grown into a national, nonprofit organization distributing free books at more than two thousand clinics and pediatric offices around the country. I vigorously applaud their success and call for an encore!

All Music All the Time

Babies often love music. I've had some mothers tell me that when lively music comes on, their babies start to dance inside. Others report that music calms their babies. I suspect it depends partly on the baby, partly on the music, and partly on the time of day.

Singing to your baby is a great way to combine the power of music with the magic of your voice. You might want to sing duets! Try to tell how your baby reacts to different songs.

Babies aren't always in the mood to listen. They tend to cycle through several "moods" each day. Sometimes they are in an active, exploring mood and the physical movement is unmistakable. Sometimes they are sleeping. Sometimes, though, they are awake but quiet (the quiet alert state, which we will learn more about later). It is when they are quietly alert that they are most interested in listening to your voices, especially if you're not too loud. They tend to react negatively to harsh and loud sounds.

Whether you intentionally read and sing to your baby or not, you are teaching her every day. Her ears are open. She is listening; observing; learning from what you eat, smell, and say. Almost anything you do is a way to tell part of your story to your baby, a way to pass along your heritage to the one who is carrying your genes.

Secure in this connection, you can both sleep. And you can dream.

13

Sweet Dreams

Weeks 28 to 32 in Baby Time

When your developing baby reaches about 28 weeks after conception, something astonishing happens. Here's the backdrop: Your baby has changed colors. No longer the reddish hue caused by blood vessels that are close to the surface, a layer of new body fat has beautifully rounded his bony contour and given him a paler color, closer to whatever his later skin tone will be. Your baby has now reached about half his birth weight. The rate of weight gain slows (if it were to continue at its recent rate, he would weigh as much as an adult before his first birthday), but brain growth accelerates.

It's getting tight inside. Hopefully, his head is orienting down toward your pelvis. The graceful water ballet is over (just in time—his fingernails are now long enough to scratch himself). But the dance of the senses is only beginning. The tiniest bones in the body, the ossicles of the ear (the anvil, the stirrup, and the hammer) are now independent and free, allowing for more precise hearing than ever before. The pupils of the eye are now able to constrict when it is bright, allowing him to look at light more comfortably. There is so much for him to learn!

Against that backdrop, something amazing happens. But before we talk about that, let's imagine the future for a moment.

A Crystal Ball

Your baby has been born. You've never felt such fierce love. Nursing for the first time was frightening and exhilarating. It became awkward and you felt sore for several days, but now it seems as natural as breathing. You've laughed, cried, and shaken your head in wonder. Now it is time to take your baby to see the pediatrician for a physical. When I see families for their

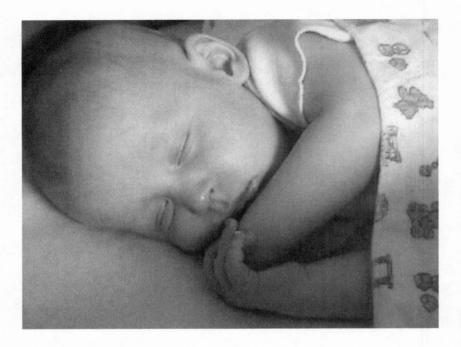

babies' two-month physical, I like to ask them what they wished they had learned before the baby was born. What, from those magical newborn weeks, do they wish they had known more about? Overwhelmingly, the most common answer was sleep!

The Most Frequent Lament
We wish we had known more about sleep.

Parents Everywhere

I remember one young couple I met just before their first baby was born. For me, it came at the end of a long day seeing children, young and old, healthy and sick. The office was still bustling, so we found a quiet spot and closed the door. We gathered around my desk and talked about how the world would never be the same once their baby was born.

They were eager, prepared, and confident. Both had successful, demanding careers, and they'd still found time to read several parenting books.

They began quizzing me on my philosophies about breastfeeding and antibiotic use. As we were ending our time together, I gave them some tips about how to get plenty of rest once the baby arrived. They laughed and said energy was the least of their concerns.

The delivery and first days were every bit as magical as they had anticipated. We celebrated together.

Two months later, I saw them in the train room of my office. Murals adorn the walls, and a small train chugs back and forth on a platform near the ceiling. When I walked into the room, I saw immediately that they were exhausted and fragile. We hugged, and tears streamed down both of their faces. They said that they couldn't enjoy their new daughter because they were so sleep-deprived.

Day-Night Reversal

Our beautiful baby daughter is five days old, and we are exhilarated but exhausted. She seems to be asleep all day long (unless she is eating), and then as soon as we want to go to bed, she's awake—*all night long*! Do you have anything you can suggest?

Nashville, Tennessee

You already know what it feels like to be grumpy, contrary, or "not at your best" from lack of sleep. Missing a whole night's sleep makes you feel rotten. The surprising truth is that sustained partial, or low-level, sleep deprivation has a bigger effect on behavior than either the short- or long-term total sleep deprivation studied in medical residents. Until recently, the effects of chronic partial sleep deprivation have been seriously underestimated.

We know that interrupted sleep makes people more moody, more impulsive, and less able to concentrate. We've known for more than 25 years that sleep deprivation makes it difficult to create lasting new memories. Recent research has verified that chronic poor sleep results in daytime tiredness, difficulties with focused attention, irritability, easy frustration, and difficulty modulating emotions.

Most families are not as deeply affected as the couple sobbing in my exam room that day, but sleep changes still loom large. By around four to six weeks after the baby arrives, the cumulative sleep deprivation becomes significant—especially for parents with more than one child! I've now changed what and how I tell families about sleep, so that most are getting more rest.

> My wife and I are in love with our new baby (we were infertility patients). But we are both sleep-deprived, and my wife is miserable. She cries all the time. She's being treated for postpartum depression, but I'm wondering how our sleep (or lack of it) is affecting things. Is this a part of it? What can we do?
>
> **Anonymous**

On the Internet, I have the joy of interacting with many families I have never met in person. One way we connect is during live chats at DrGreene .com. I've been available live online to parents for one hour each weekday for over five years. I often get to celebrate with them when the family celebrates their baby's first birthday! We sing "Happy Birthday" together and cheer as the parents help the baby blow out that one candle. I listen as the father or mother reviews the last year and looks forward to the next. One of the most common comments I hear is parents wishing that they had learned how to establish good sleep habits so they didn't have to undo sleep problems once they had developed.

> **Many Sleep Questions**
> Do babies even sleep in the womb?
>
> **Rsalkin**
>
> How much should newborns sleep?
>
> **San Mateo**
>
> My two-month-old . . . still needs a lot of sleep, but she has a really hard time sleeping for more than 45 minutes. Do you have any tips on how I can help her to sleep longer???
>
> **aslan122500**

With my girls just turning 10 weeks, my wife wants them up more during the day so they might sleep through the night. Her doctor (for her fibromyalgia) wants her to get the babies to sleep through the night so she doesn't get tired. Is this realistic?

rich

My babies are awake when we want to sleep and asleep when we are awake. We're exhausted!

VPDOT

What's a doula do? Do you recommend them?

Davina

I would like to break a habit I formed of rocking [my son] to sleep every time he wakes up in the middle of the night. Sometimes four to five times per night. I would also like to know how I can get him to go to sleep on his own, after his nighttime bottle.

Mrs. Pamela Marino, Miami, Florida

I was wondering about what age kids will start sleeping through the night. Is it too much to ask to get a seven-week-old to sleep for more than two hours?

jenniferccrn

When does a child start to dream? At what age do nightmares . . . begin?"

Tim Allen, Anchor/Producer, New Cumberland, Pennsylvania

We'll talk about undoing sleep problems later. Let's start with what these parents wish someone had told them: how healthy sleep begins. Rsalkin, like many other moms in our online community, asked me when sleep habits begin—whether babies even sleep in the womb.

Let's go back to the beginning now, when sleep patterns are first forming. Babies begin to sleep early in pregnancy. Before mothers miss their first periods, their babies are already taking naps. Lots of naps!

Napping

Adults sleep about one-third of the time; newborns sleep about three-fourths of the time; but before birth, babies sleep about nine-tenths of the time! Much of our physical and mental growth happens when we are asleep. About 80 percent of growth hormone is secreted during sleep. It makes sense that during the phenomenal growth in the womb much sleep would be needed.

If babies begin life as experienced sleepers, sleeping an average of 16 to 18 hours a day as newborns, then why do parents become so exhausted? Because each episode of a baby's sleep is brief. Moreover, most episodes occur during parents' normal waking hours rather than during the hours when parents would like to be sleeping. There is as much wakefulness at night as there is sleep during the day. Most parents get much less sleep after a baby is born. The sleep they do get is frequently interrupted. This combines to produce chronic partial sleep deprivation.

Getting the Rhythm

Our daily sleep schedule is set by something called our *circadian rhythm*. (*Circadian* means "about a day.") Each of us has an internal biological clock. The time for one complete cycle is approximately, but not exactly, 24 hours.

Our normal body temperature does not remain at a constant 98.6°F but rises and falls with the circadian rhythm. The circadian rhythm is a strong tide that carries with it many bodily functions. Blood pressure, heart rate, blood flow through the coronary arteries, urine production, white blood cell production, immune function, drug metabolism, liver function, and even cancer's susceptibility to chemotherapy and radiation all cycle with the circadian rhythm. Our hormone levels, like our temperature, rise and fall with the circadian rhythm. We tend to be born at night and to die at night.

Changing sleep schedules means swimming against this strong current. What about the baby's circadian rhythm before she is born? Does she move in gentle concert with Mom, heart rates rising and falling to the same tide? Do her mother's hormones set the baby's biological clock?

Quite the opposite! Research at the beginning of the 21st century indicates that babies develop independent circadian rhythms before they are born. They are already distinct individuals, marching to the beat of their own drum. The baby's rhythm is shifted from the mother's by an average of eight hours.

You probably already have a sense of when your baby is the most active and the most quiet. For most families this does not coincide with the parents' levels of activity.

Once your baby is born, one of your first tasks as a family is to begin the slow adjustment of your baby's and your cycles toward each other. Both sides need to change. Parents are no longer just adults, but parents affected by their child. They need to help their child learn to remain independent but to do it in harmony with the new world around him.

The circadian rhythm can be reset. Indeed, it is reset every day. In the absence of light, clocks, and other external cues, most people's cycle would last about 25 hours. A totally independent human would go to sleep about an hour later each day.

Zeitgebers

The circadian rhythm is the pacemaker of sleep. The process of adjusting one's circadian rhythm is called *entrainment*. Signals in the environment that help to entrain the circadian rhythm are called *zeitgebers*. Zeitgebers are your friends. They are the tools that so many parents with whom I interact are looking for.

The most powerful zeitgeber is light (or darkness for nocturnal species). It does more than anything else to set the circadian clock. Keep the room bright during the day, even when your baby is asleep. Open the shades and turn on the lights. Keep it dark during the hours you would like him to be asleep (even if right now you are up with the baby). Use a nightlight that is as dim as practical for nighttime feedings.

Alcohol is an anti-zeitgeber. Even though it produces drowsiness and may give you some short-term rest, it confuses your circadian rhythm. This is true even before birth. When a mom has as little as two glasses of wine during the third trimester, her baby's circadian rhythm becomes dramatically disorganized.

I believe that light also functions as a helpful zeitgeber before birth. Your baby sees a soft red glow when the room is bright. Everything in his world looks more interesting. Lots of windows, sun exposure, light fabrics, and extra lights in the room throughout the day, contrasted with keeping your belly in the dark at night, might give your family a head start at finding individual but compatible rhythms.

Arousal is another important zeitgeber. The adrenalin rush that comes from physical handling influences the body clock. Consistent daytime or evening handling of nocturnal hamsters can shift their sleep phase all by itself. After babies are born, I recommend gently, playfully, handling their hands and feet from time to time throughout the day (even when they are asleep) and using only soothing contact (cuddling, rocking) at night. Jean-Pierre Lecanuet found that before babies are born, rocking forward and backward, as in a rocking chair, has a bigger impact on them than swaying from side to side in a garden swing. You might see if this calms your baby or if the exciting ride wakes him up! Researchers at the University of Miami (including Lecanuet) found that when pregnant mothers got a three-minute foot massage, it woke up their babies. Neither a hand massage nor a belly rub had the same effect. You might try starting the day with a foot massage to relax yourself and to help your baby learn that morning is wake-up time.

Making eye contact with your baby is also a potent stimulus. After birth, when you gaze at each other, the baby's heart rate and blood pressure go up. Minimize eye contact during those hours in which you want your family to learn to sleep. Use daytime for those long looks of love.

Social cues are also important zeitgebers. Your voice and behavior can signal that it is time to play or time to rest. New parents often try to keep the house too quiet when the baby is napping during the day. Ambient noise can be helpful. Use your voice and behavior to say, "Daytime." Nighttime communication should be especially soft and gentle, with a lullaby sensibility. You can start this even now.

Food is a powerful zeitgeber at all ages, but especially for babies. By three days of age, you can make use of this by picking a time in the late evening, usually somewhere between 10 P.M. and midnight, for something called the *focus feeding*. By feeding once at the same time every night, even if you have to wake the baby up, you can help your baby establish her own cycle in a way that fits best with yours.

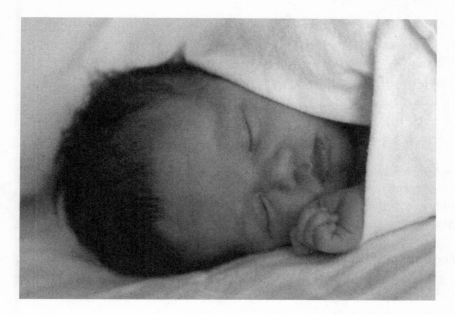

Matching Your Rhythms

Of course, your baby isn't the only one whose rhythms change as you become a family. The first thing new parents can change is their own mind-set about when to sleep. Most of us have a long-standing habit of being awake during the day and being asleep at night. When the baby is born, this will no longer serve you well.

A baby who sleeps 16 to 18 hours a day affords plenty of time for parents to sleep. However, because the baby's sleep usually comes in small increments at the beginning, parents need even more than their usual amount of sleep in order to avoid becoming exhausted over time.

When the baby falls asleep, there is an impulse for parents to use the opportunity to clean or cook or call loved ones, to spend a few precious hours with the other parent, or to gaze adoringly at their new treasure. It's time to develop a new mind-set for the first six weeks. In those peaceful moments when your baby drifts off to sleep, first consider using the opportunity to get some sleep yourself. You won't always be able to fall asleep, so if you feel you can, nap unless you have a really good reason to do something else.

Mothers who nurse find a built-in mechanism to help. Breastfeeding ties mothers to waking up at brief intervals around the clock, but it also makes mother (and baby) drowsy just after nursing. This creates a window in the circadian rhythm where sleep is easy.

Calling for Help

The first weeks at home with a new baby can be a wonderful time to have someone stay with you or be available to help out. If family or friends come, explain that their most important role is to help with the mundane tasks so that you two can enjoy your baby and each other—and get some sleep.

Alternatively, you might arrange for the services of a *doula*, someone who specializes in providing support during labor and/or during the postpartum period. Doulas "mother the mother" so that parents can focus on the baby. In addition to their invaluable support and wisdom about feeding and baby care, many doulas provide night care. This has become an important part of their services in the last few years. Doulas' fees generally run in the $20- to $28-per-hour range. If you are considering this option, you can learn more from *The Doula Book* by Marshall Klaus, John Kennell, and Phyllis Klaus or from the National Association of Postpartum Care Services (800/453-6852 or www.napcs.org). Many doulas will also help with meal preparation, errands, or housework, although you may be able to stretch your doula dollars further by hiring someone less expensive for these tasks.

The Ups and Downs of Sleep

In addition to the rhythms of sleep, the associations of sleep make a big difference for babies (and thus for parents). We are decidedly creatures of habit. This is especially true about falling asleep. If babies are eating, being held or rocked, or sung to each time they fall asleep, they will come to depend on this to aid their sleep transition. This is an excellent choice for many families, but it can present a problem for families who want to teach babies to sleep by themselves. This strong tendency to form habits is one of the reasons parents have so many sleep frustrations.

Most parents do not understand a critical concept: the desired achievement of "sleeping through the night" will not mean being able to sleep all night without awakening. Instead, it will be the skill of rousing and drifting back to sleep without a fuss.

The fact that your baby wakes up at night is not the problem. The problem is she hasn't learned to go back to sleep. Our goal is to teach babies to settle themselves down (not to leave them alone to cry it out). Many babies are able to do this by the time they are four months old, perhaps waking once to feed. About 60 to 70 percent of babies get themselves back to sleep by their first birthday. Those who still don't can be taught to do this rather than continuing to rely on outside help.

You will discover that babies often fall asleep feeding or while they are in your arms. That's fine. Nevertheless, be on the lookout for opportunities to lay your baby down drowsy—when he's almost, but not quite, asleep.

Some babies will then drift off to sleep on their own. As Marc, one of the fathers in our online community, found out, others protest loudly! Picking them up might short-circuit the learning opportunity, but leaving them alone to cry might teach them that you are not there when they feel they need you. Instead, firm, gentle patting from their parents, perhaps accompanied by lullabies, thumbs, pacifiers, or recordings of the parents' voices, might help ease them to sleep.

A baby who always falls asleep at your breast or in your arms comes to depend on this closeness, for better or worse. But each time she makes that final transition more on her own helps her to grow toward achieving the milestone of being able to fall asleep on her own.

Baby Sleep

White tablecloths cover dozens of tables bunched close together. Candles, drinks, the elbows of smiling couples rest on the tablecloths. A stand-up comedian during the late show at a San Francisco comedy club tells the eager crowd, "I sleep like a baby—I wake up screaming every few hours!" The audience roars.

Many parents wonder if their babies might be having nightmares. Parents often ask me when dreams begin. The unspoken question that follows—how about nightmares? The truth about dreams and nightmares will surprise you.

Dreams have been described since the beginning of human history, but it was only in 1953 that Aserinsky and Kleitman discovered the brain wave pattern we call rapid eye movement (REM). During sleep, we proceed through progressively deeper sleep stages (stages 1 to 4). In each of these four stages, our brains are dramatically quiet, even though our bodies may move or shift.

In a different stage, called REM sleep, our brains are highly active, but our bodies seem paralyzed (except for our eyes, which dart back and forth). This type of sleep is what we know as dreaming. As adults, we spend about 20 percent of our sleep time in REM sleep.

A mother from California told me this story about her preschool-aged child: "My son is four years old. The other night he came pattering down the hall and into our bedroom with tears streaking down his face. 'Mommy, I've had a bad dream!' he reported. 'I fell off a building and kept falling.' He reported a classic falling dream at four years old!"

At age three or four years, most children begin remarking about dreams. However, in their passion to imitate adult behavior, children at that age assert with confidence many things that aren't quite factual. Are they really having dreams? Might they just be using their fertile imaginations to describe what they've heard others talk about? Perhaps this is another way to try to maneuver into their parents' big bed ("I can't sleep. Can I get in?"). Alternatively, might children begin dreaming even earlier than three or four, but only start talking about it as preschoolers?

To solve this mystery, Drs. Roffwarg, Muzio, and Dement undertook a classic study in 1966. They began by studying brain sleep waves in newborns. The investigators believed that infants would not have REM sleep because they do not dream and intended to discover only what newborn sleep waves looked like. The team would continue to measure sleep waves throughout infancy and toddlerhood to learn when and how dreaming begins. The startling discovery was that not only do newborns dream—even on the first day of life—but they actually dream more than the college students in earlier studies did!

This study has been repeated several times, confirming and expanding our knowledge. We dream more in the first two weeks of life than at any later time. And the visual part of the brain is more active during newborn REM sleep than during adult dreams. Babies seem to have more vivid visual dreams than anyone older.

Infants who are 3 to 5 months old dream much more than 6- to 12-month-old infants. And 18-month-olds dream almost twice as much as three-year-olds. By age three, the amount of time spent dreaming per night is in the same range as that of young adults. As the wheel of time turns, we dream a little less each year.

Children dream from the moment they are born. Might they dream even before? This brings us to the amazing development that takes place at about 28 weeks after conception.

REM sleep waves have been found as early as 26 weeks after conception, and REM sleep waves accompanied by the eye movements of dreams start at about 28 weeks. Dreaming begins two or three months before babies are even born.

We now know that as babies approach term, they sleep 85 to 95 percent of the time. About 6 hours a day are spent in quiet fetal sleep (stage 1F), whereas 14 to 17 hours are spent in active fetal sleep, where they are both moving and dreaming (stage 2F). These long hours of sleep come in brief naps. The periods of quiet sleep are usually about 20 minutes; active sleep lasts about 40 minutes. Add it all up, and your baby spends most of his time dreaming!

Dreams

Dreams appear to be a kind of parallel processing by which we integrate our experience, making new connections in our brains. Most people are surprised to learn that we dream more when we are awake than when we sleep.

As mentioned earlier, when we sleep, we dream only about 20 percent of the time. During the rest of the time, the brain rests. Growing evidence suggests that we have real dreams all day long. These go unnoticed because of the "loudness" of our senses and our conscious thinking. In a similar way, we have an unobstructed view of stars in the sky all day long, but we can't see them because they are overwhelmed by the light of the sun. At night, the stars and the dreams come out. So it is in the womb.

When dreaming comes online at about 28 weeks after conception, it heralds an explosive period of brain growth. The brain and its connections are developing so swiftly that the mother's drinking alcohol even once during this time can make a permanent, measurable difference in the baby's brain function.

Babies dream more and learn more in the season beginning at 28 weeks than at any other time. In the uterus, babies probably dream about their own movements, helping them gain familiarity with the new, complex machinery of their bodies. They probably dream about the muted light they see and the sounds they hear (heartbeats, voices, and music). If you read your baby *Red Fish, Blue Fish*, he may dream about the rhyming sounds for days to come. With their many vivid dreams, it makes sense that babies recognize music they "heard" only in the uterus a full year later (see Chapter 12).

After birth, perhaps babies dream about the explosion of new sights, sounds, tastes, smells, and textures as they delight in getting to know their parents.

Nightmares

Nightmares are unpleasant dreams that awaken a dreamer from sleep. Traumatic events are known to cause a predictable pattern of nightmares: first come dreams that relive the event, then dreams that relive the primary emotion of the event using different scenarios (pictures), then dreams that incorporate aspects of the event into other parts of life. Nightmares are an important means of addressing difficult events and emotions, helping to weave them into the fabric of our minds in a constructive way.

Nightmares are generally thought to be most common at the ages of three to five years—the peak ages when children express fears—and conventional wisdom tells us that they begin not too long before then. The available evidence leads me to a vastly different conclusion: just like other dreams, nightmares are most common in infancy. Stressful events, such as injections, circumcision (which should never be done without anesthesia), being left alone, being dropped, or even feeling hungry, need to be learned about and integrated. It seems to me that anything worth crying about is worth dreaming about.

We know from older children that nightmares commonly follow surgery, tooth extraction, and motor vehicle accidents. Why wouldn't they follow the ultimate extraction—childbirth?

We don't want to believe that our little ones experience anything unpleasant. So strong is this desire that it led to the long-held (now finally and forcefully disproved) belief that newborns don't feel pain when circumcised. How absurd!

Knowing how much young babies dream and cry (and wake up crying), it seems equally absurd to me to believe that all of their dreams are happy ones. Birth is a wonderful and terrible experience. There is much to be happy about and much to learn about in the weeks that follow. Babies' dreams must incorporate and address those things that bring them pleasure and those that make them cry. I believe that in all likelihood the peak age of crying, the first six weeks, is also the peak age of nightmares.

These nightmares are not unsuccessful dreams. Far from it! They help babies learn and grow. These nightmares may even be an important reason that crying diminishes after six weeks.

Aren't They Beautiful When They Sleep?

No one can deny that there is something about seeing your child asleep that warms your soul and repays your waking efforts. Your baby is sleeping already, but now you can only glimpse this precious sight in your dreams and imagination.

This is the beginning of a new era in your baby's life. It's an era of quiet, profound change. Your baby is silently storing nutrition he gets from you as a layer of fat, a box lunch for his first trip into the outside world, because a table at the gourmet breast milk restaurant will not be available to him for at least a few days.

His rapid growth and his new layer of fat combine to keep his body temperature high—up to about 100.2°F. In some ways, you really do have a bun in the oven.

As you dream about your baby, who now has dimples and dreams, your baby sleeps the day away already dreaming about you. All the while, new connections form in his brain at an astonishing rate. Dreams create.

14

The Final Weeks

Weeks 33 to 38 in Baby Time

A time to dance? A time to learn? As we saw in Chapter 12, we are discovering more all the time about how babies notice, learn, and remember what they see, hear, smell, taste, and touch before they are born. But we saw in Chapter 13 that babies sleep up to 90 percent of the time during the third trimester. So when are they really paying attention to you?

A Question of Consciousness

Thanks to the pioneering work of Dr. Jan Nijhuis in the Netherlands, we know about four distinct states of alertness or consciousness through which third-trimester babies cycle repeatedly each day, starting after they begin to dream. They go through these states in a variety of orders depending on the circumstances. The portion of the day spent in each state varies from baby to baby and from time to time. We looked briefly at two of these states in the last chapter. Let's look at them in a little more depth now and then consider which state a baby is in during labor.

State 1F is the period of quiet sleep or deep sleep. Just before their due date, babies average about 25 percent of the day in quiet sleep, in 20-minute naps. Babies don't move much during this level of sleep, except for the occasional small, sudden jerk. Lights and noises don't easily awaken them, which at first led researchers to conclude that they didn't learn much during this state.

Recent evidence has proven, however, that even in deep sleep babies are aware of the outside world. They learn what they hear and respond differently in the future based on what they have learned. When five piano notes

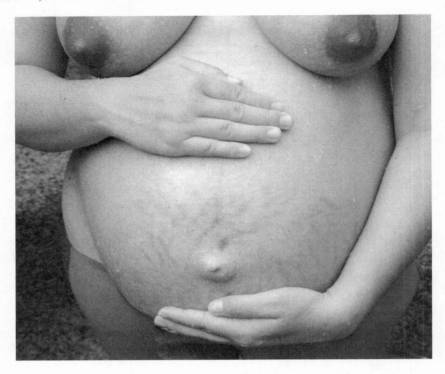

were played for babies in state 1F, their heart rates responded differently depending on how familiar they were with the order in which the notes were played—even though they first heard the notes when they were deeply asleep. This is also true after birth. Three-week-old babies also learn piano note sequences during quiet sleep. Your baby is actively absorbing what he hears. Reading to your baby, before and after birth, makes a difference even when he sleeps.

As the due date approaches, babies spend 60 to 70 percent of the day in 40-minute state 2F naps, also called dream sleep, rapid eye movement (REM) sleep, light sleep, or active sleep. Babies usually pee as they switch from state 1F to state 2F. Even though dreams are mostly about learning from past experiences, I know that occasionally when I'm dreaming I incorporate sounds or smells from the outside world into my dreams. I suspect this is true of babies before birth as well. While we don't know this to be true, we do know that they respond to lights, sounds, and vibrations experienced during state 2F, sometimes with changing heart rates, sometimes with changing states.

Babies do stretch and writhe a bit during 2F and sometimes have brief jerking movements. Their breathing is also more pronounced. But even when they dream, they are aware of our world.

State 3F is the quiet alert state. Babies spend less time in 3F than in any other state. Here they seem to be paying undivided attention to the world around them, trying to learn. They are silently observing and more responsive to the world around them than at any other time.

State 4F, the active alert state, is the easiest to recognize. Here babies seem like battery-operated bunnies, always on the go. But even then, they will pause and look or listen if something from the outside attracts their notice. Or they will dance in rhythm to the music they hear.

And the Answer Is . . .

Babies can notice, learn, and remember events that occur in any of their four states. They respond differently depending on which state they're in, but they can respond in all of them. In one study, a normal household flashlight shone at Mom's belly was noticed by about 4 percent of babies in deep sleep; none of them awoke. A full 82 percent of the dreaming babies noticed the light; none of them awoke either. And 83 percent of the quiet alert babies noticed the light; many of them became active. Active babies who noticed the light often became quiet. Some became even more active. Strong, vibrating sound waves were noticed by 100 percent of babies in each state and frequently caused their state to change, no matter where they started. At home, you may notice that light, sounds, meals, or activities start your baby dancing or calm her down.

Interestingly, boys and girls are very similar in their prenatal responses, except that on average boys tend to be awake more than girls. Second and third children tend to spend about the same percentage of time in different states as do firstborns, but they tend to learn all of the states earlier in pregnancy—and it's not just that Mom notices them earlier.

As you might expect, if Mom is taking stimulants, it changes the amount of time the baby spends in different states. Cocaine and caffeine both significantly increase the time spent in state 4F. Cocaine does this by reducing deep sleep. Caffeine also reduces deep sleep, but it reduces dream sleep even more. Alcohol, nicotine, and some prescription medicines disrupt the states and blunt learning.

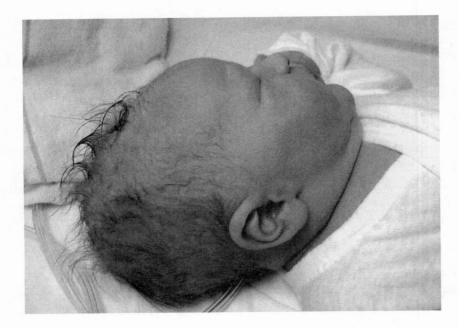

Does your baby's round-the-clock awareness mean you should feel pressured to be perfect? Should you feel guilty if you fail to read Shakespeare to your baby in seven languages or forget to play chamber music while eating your vegetables? Does the thought that your baby may be noticing what you eat and how much you exercise feel oppressive? As if you *should* be doing more?

Relax! Babies' gradual learning by observation and imitation is very freeing. You don't need to try to pretend you are who you aren't; your baby is designed to get to know the real *you* and to learn from your life. You couldn't keep up a pretense if you tried. Your kids will be watching and learning all the years of their childhood. You don't have to worry about missing a particular opportunity. And they aren't supposed to be perfect. They're supposed to be human. Babies have been learning in this way for generation upon generation, without parents knowing or making extra effort. The way babies learn is beautiful. You can really relax.

If you want, you can let their closeness bring out the best in you, like those wonderful days at the beginning of falling in love. You can use this feeling as motivation to carry through on choices and changes you wanted to make anyway. And you can feel encouraged that your connection with your baby is already making a difference. But the baby's ability to learn quietly from what you say and do takes away the pressure of having to perform. If your baby can learn to relax during labor, perhaps you can learn to relax as a parent.

So what about labor? A healthy baby not exposed to medications tends to spend most of labor asleep, both quiet sleep and dream sleep, in spite of increasing contractions and the dramatic breaking of the bag of water sweeping away the world as she knows it. Cycling of states continues during labor. Some of labor is spent relaxed in the quiet alert state. Only the agitated state 4F has not been observed during this momentous occasion.

I remember falling asleep once during a slow lecture in medical school. But I was so sleep deprived that I remained asleep as the lecture ended and my classmates all filed out of the hall. I continued to doze as the next group of students filed in and awoke in the middle of a dental school lecture. I sheepishly slipped out the door, and the room erupted in laughter just as the door closed.

But to sleep during labor?! Your baby doesn't sleep through the cataclysm of labor because of sleep deprivation. She may be as well rested right now as she will ever be in her life. Labor-sleep seems to be nature's own anesthesia.

Where Will Your Baby Sleep Next?

Once your baby has slept for months in the cozy nest of your uterus, and then perhaps slept quietly through the avalanche of labor, where will you put your baby to sleep next? Whatever you choose, your baby is likely to become accustomed to it.

Family Matters

To save money my husband wants to use a laundry basket for our baby to sleep in for the first month or so. I think a bassinet is the way to go, my mom says to use a crib, my mother-in-law says to use the car seat. I'm so confused. Where is the best place for my new baby to sleep?

Kcdokins

Many families throughout history have chosen to have the baby sleep with the parents, a "family bed." In fact, for most people around the world today such a bed is the norm. If that is a family's choice, it can work very well. It may be easier to fall asleep, and it tends to foster closeness.

Learning to sleep in a crib can also work well. It tends to foster independence. Some parents sleep better if the baby is in another room, and some feel that this distance allows them to feel closer to each other. Many babies sleep in a crib most of the night and then join their parents after the last feeding for some snuggle and sleep time together before starting the day.

Having watched many young babies maneuver toward a side or corner of the crib has given me a renewed appreciation for bassinets or cradles for the first three or four months. Some babies seem to prefer having a small, enclosed space for sleeping. Many parents enjoy having a bassinet or cradle next to their bed, because when the baby wakes up and calls for room service, it is easier to scoop him up and hold him next to you to feed in bed than it is to traipse down the hall to another room several times a night. Also, many bassinets are portable, so your baby can sleep in a familiar spot wherever you happen to be. A disadvantage of bassinets is that babies will need to form new sleep habits when the bassinets are outgrown. Of course, by then many babies start preferring a new place to sleep.

The American Academy of Pediatrics (AAP) recommends that if you choose a crib, it should conform to the latest safety standards of the Consumer Product Safety Commission (CPSC). There are no official safety standards for bassinets or cradles. The CPSC does have, however, guidelines for families who use bassinets or cradles. If you choose a bassinet, be sure the mattress is firm and fits snugly. If the legs fold, be sure they have effective locks to prevent folding while in use. Be sure that the bassinet or cradle has a sturdy bottom and a wide, stable base. And check to see that the bassinet or cradle has smooth surfaces—no protruding staples or other objects that could injure the baby. Don't use a bassinet or cradle beyond the age or weight recommended by the manufacturer.

In 2002, the CPSC and the Juvenile Products Manufacturers Association (JPMA), the association for crib manufacturers, launched a new national safety campaign urging parents to never have babies sleep with them but to always put their children in cribs that meet current safety standards. This warning was issued because a total of 180 children (out of more than 12 million in the age range) died in an adult bed during the three years studied.

This is certainly tragic. *But,* during the same period, many thousands of babies died in cribs!

In 2003, a major study hit the news showing that babies who sleep with their parents are 10 times more likely to suffocate than their peers. Reporters everywhere parroted the press release: beds are dangerous; cribs are safe. But suffocation is far rarer than sudden infant death syndrome (SIDS). There was no overall safety advantage in cribs as long as babies were put to sleep correctly.

A review of all the SIDS cases in Alaska over a period of six years was published in the October 2001 issue of *Pediatrics.* It was consistent with previous studies. Far more important than where a child slept was the sleeping position and the parents' use of tobacco, alcohol, antihistamines, or other drugs. During six years, 130 children died of SIDS. Only two children died faceup in a crib; only one died faceup in bed with a non-drug-using parent on a nonwater mattress. Fully 98 percent of cases were associated with other risk factors.

I recently spoke with Professor Robert Carpenter, an internationally prominent SIDS researcher at the London School of Hygiene and Tropical Medicine. Putting together all available evidence, he concludes that sleeping next to the parents' bed for the first 8 to 16 weeks is safer than either in the parents' bed or in a crib in another room.

Parents who choose to sleep with their babies should be taught how to do it safely. Anything that makes it more difficult for parents to wake up or anything that hinders a baby's ability to breathe should be avoided.

Babies are safer if the person next to them is aware of their presence and easily awoken. Usually, this is the mother. Fathers, siblings, and babysitters may not wake up as easily, though there are exceptions.

Whoever you are, don't sleep with a baby if you are taking something (alcohol, antihistamines, or other drugs) that makes you less aware of the baby when you sleep. The same holds true if you are so sleep deprived that you would have difficulty waking up if the baby were in need.

Tobacco smoke, adult obesity, overbundling, excess bedding, waterbeds, couches, and chemical irritants (fragrances that might irritate a baby's nose and clog the air passages) could all make breathing dangerously difficult for babies. Choose a bed that avoids places the baby could get trapped (headboards, footboards, railings, or bed frame), and avoid positioning the bed next to a wall or other furniture.

Teaching babies to sleep in their own cribs, bassinets, or cradles is a good option for some families; having them sleep with their parents is a good option for others. Soft mattresses are not good choices for babies. Nor are soft pillows, quilts, comforters, sheepskin, or stuffed toys. I prefer cozy sleep clothing to blankets to more easily avoid blankets covering babies' faces.

Wherever he sleeps after being born, don't put him to sleep facedown. Tummy time while awake is a great workout. Tummy time while asleep is a hazard. Devices to hold babies in place while they sleep, however, have not been shown to be helpful. Pacifiers, though, may decrease the risk of SIDS (and breastfeeding cuts it in half).

As long as you provide your child with a safe environment for sleeping, the place you select is a choice about how you want to live as a family during these early weeks. You might use the bi-empathy you learned about in Chapter 10, paying attention both to your needs and desires as parents as well as your baby's needs and desires. As you choose where your baby will dream after being born, he continues to add a little more baby fat from the foods you eat.

A Care Package

As you are preparing several meals for your baby's first few days (by way of the extra fat), you are also slipping a few other important gifts into your baby's birthday "care package."

Your baby already has an extraordinary immune system of her own. She has been making specialized white blood cells called *T cells* and *B cells* for some time. She is already a pro at making *natural killer cells*. Her immune system is in great shape, except for one very important thing: it lacks the wisdom that comes from experience. And that is exactly what you are going to loan her until she gains experiences of her own.

Ever since you were a little girl, even before you took your own first steps, your body has been learning about the infections you've encountered. When you had chickenpox and stayed home from school covered in itchy spots, your body remembered. You made antibodies to the chickenpox virus. When you had each sniffly cold with a stuffed-up nose, your body remembered. You may have made antibodies to a hundred different cold viruses by

The Dangers of Car Seats

Have you ever noticed newborns in car seats with their heads all the way over to one side? Have you ever wondered what it was doing to their necks? An important study in the September 2001 issue of *Pediatrics* measured how well newborns breathe in car seats. The researchers compared 50 healthy, slightly preterm babies (born at 35 to 36 weeks) to 50 healthy, full-term newborns. Surprisingly, the amount of oxygen in the blood (and getting to the brain) declined in all of the babies in both groups as they rode in car seats. The lowered oxygen levels were significant but not dangerous for most children. Among the premature babies, 12 percent had periods of apnea (absent breathing) or bradycardia (depressed heart rate), accompanied with significantly decreased oxygen levels (this would endanger about 20,000 near-term babies in the United States each year).

Conclusions? This study supports the American Academy of Pediatrics' too-seldom-followed recommendation that all preterm babies be checked in a car seat for proper fit and breathing stability before discharge from the hospital. The findings also suggest that car travel be minimized for all babies (especially preterm babies) until they are able to support their heads, unless flatbed car seats are used. Car seats and baby swings have become convenient spots for babies between car trips. Likewise, extended nontravel use of these nonflat seats should be discouraged until the babies are able to support their heads.

now. Your collection of antibodies is a personal history of your body's wisdom gained through a lifetime of experience.

During the final weeks of pregnancy, you will actively deliver your antibodies to your baby through that incredible exchange organ, the placenta. By the due date, your baby's antibody levels will be the same as yours.

Your gift will help protect her against important infections she encounters during her otherwise vulnerable first months on the planet. These antibodies will disappear during the next several months as her own antibodies are forming in earnest. The window between 6 and 12 months, as your antibodies are leaving and hers are taking charge, is the most common period for ear infections, colds, and so on. If you continue to breastfeed, you will continue to give her immune support during this window.

By the time she takes her first step, your birth gift will have completed its course, and she will toddle into the future ready to take on the world.

The Gift of Hormones

Breast Lumps

My three-week-old baby girl has small lumps of tissue under her nipples that are fairly firm, almost like tiny developing breasts. Is this normal? How long do you expect that it might last?

Amy, Los Angeles, California

Often parents are dismayed to discover small firm lumps under one or both nipples in their babies. These little nubbins of tissue are not a cause for alarm but a tangible reminder of another gift you have given to your baby.

Several times throughout childhood, situations arise where the past and future collide. No, not really collide. It's more like a triple-exposed photograph with the past, present, and future superimposed. I can remember seeing my children toddle across the family room wearing my loafers, many sizes too big. Conjured up in my mind is an image of myself as a toddler, tromping about in my dad's shoes. While watching these scenes, one in my family room, one in my mind, I recognize that someday my children will really fill those shoes—perhaps with children of their own.

For me, breast buds in an infant is another one of those precious times. A burst of your steroid hormones delivered to your baby shortly before birth is one of the finishing touches in preparing her lungs for chestfuls of air in the outside world. These hormones include estrogen and androgens, like the hormone surge during puberty. Besides literally giving the gift of breath, this prebirth pulse of hormones can have several transient side effects.

Real, mature breast tissue forms, creating temporary firm lumps under the nipples. Some babies even leak some real milk from their breasts. This is colorfully named *witch's milk*, a term that captures the magic of the situation but inappropriately attributes sinister and supernatural overtones to it. Breast buds commonly occur in both girls and boys.

Many little girls develop a cloudy vaginal discharge. Some will even have miniperiods, with blood appearing at the vagina during the first week as estrogen levels fall rapidly. Some boys and girls will have swollen genitalia.

Baby Acne

My one-month-old son's cheeks are very rough. There are small bumps that are sometimes red and irritated looking, and other times it looks very clear, but the roughness is still there. Is that baby acne? Is there something I can do to treat it?

Beckie, San Bruno, California

Many boys and girls will have their first experience of teenage acne, with real pimples appearing on the face and upper chest, at around three weeks and typically at their worst for three or four weeks. It tends to occur at about the same age as the baby's peak gas production and fussiness. How attractive! (And all this coincides with parents' time of maximum sleep deprivation.) Parents are often quite concerned about both how these bumps look and their significance.

The pimples occur predominantly on the cheeks, but they are also quite common on the forehead and chin. Whiteheads are sometimes present. This condition often comes and goes until the baby is between four and six months old.

The acne will be most prominent when your child is hot or fussy (increased blood flow to the skin) or when his skin is irritated. If his skin comes into contact with cloth laundered in harsh detergents or becomes wet from saliva or milk that he has spit up, the condition may appear worse for several days.

Gently cleanse his face once a day with water and perhaps a mild baby soap. Oils and lotions do not help and may aggravate the condition. If the acne is severe or lasts beyond six months, your pediatrician may prescribe a mild medicine to help.

Otherwise, you can expect that the rash will soon be a memory. The oil glands will diminish, and you won't see the acne again until you turn around and he's a teenager. This time the acne will be evidence that his own hormones are turning him into a man.

Your hormones and most of their effects disappear gradually, usually over the first several months after your baby is born. Typically, the breast buds are the first signs to form and the last to go. Unless the breasts become red, hard, or warm (indicating possible mastitis, or breast infection), savor the weeks the firm lumps remain.

Budding breasts, a face full of pimples, and her first period are all visible reminders of a moment not long ago when your baby was still inside your uterus. They might even remind you that not terribly long ago, you were inside your own mother and receiving these same hormones. And these little bumps are a glimpse of a future that seems so far away right now (especially on those sleepless nights) but will come all too soon—when your teenage daughter becomes a woman.

Cherish moments like this when they occur. It might be when she stands in front of a mirror putting on makeup or delights to play with a briefcase, or it might be her graduation from kindergarten. Notice those junctures when, for a fleeting moment, she looks grown-up—and appreciate the brief double-exposure of the future and the past.

After this set of side effects and the hormones are long gone, the real gift remains. Each breath she takes is a reminder of your connection. As her chest quietly rises and falls in peaceful sleep or struggles during a childhood illness, it points back to this secret gift in the quiet before birth.

In the next chapter, we'll look at other things to consider as you and your baby get to know each other face-to-face. But first let's consider one more gift, a gift you can help your baby give.

Cord Blood Banking

I love being able to help my children give gifts. For Mother's Day and my wife's birthday, it's a treat for me to get a sense of what the kids want to give and to provide what they need to make it happen. Perhaps all it takes is a few markers and a nicely shaped stone. Sometimes it would require an extravagant sum of money, far beyond my means. Then we look for something else for them to give.

What does a brand-new baby have to give? When a baby's umbilical cord has been cut, the blood that remains in the cord and the placenta is usually thrown out. But this blood is very special, not only because it is genetically new and unique, but also because it contains special stem cells, the center of much exciting medical research. Stem cells are cells that haven't yet committed themselves to remaining a single type of cell. They are full of potential! They can reproduce into other types of blood and immune cells. They can also reproduce into other types of cells including bone, heart, muscle, and nerve.

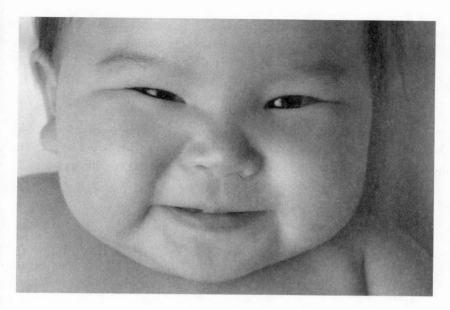

Stem cells are like master keys, unlocking different paths of development. Throughout your pregnancy, they have been making the marvels of development possible. Are they useful after a baby is born?

Cancer Treatment

Stem cell transplants are currently an important, lifesaving treatment for some types of cancer. One of my best friends is having a stem cell transplant as I am writing this chapter. The odds that your child will need this are small. About 99.96 percent of children will have no need of this before their 21st birthday. And 99.93 percent of families won't need them for another family member. About 1 in 1,400 will.

In the unlikely event that such a transplant is necessary, the cells could come from a public stem cell bank or from a bone marrow transplant. Often this solves the problem. But if stem cells from your baby were available, they might be preferred. Not only are they unique to your baby, they are the stem cells most likely to be a match for other people in the family. Using cord blood stem cells decreases the chance of a patient rejecting the transplant and increases the survival rate. And they are available without a search. Your baby's cord blood is unique and can only be collected in the few minutes after he's born.

Stem cell transplants are also currently used to treat diseases such as aplastic anemia, severe combined immunodeficiency, and rare metabolic diseases.

Other Potential Benefits

Stem cell research is a hot area. It's likely, but not at all certain, that in the next decade exciting new uses will be found for stem cells. It's also likely that some of the areas scientists are investigating will not pan out when more is known. Here are some of the most promising possibilities:

- **Heart repair.** Human trials have already shown improved heart health within weeks when stem cells have been given after a heart attack to repair damaged muscle.
- **Blood vessel repair.** Human trials have already shown some success with giving stem cells to help grow new blood vessels and improve circulation. This has worked even on coronary blood vessels, with people growing their own bypasses. Perhaps they could even be used to prevent or treat strokes.
- **Brain repair.** Because stem cells can transform into nerve cells, researchers are actively looking at ways to treat, and perhaps reverse, diseases like Parkinson's and Alzheimer's with stem cells. I recently went to a dinner where Christopher Reeve spoke with power and passion about the possibilities of stem cell research for repairing spinal cord injuries.
- **Other organ repair.** Scientists are also looking at other possibilities, including trying to cure diabetes by repairing the insulin-producing cells of the pancreas.

A Second Chance

Cord blood companies often emphasize that you only have one opportunity to collect cord blood. This is true, to a degree. You might, of course, store cord blood from a future child for your family. Or you might store stem cells from another source. Cord blood cells are unique because they are so immature that they allow a greater degree of mismatch while still being compatible with someone in the family. But stem cells that have incredible power may also be collected later.

My youngest son, now eight years old, put his tooth under his pillow this weekend, giggling with anticipation of what the tooth fairy would bring.

Across the country, Songtao Shi, a pediatric dentist at the National Institute of Dental and Craniofacial Research, has been putting the teeth of his daughter of about the same age into a glass of milk in the fridge. Why? Shi and his colleagues have discovered that recently lost baby teeth contain powerful stem cells. They could prove to be an excellent alternative to fetal stem cell harvesting, which is understandably controversial despite its enormous therapeutic potential. Baby tooth stem cells may one day be used to repair damaged teeth—or perhaps even spinal cord injuries, diabetes, or degenerative diseases. I asked Dr. Shi about this. He said that baby teeth stored overnight in milk at about 40°F are still loaded with living stem cells in the morning. One day soon, people may well drop off their children's baby teeth at the dentist's the next day. The stem cells could be frozen and stored for years and years, available for transplant or treatment if needed. My guess is that this will become practical while my son is still losing his baby teeth. I hope so.

What to Do About Cord Blood Banking

Parents are often confronted with brochures asking them to make an expensive investment in collecting and storing their baby's cord blood. How do you decide?

It's clear that if money weren't an issue, this would be an easy choice. I would resoundingly endorse it and enable children to give this amazing gift to themselves and their families. But the real question is whether the definite cost is worth the possible and potential benefits. The answer will be different for each family, depending partly on the family history and economic situation. Many investments may be better choices than this one, such as a safe home or car or food. But reducing from a daily 20-ounce latte at a popular coffee joint to a 12-ounce latte six days a week could cover the cost of storing the cord blood and may be a sacrifice worth making. This is a wonderful topic to discuss with your doctor before the birth to help you sort out what is best for your family. You might also discuss the option of donating your baby's cord blood if you choose not to store it yourself.

Whatever you finally decide, be sure to keep the situation in perspective. My daughter was born on Christmas morning, and I can tell you that she is a greater gift than anything she could have given (including stem cells).

Part III

Steppin' Out

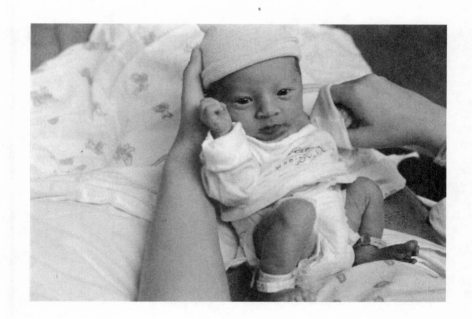

15

The World Will Never Be the Same

Labor and Baby's Arrival

When the contractions of labor begin, you know that the moment you've all been waiting for is finally approaching. Very soon now, the unfolding drama of development will shift to a baby you can see and who can see you, to baby feet you can press on an inkpad and touch to a piece of paper, instead of feel dancing inside your belly.

In many ways, though, the wonder of your baby's continuous development does not change at birth. The same natural choreography continues without your causing it or even necessarily being aware of it. It's an everyday miracle you get to watch and nurture and enjoy, but that you don't have to work to make happen. Our roles as parents adjust with each new phase of development, but they all come down to new ways of doing the same things we did during pregnancy—providing a safe, nurturing, and gently stimulating environment for our children. But it's different when you are caring for a baby who's made his grand entrance.

Who Starts This Party, Anyway?

Back at the time of Hippocrates, people believed that the reason babies turned head down in the uterus was so that they could push with their legs to start labor and propel themselves out. At many points in history, people assumed that labor began when a woman was ripe, and it didn't depend much, if at all, on the baby.

Then in the 20th century, studies involving sheep and cows proved that labor was started by hormones released by the lambs and calves. But it turns out that humans are different.

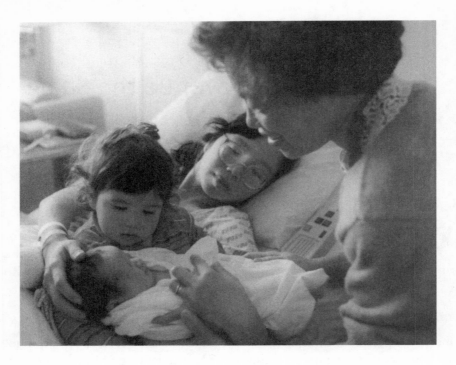

The decision to start labor appears to emerge from a silent, dynamic dialogue between Mom and the baby. Complex biochemical signals race back and forth until the two are in agreement. Regardless of who makes the initial suggestion or asks if the other is ready, fetal hormones send the signal to get the process going in Mom's uterine muscles where labor begins.

Labor Pain

Childbirth classes are one of the most common types of parenting education that couples get. I still remember people from the childbirth classes I've attended as a parent. When my first son was on the way, Joel Lavine, a physician friend was in the class. Always the jokester, when he signed into the building security log for the evening class, he calmly wrote *arson* under "purpose of visit," commenting that "Nobody ever reads these." Back then, apparently no one did.

But the joke stuck in my mind in a way he didn't intend, because in some ways labor is a purifying fire, the quintessential rite of passage that changes you as much as any science fiction teleportation or transformation. The world will never be the same.

But the passage can really hurt. So while these classes include choices you can make to try to have the labor you want (understanding that all choices are subject to change), the main focus is on strategies to reduce pain and discomfort. In the classes I've attended, the focus has been on the mother's discomfort, not the baby's.

Labor is another opportunity for bi-empathic vision, a chance to make choices that honor your needs and that also consider the needs of your baby. You might want pain relief during your labor, or you might want to experience the full brunt of it, aided only by breathing techniques.

My question is, what does your baby want? His body will be going through mirror-image contortions of your own, shrinking where you are expanding, bones pressing together where yours stretch. He will experience pressures unlike anything he has experienced before or will again, as he is permanently expelled from his paradise, into a wonderful world he has not yet seen.

If death is permanently leaving this world, then this experience may feel like dying. His world collapses as he moves toward the light of the outside world. The fish tank wall breaks; the water rushes out. The umbilical cord, his source of oxygen and food, is stretched taut and finally severed. His lungs are squeezed shut. For an instant he is poised between two worlds, no longer able to breathe underwater, not yet having breathed air. And then comes the first cry—a sound that changes you forever.

Meanwhile, inside, a quiet series of events like silent dominoes toppling in a row forever change his heart and his blood vessels so he can join your world. Some blood vessels close off, others open, flaps change in the walls of his heart, the direction of his bloodstream changes momentously. Now oxygen will come from the air, not from you. And food will go through his lips, not through a living tube protruding from his stomach. His waste carbon dioxide will vent directly into the air, rather than into your bloodstream. And his food waste—well, you will still get to remove that. At least now, perhaps, you can share the responsibility.

Your Baby's Perspective

Does your baby want pain medication or drugs to make her numb during the earthquake passage? I can see why she might—or might not. I don't know the answer to this question, but I think that it's an important question to consider. We do know some things from scientific research, and I hope more will be understood in the future.

As we saw in the last chapter, we know that most healthy babies sleep through the greater part of labor on their own. Even though loud, vibrating sound is enough to awaken babies from any stage of sleep before birth, labor is not. Perhaps they are not as uncomfortable during labor as we might imagine. They usually do cry shortly after birth, but as we'll see in a bit, most babies quickly become calm and curious. They seem eager and alert, not traumatized or exhausted. Unless they get narcotics.

One of the common ways to reduce labor pain is to give the mother shots or intravenous (IV) doses of narcotic pain medications. Especially popular are the forms where mothers can adjust the dosage themselves to get just the amount they need. And when mothers get narcotics, so might their babies.

But these drugs can affect mothers and babies differently. A popular pain medicine called meperidine (Demerol) is halfway gone from mothers' bodies within three to six hours. However, half of it is still in their babies after 15 to 23 hours. Most of these babies do quite well. Nevertheless, a number of subtle effects are commonly seen. On average, these babies are measurably less alert or eager to discover their parents and the world around them after the big event. They also have a higher risk of breathing problems, although an antidote can be given if there is trouble. And the one-minute Apgar score tends to be lower. (The Apgar test is used to check that the baby's color, breathing, heart rate, muscle tone, and response to stimuli are normal.)

One large study gave a placebo or varying amounts of meperidine to 920 women during labor. The people who examined the babies did not know which came from which mothers. They found that those babies who were exposed to meperidine scored significantly lower on an early neonatal neurobehavioral test on their first and second days of life.

The larger the dose of meperidine, the greater the effect. The timing also makes a difference. Those who get the medication within an hour of delivery have minimal effects. If it comes three hours or more before delivery, the effects are generally larger.

Babies whose mothers have had meperidine also tend to have depressed sucking and rooting reflexes. It's not surprising then that there is a measurable delay in establishing breastfeeding. However, when babies are six weeks old, there is no detectable difference in nursing between those whose mothers were given meperidine and those mothers who did without it.

There are a handful of studies that suggest the possibility of longer lasting consequences. Researchers in Sweden found that among drug-addicted adults whose birth records were available, a higher percentage had mothers who had received narcotics during labor. This could be just a coincidence.

There might be many differences in the families of these people other than just the choice of anesthesia during labor. So the researchers did another study, looking at families in which some siblings became drug addicts and others in the same family did not. Why do kids in the same family turn out so differently? The study found that siblings who had narcotics during labor had a 4.7 times higher chance of becoming addicted than their own siblings who did not. A subsequent study in the United States came up with the same level of risk. Perhaps babies are learning even during labor.

Some people suggest that newer narcotics are a better choice than meperidine for a variety of reasons. Some of these medications leave the body more quickly, but more gets into the brain, giving Mom more pain relief with a smaller dose. In the United Kingdom, an old narcotic (heroin) is often prescribed in maternity wards for similar reasons. But there remains a lack of evidence to show any better short- or long-term effects on babies than those encountered with meperidine.

Again, most kids who have narcotics during labor will be fine, but it's important to consider the risks and benefits to the baby as well as to the mother. It's a question that should be asked.

What About Epidurals?

Many women love their epidurals and speak of them in glowing terms that would be hard to exaggerate. Others dislike the numbness or the effect on the pace of their labor. These feelings may be so strong either way that it might be tough to imagine what your baby's perspective would be.

What do we know about the baby's point of view on epidurals and similar techniques of regional (as opposed to general, or all-over) anesthesia? The big difference they experience is that these drugs tend to make labor last longer. But not all of labor.

The first stage of labor lasts from the beginning of contractions until the cervix is completely dilated. This includes the slow dilation up to 3 or 4 centimeters during the latent phase of labor, when Mom and the baby can relax between contractions. The first stage also includes the mighty muscular contractions of the active phase as the cervix dilates to about 9 centimeters. And it includes transition—the short, exquisitely emotional period as the cervix finishes dilating and the end is finally in sight. I've seen more than a few labor coaches panic during the brief, intense transition.

On average, the first stage of labor takes almost 10 hours in first-time mothers, but this can vary considerably. Of this, the latent phase averages almost seven hours and the active phase almost three. During this time, the baby is still in the uterus. The work has been to change the shape of things inside. Taking together all of the major research studies on epidurals, it looks like they generally don't lengthen the first stage of labor appreciably, if at all. And they do make it much more comfortable for moms.

When someone says, "OK, push!" the second stage of labor has begun. During this stage, the baby makes his skintight journey through the eye of the birth canal needle. Within an average of 33 amazing minutes (of pushing for Mom and of being forced through a conehead-making machine for the baby), labor ends in the glorious birth.

It's the second stage of labor that an epidural tends to lengthen by an average of 15 minutes. What are these 15 extra minutes in the birth canal like for the baby? We don't know.

We do know that babies' heart rates tend to race during this long transit if their mothers have had an epidural. This might be from an emotional response, from physical stress, or because their mothers often have an elevated temperature during the second stage. And we know that there is a higher chance of instrumentation use (a vacuum or forceps grabbing the baby's head to pull while you push). But various measures of newborn health tend to look great in babies with epidurals just after they are born, including Apgar scores and blood pH. There is no increased risk of meconium (fetal stool) entering the amniotic fluid. The cesarean section (C-section) rate was also similar for women who did and did not have an epidural.

Studies looking at the breastfeeding experience after an epidural found interesting results. In the event of a cesarean section, women with an epidural are more likely to breastfeed than those who have any other kind of anesthesia. Among women who want to breastfeed and who deliver vaginally, there is no difference in breastfeeding between those who choose an epidural and those who choose no medical pain relief.

And mothers who have an epidural report experiencing less pain during labor, and feeling better immediately afterward.

Doulas — A Powerful Alternative

We discussed doulas briefly in Chapter 13 for their support after your baby is born. Having a trained labor companion supporting you during the intensity of delivery can be especially powerful. In many delivery settings, professional assistance is available only intermittently during the tumultuous hours of labor. The continuous, empathetic, unobtrusive presence of an experienced doula has many proven advantages. It's not surprising, perhaps, that the ministrations of a doula measurably reduce anxiety, discomfort, and pain. This is true even though narcotic and epidural use is significantly less when a doula is present. Using a doula shortens labor by an average of two hours! Doulas dramatically decrease the need for oxytocin, forceps, and vacuum-extraction. The chance of an unplanned cesarean section is 45 percent lower. Fevers in Mom are less common, and babies are ready to go home from the hospital sooner. Twenty-four hours after the delivery, mothers who used a doula still report less pain and are less anxious about caring for their babies. They also report a more satisfying first 24 hours as a new family.

When interviewed six weeks later, mothers who used a doula were more likely to report that becoming a mother was easy, and that they can look after their baby better than anyone else could. They are more likely to view their baby as clever, beautiful, and easy to manage. They tend to believe that their babies cry less than others do.

Parents are sometimes concerned about using a doula because they are afraid that the doula will come between them or make the father feel peripheral. On the contrary, doulas are trained to support and include both parents, providing a reassuring, seasoned presence to allow the parents to relax and connect with each other and the new baby.

There are wonderful ways to have a baby without a doula, and many parents who do not use a doula still experience the benefits described above, but parents deserve to know about this valuable option.

Zero Hour

Whether your delivery is by C-section or vagina, whatever anesthesia choices you make beforehand, and whatever is actually done, the moment arrives when you and your baby glimpse each other for the first time. You are hungry to get to know each other.

The baby is quickly dried and given the Apgar test to make sure she's OK. Then the baby is brought to Mom, and the new family can marvel together.

In some ways, this is a strange new world for your baby. But some things are familiar. Babies recognize their mothers' smell, and they recognize the sounds of voices that are familiar to them. Skin-to-skin contact and quiet conversation are a warm welcome to this side of the cervix.

Dr. Marshall Klaus, the author of *Your Amazing Newborn* and one of my heroes, points out that when healthy babies enjoy skin-to-skin contact with their mothers, they are usually amazingly content during the first 90 minutes of life, with little or no crying. If they are wrapped warmly and placed in a nearby bassinet, however, they cry an average of 20 to 40 seconds every five minutes for the next hour and a half. They want to feel safe and warm next to you. And to start getting to know you from the outside.

Bonding

Dr. Marshall Klaus and his colleague Dr. John Kennell were the first to describe the powerful bonding that can occur between parents and babies soon after birth. When the baby is healthy and the room is not too bright or too busy, something magical happens. The baby enters the same quiet alert state that we talked about before birth; his mind and body are ready to drink you in. This first quiet alert moment is several times longer than any that have come before, usually lasting about 40 minutes. Your newborn is still and quiet, with wide-open eyes gazing at you, perhaps with a hand touching your skin. This is not the time to make your phone calls and announcements to the world. It's not the time to run down to move the car (even if that means getting a traffic ticket or being towed). It's a time to enjoy quietly being together as a family.

A baby in the quiet alert state may follow your face or your voice as you move and may even try to imitate you if you stick your tongue out or make a funny face. It's a time for connecting, for learning about each other.

Drs. Klaus and Kennell have commented that hospital procedures may interfere with this golden time. I agree that hospitals should not intrude unless necessary. But neither should this bonding time be forced. Sometimes labor has been physically or emotionally trying for the parents or the baby, who may need some extra care or time to recover. When both parties are

ready, they can take the time to bond. Bonding is a long process. Some parents feel overwhelmed with love and connection immediately. Others (even excellent ones) feel numb or sad at first, and don't feel the connection for days or weeks or months.

This first quiet alert state is by no means your only chance. Quiet alert states will come again soon. On average, babies are in this magical mode about 10 percent of the time. When you notice one, it is a precious time to connect. But they will continue to occur in various forms throughout your child's life, although they may be less predictable. Just yesterday, my 14-year-old son and I sat quietly looking into each other's eyes, listening to each other's hopes and fears.

Baby's First Date

The very first quiet alert is usually the longest one that a baby experiences. Each baby is unique, but typically your baby will want to see your face, to gaze at your eyes, to watch your lips when you talk, to learn who you are. They can see best at a distance of about 8 to 10 inches, perfect when you're holding them lovingly. Babies can learn to recognize their mother's faces as early as four hours after birth and can pick out her picture from similar pictures of other women's faces. Soon they can recognize the smell of their mother's breast pads and pick them out from the pads of other women.

And babies can start putting parents' voices with their faces. Researchers in Canada tested this by presenting toys to brand-new babies, along with consistent accompanying sounds (randomly chosen but consistently paired). When this was repeated several times, the babies quickly learned the correct sight-sound pairings. They expected the correct sound with each toy, even if the toy was moved to another spot in the room. If the sounds were switched the babies knew something was wrong.

While your baby's senses are flooded with the new sights, sounds, smells, textures, and perhaps tastes of his parents, it's a wonderful time for you to also get to know him.

Research has shown that by the end of the first hour together, 60 percent of fathers are able to pick out their own baby from other newborns *by touch alone*! Blindfolded, and in the absence of sound, they recognize their children simply by touching the backs of their hands.

Things You Might Notice

Parents are quick to notice whether their baby's a boy or a girl. The number of fingers and toes are rapidly counted. However, some things are easily missed—my wife didn't see that our son had a dramatic conehead until she looked back later at his newborn pictures. All she saw was that he was gorgeous. Here are a few things you might discover on your first date with your baby.

The Eyes Have It. Many babies are so taken with eyes, that you can play a little game. If one of you closes your eyes, your baby may turn to look at the parent whose eyes are open. What happens if only one eye is open? Most babies are not very interested.

Seeing Red. The dazzling experience of color begins when light strikes a canvas of tightly-packed nerve cells in the back of the eye. The rods are the "black-and-white" receptors; they photograph the ever-changing patterns of light and darkness that are before our eyes. The cones are responsible for the wonder of color vision. Usually. We humans are born mostly color-blind. The cones don't begin functioning until a baby is about four months old. The color tones of the world begin as black, white—and red. For reasons we don't entirely understand, right from the start babies are able to pick out red objects. They love faces (especially eyes), high-contrast patterns (especially target or breast shapes), and things red.

Boys Will Be Boys. We've known for a while that boys and girls tend to have different interests by the time they are taking their first steps. For instance, if you show one-year-olds videos of cars moving or of faces moving, the boys are more likely to be captivated by the zooming cars, the girls by the animated faces. Is this the way they are built? Or is this what we have taught them?

Researchers at Cambridge have discovered that when newborn babies are shown both mechanical mobiles and human faces, boys tend to show stronger interest in the toys, while girls show stronger interest in people.

A Face a Baby Could Love. On the first day of life, most babies already prefer looking at attractive faces. When photographs of two women are put in front of them, babies will tend to spend more time looking at the one that adults judge to be more attractive. Are they born with an idea of beauty? Or do they learn quickly from the faces they see? Either way, to babies their parents are the most beautiful of all—with faces a baby could love, whether or not there are imperfections. Of course, babies may have beauty marks of their own.

It's Not Acne. When you first meet your baby, there may be tiny bumps on her face. These may catch your attention, or you might look right past them and not even notice at first.

Milia are little plugs of keratin (a kind of protein) in the glands of the facial skin, and they are found in up to half of newborns. These bumps are yellow or white (unlike the red bumps of baby acne). The tiny bumps of milia are no larger than a millimeter or two. They are most common on the tip of the nose or chin and are frequently seen on the cheeks and forehead. Less commonly, they will be found on the upper trunk or limbs—and even on the penis. Most milia disappear within the first few weeks of life. Sometimes they last for the first three months.

> ### Skin Deep
> What is a Mongolian birthmark, and what causes it?
>
> **Jmill1948**
>
> What caused the "stork bites" on my newborn's face, and when will they go away? I assume they are stork bites; they are patches of reddish spots on each eyelid, between her eyes on the brow bone, under her nose on the area above her upper lip, and at the base of her spine.
>
> **Sea**

Salmon Patches. "Angel kisses" and "stork bites" are among the other picturesque names given to these very common birthmarks. Salmon patches appear as flat, dull pink splotches. Most commonly they occur at the nape of the neck (stork bites), between the eyebrows or over the eyelids (angel kisses), or around the nose or mouth. Parents often worry that these will last forever or get darker with time, but the opposite tends to be true. They are tiny windows into the past.

Salmon patches are dilated capillaries in the skin. They are not new capillaries or new growths, but leftover patches of the way the blood vessels looked during fetal circulation. Before birth, every child has salmon patches. By the time a baby is born, only about one-third do. The great majority disappear, usually within the first year. Those around the hairline at the back of the neck (called "Unna's nevus") are the most likely to remain.

Because these birthmarks are collections of blood vessels in the skin, they tend to look darker or redder when a baby is crying, excited, or upset. This may even be true after the patch seems to have disappeared.

Pustular Melanosis. With a name like "pustular melanosis," this interesting quirk of baby skin sounds nasty. Instead it is clean, cute, and as temporary as those oh-so-short first days with your baby. This birthmark makes a grand entrance! Small blisters are usually present at birth, most commonly under the chin, at the back of the neck, on the forehead, the lower back, or the shins—but they can occur in other locations as well. The small blisters peel open within the first 48 hours of life, revealing a small "freckle" inside. When the blister roof is gone, a small white collar of skin may surround this dark spot for a while. Some babies have only the spots (the blister event happened before birth). The "freckles" fade within three weeks to three months.

Gray Slate Patches. These flat birthmarks, sometimes called Mongolian spots, can be deep brown, slate gray, or blue-black in color. They sometimes look like bruises. The edges are often, but not always, indistinct. They are most common on the lower back and buttocks, but they are often found on the legs, back, sides, and shoulders. They vary from the size of a pinhead to six inches or more across. A child may have one or several.

These spots are nothing more than dense collections of melanin, the normal pigment of the skin. When melanin is close to the surface, it looks brown. The deeper it is in the skin, the more bluish it looks. The spots do not predispose the baby to skin cancer or any other problem.

At least one Mongolian spot is present on the great majority of darker skinned babies. They are also present in about 1 in 10 fair-skinned infants. Present at birth, most of these spots fade (at least somewhat) by age two. Most have completely disappeared by age five. If Mongolian spots remain at puberty, they are likely to be permanent. Fewer than 5 percent of children with Mongolian spots still have them by the time they reach adulthood. Those who keep them tend to have multiple, widespread spots or spots in unusual locations.

Lanugo Hair. Before birth, your baby was covered with fine, soft hair over most of his body—everywhere except his palms, soles, lips, penis, nails, and the sides of his fingers and toes. Most of this hair is usually shed during the seventh or eighth month of pregnancy. Sometimes it is still present for a few months after birth, especially in babies born early. This soft, leftover hair is called *lanugo* hair.

Parents are concerned that this hair will stay, but lanugo hair is shed, never to return, within weeks. Some people advocate rubbing the hair to speed its shedding. However, this reminder that your baby is in the fleeting newborn period will soon disappear with no treatment.

Heat Rashes. Children's skin can be quite sensitive to heat. Nursing moms often discover this, especially in the summertime, when their baby's face turns red where it is against the mother's skin. This redness comes from blood vessels in the area dilating to cool the skin down. Cooling the skin usually makes the rash disappear within hours, or even sooner.

Miliaria is a type of heat rash that lasts for days. It is also a classic newborn rash. The pores of their immature sweat glands plug easily, leading to tiny pink bumps or water blisters. These are most common in the first few weeks of life. It is especially common in hot, humid weather but almost any baby can get it. It is more common in babies who are bundled too warmly.

Older children can also get miliaria, in which case it is often called "prickly heat." Either way, miliaria tends to show up on covered parts of the skin, especially where there is friction from clothing. The forehead (under caps or visors), body folds, the upper back and chest, and the arms are the most common locations. Often prickly heat itches in older children, and they often describe a "prickly" sensation. What newborns feel remains a mystery.

Erythema Toxicum. Toxicum? That doesn't sound good! And the rash itself looks frightening to many parents. Nevertheless, this common splotchy rash in newborns is an entirely benign condition. It seems to be a result of the skin's regulatory mechanisms adjusting to life outside the uterus.

Erythema toxicum is found in about half of all babies. Some have splotchy red patches. Some have firm yellow or white bumps surrounded by a flare of red. The rash tends to come and go, shifting its location across the body. The palms and soles of the feet are often exempt.

It is most common on the second day of life but can first show up at birth or within the first two weeks. The individual splotches may remain in place for only a few hours or for a number of days. The entire rash may come and go over a couple of weeks.

Personalitorum Persistus. OK, I made that phrase up. But beyond the skin-deep birthmarks, you will see something of your baby's personality. And while life changes us all, there is a tendency for babies' temperaments on the first day of life (if they are healthy) to be noticeably similar to children's temperaments years later. As you say hello to your baby in this first golden hour, you can get a glimpse of the kindergartner who will wave good-bye on her way to class.

The First Supper

At some point, babies will want to try their first meal by mouth. Studies have shown that if breastfeeding is attempted before the baby is taken out of the room, the chances of ongoing breastfeeding are much higher. Because of this, nurses may be eager to put the baby to the mother's breast. This may work well, but often babies will lick the nipple and not latch on correctly.

But one of the most surprising things I've learned from Marshall Klaus is the wonder of letting a baby decide when to sample that first meal—and of letting him make the journey to the breast on his own.

Dr. Klaus describes how, around 40 minutes after birth, the great delight a baby may have been experiencing at looking at your faces often gives way to concentration on his own lip smacking or other mouth movements. Saliva may start to flow. And if the baby is placed on his mother's belly, he may try to maneuver in his own way toward his mother's nipple.

Babies are born with what we call a *stepping reflex*, the ability to push with their legs, as if they were walking. It has been assumed that this reflex prepares them to walk months later. But the reflex disappears after a few weeks. Perhaps it is present to enable them to push their way to Mom's nipple. Babies can take their first "steps" against Mom's belly.

With stretches and pushes, the baby makes slow progress. He may even do his first push-up on the way. Rest breaks are frequent, as are stops to check the map. In this case, the map is the baby's own hand. Babies will lick and suck their hands to get their bearings, using the taste and smell of the amniotic fluids on their hands to navigate toward the breast, which secretes an oily substance containing some of the same ingredients. If babies' hands are washed before this journey, they probably will not succeed. Similarly, if one breast has been washed, the baby will head toward the other one. If both breasts have been washed, the baby will head toward one breast if you splash it with amniotic fluid.

If parents (and hospital staff) are patient and all goes well, the baby may latch on perfectly and begin to feed on the colostrum. Babies who work to get there on their own are more likely to take the whole areola into their mouth, nursing more efficiently and hurting the nipple less.

And when you see the power of your baby's instincts and reflexes, you may begin to trust yourself more deeply. Not that long ago, you were the baby. Now a whole set of powerful parenting instincts are being activated in you, every bit as strong as the instincts in your baby, even though they're sometimes hidden from view by layers of conscious thoughts and fears. This will become very obvious soon when Mom's breast milk has come in and lets down in response to her baby's cry.

This first supper is an Olympic achievement for all of you. And for most healthy babies, it's a reason to delay washing, eye ointment, weighing, measuring, shots, or procedures for the first hour. Just take an ounce of drying, a cup of skin-to-skin contact, a teaspoon of soft lights and eye contact, a tincture of time—and enjoy! Serves 2–3.

16

The Babymoon

What to Expect from Baby's First Few Weeks

What comes after the triumph of birth and the very first meal? When an athlete is named Most Valuable Player of the Super Bowl, his next stop is a celebration trip to a famous theme park. When a couple gets married, they often enjoy a honeymoon to celebrate their new relationship. A friend of mine named Ann Douglas, a parenting author who's chock-full of practical wisdom, recommends a "babymoon" to celebrate your new family.

I like her name for this important idea. On a honeymoon, the couple sets aside ordinary responsibilities to focus on enjoying each other and building a foundation of closeness for the years ahead. During a babymoon, the couple likewise sets aside other work and home responsibilities to focus on learning about and establishing their new family. Both can be magical, unique times, building memories to last a lifetime.

But I contend that a honeymoon and a babymoon are also very different. While honeymooning, your time is spent on some combination of intimacy, adventure, relaxation, and indulgence. It's a very special kind of vacation. But on a babymoon, time is spent in the seemingly ceaseless cycle of caring for your baby's most basic bodily needs: feeding and burping and changing diapers. It's a very special kind of work.

A honeymoon is a going out, a break from everyday life. A babymoon is a drawing in, a concentration on the very core of day-to-day life. And as you get to know each other in the mundane, you grow a new dimension, a new depth.

One of my vivid memories from childhood (back before DVDs and Tivo) is watching *The Wizard of Oz* on TV. (Don't tell, but I used to hide behind the couch during the part with the flying monkeys.) I remember my won-

der at the sudden transition from the dull, sepia landscape of Kansas to the dazzling Technicolor of Oz. And I had mixed feelings about Dorothy's insistent longing to leave the boldly colorful magical land as she repeated, "There's no place like home."

A babymoon is having Oz and Kansas rolled into one. It's learning to see you're a hero on a quest, while being stuck in one place with a burp cloth on your shoulder. It's finding vibrant color and magic in the everyday world of home.

The Blue in the Rainbow

You may feel a rainbow of emotions during the days following your baby's birth. Sometimes they may follow each other in bewildering succession; sometimes several conflicting emotions surface at the same time.

As magical as the journey of parenthood is, it often begins with a period of feeling blue. Women's bodies are the scene of a powerfully changing tide of hormones in the days and weeks after their baby is born. The rising hormone levels that gradually produced the incredible changes in your body during the time you were carrying your baby have now dropped precipitously.

Blue and Red

My wife and I have a beautiful new baby girl. We were both excited about having her (we were infertility patients). Now that she is here, my wife is miserable. She cries all the time, and I am at my wit's end. I find myself feeling angry, which I don't want to do. Is this just postpartum blues? What should I do?

Ron from Nashville

Most new mothers (perhaps as many as 90 percent) will have a period of weepiness, mood swings, anxiety, unhappiness, and regret. Usually this lasts for a few days or less and is quickly forgotten. It's not unusual, however, for the blue period to come and go for six weeks. For some moms, the blues don't begin until the baby stops nursing (another time of major hormonal shifts). Hormones, however, are not the entire story.

Moms who have adopted their babies also commonly go through a blue period. And now that investigators have begun to look into it, we know that most dads (though less weepy) go through a time of feeling unhappy, insecure, left out, and moody. One day I expect we'll discover that even dads and adoptive moms have sudden hormonal and chemical changes in response to a new baby—but this has not been proven. We do know, though, that even at this exciting time of having a newborn, there are good reasons to be blue.

Every new beginning is also an ending of what came before. Whenever a baby is born, the world will never be the same. This is wonderful. It's also OK to grieve for the loss of the way life was before.

You no longer have control of your own time the way you once did. Perhaps you miss the challenges and rewards of work. Hobbies may have to be put on hold for a while. The romance of your relationship is also different—it's no longer just the two of you.

Whether pregnancy was comfortable or not, Mom may be mourning the special intimacy of feeling her baby kicking. Many new mothers describe feeling empty inside. Pregnancy is a time of looking forward to an eagerly awaited moment. Now the anticipation is gone. Also, pregnancy breaks down barriers in society. Complete strangers used to beam at you, want to pat your tummy, and remark on how you glowed. They might have leapt up to give you a hand. Now your baby is increasingly the focus of attention, and even though you would probably benefit more now from encouragement and practical aid, you are less likely to get it.

You may also be mourning the loss of your ideal appearance; you may still look pregnant. When my youngest child was one month old, a door-to-door saleswoman greeted my wife and asked when the baby was due. (Needless to say, no sale!) Wearing maternity clothes when pregnancy is over just isn't as fun, but usually nothing else is comfortable yet.

Now add sleep deprivation to all this! You may be more exhausted than you have ever been. Whenever people are sleep deprived, they are more subject to swings of emotion and feelings of inadequacy. This by itself is enough to cause a blue period (ask any practicing pediatrician).

To make matters worse, research has shown that women with postpartum blues tend to have babies who cry significantly more than those of their happier counterparts. It hasn't been proven whether the fussy, crying babies make moms sadder or whether the sad moms make the babies less happy, but it seems to me that both are true and that the crying can become a vicious cycle.

A true grief reaction at a time of great stress (and insistent noise) in a person who is chronically sleep deprived and has tremendous hormonal surges—it's a wonder that postpartum blues aren't more of a problem. Most of the time, though, the powerful, positive feelings that also accompany this time of new beginnings soon displace the sadness.

If a plane ride is turbulent and the oxygen masks fall from the ceiling, you need to put on your own mask first so that you will be able to help your children. If your emotional sky is falling, do the same thing: taking care of yourself is often the first step to being better able to love your baby. This is also a good principle to follow if you are having the best time of your life.

Get as much sleep as possible. If you are breastfeeding, you will probably feel sleepy just after nursing. Sleep when the baby sleeps. Once nursing is well established, you may want to give your baby some bottle-feedings (ideally of pumped breast milk), both to give you a break and to allow Dad the treat of feeding his baby. If you are bottle-feeding from the beginning, share the responsibility when you can.

Eat delicious, healthy food—hopefully that somebody else prepares! And be sure to get enough omega-3 fatty acids; low levels of this nutrient make postpartum blues worse.

Get out of the house. Even brief breaks (particularly if it's time the two of you can spend together) can be very restoring, especially if you get outside. Or treat yourself to a massage. It's not a guilty indulgence, but a valid treatment supported by scientific literature.

Clearly, this requires teamwork. Teamwork in the form of a couple, an extended family, a community, or baby care support such as a doula. An online community can be another source of support and wisdom. We've found the online community at DrGreene.com to be a great way for new parents to connect with other first-time and experienced parents when they need it most, right from their own homes, without having to get dressed, go out, and look presentable.

Wherever you turn for help, you don't need in-laws or anyone else to come in and seem to be bossing you around. On the other hand, little is more valuable than concrete, loving assistance in caring for your baby—on your terms and in your time.

Would you like someone to change more diapers? Join you in reading baby-care books? Do the laundry? Call your pediatrician with questions? Rock the baby to sleep? Run out and buy supplies? Ask.

You have just done something magnificent in creating a new life. It's normal and fine for parenthood to be an unfolding process. It doesn't have to feel great right now to feel great in the future. You might feel like smiling all the time; you might not. But take time to smile at your baby even if you don't feel like it. Smiling may make you feel a little better and your baby a lot better, which in turn will help you. You might also try laughing until it is funny. Seriously—try laughing out loud until your funny bone gets tickled. If you have a hard time doing it, grab your partner by both hands, look into each other's eyes, and laugh. Soon you won't be able to stop.

Blue is a normal color in the rainbow of parenting emotions. Postpartum depression is much less common than the blues. But if the blues are lasting more than a week or two, if you find you can't sleep (because you *can't* and not because the baby *won't*), if you don't want to eat, if you lose interest in life or feel hopeless, or if you are having disturbing thoughts of doing yourself or someone else harm, this might be more than postpartum blues; you might have true postpartum depression. Seek professional advice right away. Your obstetrician or family doctor is a good place to start. Don't let anyone brush this off. Professional treatment is important and is usually quick and effective.

The weeks following your child's birth are different from any other time in your life. So whether you are flying high, plunging low, or circling in a holding pattern, take a deep breath and go on a babymoon together.

Parental leave from work and having someone else to do the household chores is wonderful. But most important, a babymoon is a state of mind. It can begin in a hospital or at home. Draw a circle around your family. Notice and appreciate each other. Work and relax as a team. Pamper yourselves. This amazing experience of having a newborn will soon be over. Though life will never again be the way it was before your baby was born, things will settle down.

Munchkin Lore

Child psychologist Peter Wolff, psychologist Heinz Prechtl, and pediatrician T. Berry Brazelton were pioneers in understanding the behavior of newborns. They carefully observed babies' sneezes, glances, kicks, twitches, eyelid movements, and other actions and noticed that young babies tend to spend their time in one of six specific states of consciousness (similar to the four we talked about before your baby was born). The first two states are the same two sleep states your baby experienced before birth.

On average, newborns sleep about 16 to 18 hours a day, with a sleep session starting at least every three to four hours. During quiet sleep, your baby's face is relaxed and her body is still, except for an occasional twitch or jerk. She ends a cycle of quiet sleep in the same position in which she began it. Babies don't wake up easily during quiet sleep (it can be a good time to trim their nails!). But they can continue to learn from the sounds they hear while they are sleeping.

During active sleep, you may be able to see your baby's eyes moving under her eyelids as she dreams. You may see her make funny faces or sucking movements with her lips. Her limbs may move about as well. Babies dream during this active, or rapid eye movement (REM), sleep. They also may move to get closer to the side of a crib or bassinet or closer to you. In one study, babies moved to get closer to a breathing toy bear than to a non-breathing toy bear while asleep. (I do not recommend toys sleeping babies can reach whether the toys breathe or not.)

Complete sleep cycles of both states tend to last for about 50 to 60 minutes in most babies. In the first months, about half of each sleep cycle is spent in quiet sleep and half in active sleep. When you are familiar with sleep cycles, you may not need to go to your baby who is whimpering and moving while asleep. You may know that she is in active sleep and likely to cycle back into quiet sleep soon on her own.

Usually, when a baby awakens, it is out of active sleep. Watch your baby. Into what type of sleep does she usually fall?

Another state of the newborn is crying. For young babies, it is obviously their main way to signal their parents. Some babies will awaken to the crying state to signal their parents that they are awake. Babies will also enter into the crying state if they are hungry or uncomfortable or lonely or bored. If you respond to a crying state within 90 seconds, it will often stop quickly when you pick your baby up. This will not spoil your baby. On the contrary, when parents respond quickly, babies tend to learn to comfort themselves more quickly.

A Babymoon Treasure Hunt

An important task during the babymoon is to begin to discover which actions are most comforting to *your* baby. Dr. Marshall Klaus taught me that the gentle swinging of a baby into the upright position as you scoop him up can be a powerful calming signal for many babies.

Often, things that remind a baby of the cozy connection before birth are the most soothing—recreating the sights, sounds, smells, taste, touch, and motion of the womb. Nursing provides physical closeness, warmth, familiar tastes and smells, closeness to Mom's heartbeat, and the sucking action he was practicing before birth. You might also experiment with other kinds of suckling, snug swaddling (reminiscent of the tight fit before delivery), soft lighting, rhythmic or swooshing sounds (white noise, fans, heartbeats, or your own shushes), music (especially familiar songs in your own voice—lullabies are great), reading rhyming books your baby has already heard, carrying (perhaps in a snugli), swinging or rocking your baby (I love rocking chairs and gliders), gently folding your baby's legs up on his belly, or maybe giving a warm bath (later, after the cord has fallen off), which is reminiscent of the warm waters of the amniotic fluid.

As you try these and other ideas during and after the babymoon, you will observe which are the most soothing to your own baby. These observations are valuable treasures. Weeks later, when the fussy period sets in, you'll be

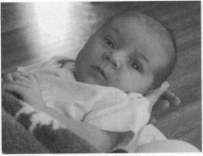

Quiet alert

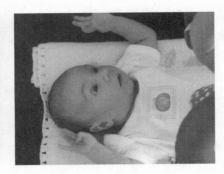

Active alert

prepared. Often combinations of your baby's favorites (perhaps rocking, swaddled, in a candlelit room, with your baby sucking on your little finger while you sing a lullaby) are far more powerful than any single maneuver.

Another task of the babymoon is to start trying to guess what your baby is signaling with each cry. These observations are also treasures. As you begin to guess correctly and respond appropriately, you will grow more adept at communicating with each other.

We've already discussed the quiet alert state, in which babies are especially attentive to faces and personal interactions. It's my favorite time to connect with babies. Babies also have an active alert state, in which they want to move their arms or legs or heads. During this state, they are often more interested in toys and objects than in people. They are learning more about the world and how it works as they look about the room and try to move.

During either of the alert states, you can play games with your baby. Tracking games are great. Depending on what your baby is interested in looking at, move your face or an interesting toy back and forth. At first, he will enjoy following with his eyes, later with his whole head. What toys fascinate him the most?

Babies also delight when they see objects and then have those objects placed in their hands for them to explore. Already babies are able to tell the difference between two otherwise identical toys with slightly different textures—and even pick out a picture of the one they are touching!

Your baby won't try to communicate by cries alone, but by facial expressions, quiet sounds, and gestures. He may say that it's time for a break just by breaking eye contact with you. He may say he wants something to change

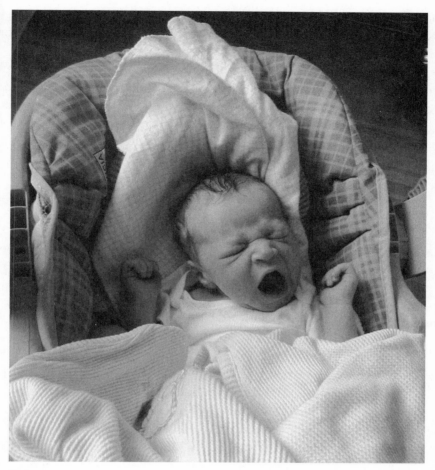

Fussy

by arching his back as you hold him. You get to "learn baby" at the same time he is learning you.

The sixth state is a transitional one, called the semi-alert state, drowsy state, or fussy state. Her eyelids may be droopy or her eyes may look dull, unlike the bright-eyed curiosity of the quiet and active alert states. But here the baby continues to move, sometimes smiling, sometimes frowning. Usually she is getting ready to change states. She may want to wake up, fall asleep, or feed.

As you learn to recognize your baby's six states, you will have a growing sense of how to enjoy and interact with her. While all states are common to healthy babies, the ways they transition between the states reflect their unique personalities. The landmarks of the six states will help orient you on your voyage of discovery.

One thing you might discover is that the quiet alert times often come around feedings. (This can still be true of elementary school students and teenagers, by the way. Relaxed meals with the whole family can be powerful times for connecting, one of the reasons I am a fan of the Slow Food movement, which is an effort to restore the healthy kitchen and table as centers of the family and community.)

Dining in Oz and in Kansas

Back before the cyclone of labor carried you to a new land, mealtime happened only a few times a day. A newborn baby may want to eat 8 or 12 times a day—or even more. The rhythm of these early meals draws you together in your new world. Feeding is perhaps the most prominent feature of a babymoon.

We saw previously that what you ate during pregnancy will have an effect on your baby's food tastes much later on. This is an example of a part of development called *imprinting*. What and how babies eat now and throughout the first year will teach their bodies even more about food.

Have you ever noticed that some people really seem to enjoy eating healthy foods, and for others it feels like a sacrifice? And some people seem to be able to eat what they want and stay slim, whereas others are careful but easily pack on the pounds. Some of these differences are genetic. But many of them are created during infancy by a process called *metabolic programming*. This helps to set not only what foods your child will enjoy throughout life, but how her metabolism will use those foods.

When my first son was born, Dr. Melvin Heyman was one of the first of my friends to hold him. I soon moved and didn't see Mel again for years. A long time later, when my second son was 14 years old and had a confusing illness, I took him to see Dr. Heyman, not only because he was a leader in the field (a smart choice), but because I was comfortable with him from that special time in the past (an instinctive choice). Adults tend to return easily to the foods that comforted them in their first years. Isn't it great when the instinctive choice is also the smart choice? Coincidentally, the best book on metabolic programming and my favorite nutrition book for parents with young children is *Feeding Your Child for Lifelong Health (Birth Through Age Six)*, by Susan Roberts and Melvin Heyman.

We know that foods eaten in the first year can have a life-long effect on your child's intelligence, height, weight, strength, and immune system. The developing brain, for instance, saw incredible growth during the third trimester which will continue straight through infancy and toddlerhood. The building blocks for this new growth, though, will no longer come through the umbilical cord but entirely from the foods your baby eats. About 60 percent of the brain is fat. The fats in breast milk are different from the fats used in some formulas. As a result, the brains of breastfed kids are structurally different from those of kids fed traditional formulas. And they function differently as well. In one study, premature babies who were fed their mothers' milk for just three weeks had an eight-point IQ advantage over their peers who got traditional formula—measured years later when they were all in the second grade. Similar studies have shown a breastfeeding advantage to healthy term babies as well, which lasts into adulthood.

How they eat also makes a difference. Healthy babies are born with a wonderful instinct to want to eat just the right amount for their needs. We want to encourage and hone that instinct, not confuse or deaden it. How I wish I still only wanted to eat the right amount! Feeding babies when they are hungry helps to do this. In the recent past, scheduled feedings were very popular to teach babies to fit into their parents' lifestyles. But this can set up the wrong relationship to food. It can teach babies to eat when they are not hungry. And when they are hungry and have to wait for the schedule, it can increase their cravings for food and teach them to be afraid they might not get enough. Another way to short-circuit the inborn instinct to eat the right amount is to trick babies about how many calories they are getting. This can happen early by putting rice cereal in a bottle or later by feeding them high-calorie snacks that lack valuable nutrition.

Meals during the babymoon have one foot in the present and one in a future you can only imagine. Let's talk about breast banquets first and then formula feasts.

Rainbow-Flavored Milk

I'll never forget when my first son was still nursing and we went out to a popular San Francisco restaurant named Café Sport. It's known for brash waiters, fantastic food, and an immense amount of garlic. The look of surprise and protest on his face when he nursed the next morning was priceless! Sure enough, Mom's milk smelled and tasted like garlic. And after his first shock, he was rather taken with reasonable amounts of garlic.

Apart from strong flavors like garlic, we may not be able to tell easily what Mom has eaten from the taste of her milk. But to babies' enhanced sense of taste, each serving of breast milk is a subtle sampling of the foods that Mom enjoys. It's another way that you pass on your life to your child and prepare her to enjoy a variety of the foods you like.

Nutrients. It's not just your tastes that you give to your baby, but the substances that will be the building blocks of her body. Nursing women have differing amounts of DHA, an omega-3 fatty acid, in their breast milk, depending on where they live and what they eat. As you might expect, babies whose mothers have lots of DHA in their milk use lots of DHA when building their new cells. Babies whose mothers have little DHA tend to substitute other fatty acids when building their cell membranes. DHA is designed to be an important component of the brain and the retina of the eye. In the first year, breastfed babies' vision varies (by about as much as one line on an eye chart) depending on the amount of DHA in Mom's milk.

You will give the best of what you eat to your baby. A normal, varied diet will give your child wonderful nutrition for good health. If you continue to eat about as much as you did when you were pregnant (an extra 330 calories or so), you can expect to have plenty of calories to give your baby and to lose your pregnancy weight steadily over about six months (with healthy amounts of physical activity). Once you've lost the weight, you can even eat a bit more if you're nursing and still stay trim. You don't have to give up any of your favorite foods. Even if you don't pay any attention to your diet, breastfeeding is likely to be a very healthy choice for both you and your child. You can relax.

Sharing: For Better or For Worse. In the same way that you share what you eat with your breast-fed baby, you also share the medicines you take, the mind-altering substances you use (including caffeine, chocolate, nicotine, and alcohol), the herbs you try, and the toxins to which you are exposed. You remain linked in a profound and beautiful way.

Does this mean no caffeine? Not at all! But it does mean paying attention. Caffeine can make babies more fussy and more awake. But only a lit-

Extra Nutrients for Nursing Women

I want to tell you about some extra nutrition that can have an added benefit to you and your baby. You can get most of the vitamins and minerals mentioned by continuing to take your prenatal vitamin, but it's still nice to know what they are to get a sense of the foods that nursing moms are designed to eat. After all, supplements only contain a few of the many complex nutrients you can get in foods.

- Calcium. Even though calcium requirements do not go up during nursing, this mineral deserves special mention, because most American women do not get the 1,000 milligrams they need each day from their diets. This is important during nursing, but even if you get an optimal amount, some calcium will be removed from your bones. It is especially important to get plenty of calcium (and plenty of exercise) in the months after you wean, when your bones are primed to absorb calcium. This is one of the best times in life to add calcium to your bones.

- Chromium. Optimal intake of this mineral shoots up by 80 percent while you're nursing, to 45 micrograms per day, far higher than the levels needed in pregnancy. Larger amounts are still safe. It's not found in most prenatal vitamins, but look back at Chapter 6 for a long list of chromium-rich foods. Chromium is important for stabilizing swings in your blood sugar. We don't have much data on the amount that typical Americans get from their diets, but the best numbers available suggest about 25 micrograms a day (for women). One small study of nursing women found that they got 43 micrograms a day without even trying. Nevertheless, if blood sugar problems are an issue in your family, then pay attention to chromium. I recommend a small extra supplement of glucose tolerance factor (GTF) chromium as a safety net; 200 micrograms a day is a good amount.

- Copper. Copper levels are high in early breast milk and gradually decrease as the months go by. Babies use this metal as an enzyme to help in connective tissue growth, skeletal growth, brain growth, and the production of new blood cells. Copper deficiency in babies most often shows up as immune system or heart problems. Copper is found in a variety of popular foods, including nuts, seeds, wheat bran, whole grain products, and cocoa. Seafood is another good source. The average American woman gets about 1,000 micrograms a day. This is plenty for pregnancy and prepregnancy life, but nursing women are better served to get 1,300 micrograms a day. Your body is smart enough to absorb more of the copper you eat if you are nursing, making up most of the difference. Women who get at least one serving a day of a copper-rich food probably get plenty. Prenatal vitamins vary quite a bit in the amount of copper they contain, if any.

- DHA (and other omega-3 fatty acids). As noted earlier, the amount of DHA in mothers' milk varies widely and has a measurable effect on their babies. The recommended daily allowance (RDA) during nursing is about 18 percent higher than for most women, but not as high as it was during pregnancy. Fish is the best source, but again you must be careful about mercury, PCBs, and other toxins. Precursors (building blocks that become DHA) can be found in walnut, soybean, canola, and flaxseed oils. There is also a small amount in eggs (more in DHA-enriched eggs).

- Iodine. No nutrient requirement increases more during nursing than the one for iodine (up 93 percent from your prepregnancy amount). You need more iodine during nursing than at any other time in life. It's used by your baby's thyroid to regulate the developing brain, heart, kidneys, muscles, and pituitary gland. It's found in seafood, plants grown in soil that was once covered by the sea, and iodized salt. Most pregnant women get enough; many nursing moms don't. The average American woman gets about 200 micrograms a day from all sources. A nursing mom needs 290 micrograms. Eating more iodine-rich foods may help (but watch out for fish that are high in mercury). Many prenatal vitamins have no iodine. I recommend choosing one that contains at least 100 micrograms.

- Protein. During most of life, women need about 10 grams of protein per day less than men do. During nursing, however, you benefit from about 15 grams more. The proteins you give to your baby in your milk will become the major structural components of all the new cells in his developing body. They will become many of his enzymes, hormones, and gatekeepers on his cell membranes. Even undernourished women will tend to give plenty of protein to their nursing babies, but they may do this at a cost to their own protein stores. Both mother and baby do best if the mother gets at least 0.5 grams of protein each day for every pound she weighs.

- Vitamin A. Optimal amounts for this vitamin shoot up to 1,300 micrograms per day during nursing, far higher than at any other time. But 3,000 micrograms is the maximum amount known to be safe. Many people know that vitamin A is important for vision. It's also important for growth and development throughout the body and for the proper functioning of a baby's immune system. Vitamin A is found in many foods, including darkly colored fruits and vegetables and in animal sources such as dairy and fish. The average American woman gets about 600 micrograms per day. Some prenatal vitamins have no vitamin A; others have 1,000, 2,500, or even 3,000 micrograms. I do not recommend taking any supplement with 3,000 micrograms, but it is important to have some vitamin A in your supplement unless you are sure you are getting plenty through your diet.

- Vitamin B_6. This B vitamin is a coenzyme that your baby will use to process amino acids and other compounds. The amount of this nutrient in your milk closely parallels the amount in your diet. A nursing mom should get 2 milligrams per day—more than she needed when pregnant. The average American woman only gets about 1.4 milligrams a day, which can lead to babies getting too little. Chapter 6 has a list of many delicious food sources. Prenatal vitamins also contain plenty of B_6. Some contain too much for nursing women, who should not get more than 100 milligrams in a day (from all sources combined). Too much can cause problems with the sensory nerves, and at higher levels can decrease the milk supply (perhaps as a protective mechanism).

- Vitamin C. Helping in the creation of everything from collagen to neurotransmitters, this vitamin is very important for growing babies. Ideally, nursing moms should get at least 120 milligrams per day, far more than they needed during pregnancy. The average American woman gets more than this, but the range is surprisingly wide. Some women get nowhere near enough. And the amount in the milk reflects the amount in Mom's diet until intake tops 200 milligrams per day. All the extra vitamin C heads to her urine, not to her milk.

- Water. Your water bottle should become one of your best friends. Take it with you everywhere, and drink whenever you are thirsty. Don't feel the need, though, to force more liquids than you feel like drinking.

- Zinc. The zinc story during nursing is similar to the zinc story during pregnancy (see Chapter 6). You need a tad more zinc during nursing, but you can usually get it from your diet and/or your prenatal vitamin. Zinc is important for many things, including babies' heightened sense of taste and smell. The amount of zinc in breast milk is very high during the first two weeks and then steadily drops a bit every day, until the baby is about six months old. As your uterus goes back to its normal size, it donates about 30 milligrams of zinc to your breast milk to provide for some of the baby's extra early needs. Most women need to take about 12 milligrams per day to cover the rest. The average American woman gets about 9 milligrams a day from her diet, and most prenatal vitamins have 15 milligrams. Vegetarians need extra zinc, because it is not as well absorbed from plant sources. I prefer that strict vegetarian women get a prenatal vitamin with 25 milligrams of zinc while nursing (as well as the B_{12} most vegetarians hear about).

Whatever you eat, your body will likely make better food for your baby than anything you could buy. You can give the very best by eating a healthy, varied diet—usually of whole grains, fruits, vegetables, lean protein, and good sources of calcium. A good prenatal vitamin can help you fill in any gaps.

tle comes through in the breast milk. One study found that it takes the amount of caffeine in five 5-ounce cups of coffee (that's bigger than the largest cup in most coffee boutiques) before a baby is visibly affected. *But* half the caffeine from a cup of coffee leaves the mother in about five hours; half of it is still there in a newborn after 96 hours. Caffeine can accumulate in babies. By three to five months, the half-life of caffeine in a baby has dropped to 14 hours, meaning he'll stay wired only about three times longer than you will!

Most babies are able to tolerate a moderate amount of chocolate in their mothers' diet. But if your baby is fussy or having trouble sleeping, it's worth considering whether chocolate may be the culprit. Don't fret, though. If you feel you should cut back on chocolate, you will probably be able to start eating it again by the time the baby is three months old.

What about alcohol? It used to be recommended to help nursing moms relax in order to increase milk supply. But research has failed to demonstrate a true advantage. It may even decrease milk supply. The American Academy of Pediatrics has concluded that light alcohol consumption is compatible with breastfeeding. The short-term risks appear to be negligible. But we don't yet know if there are long-term effects from imprinting. We do know that heavy alcohol use (two or more drinks a day) can have a negative impact on the baby's development.

If you have one glass of beer or wine after nursing, all of the alcohol that would go into your milk will likely have gone through your system within two or three hours. If you pump and discard after that, your baby should not be exposed even if you have a drink.

Nicotine leaves the body even sooner. A cigarette has a half-life of 95 minutes. Nursing is a wonderful time to give yourself and your baby the gift of not smoking. But if you don't want to stop, or if you can't, you can decrease your baby's nicotine exposure by 10 times just by smoking only immediately after nursing and only outside.

Polychlorinated biphenyls (PCBs) are an example of environmental toxins known to be transferred from mothers to babies across the placenta and to damage babies' mental and motor development. We know that PCBs are present in even higher levels in breast milk. A study reported in the November 10, 2001, issue of *Lancet* detected small but measurable damage after birth from ongoing exposure to PCBs in breast milk. Among breast-fed babies, those who received more PCBs in the milk had more damage. So

Herbs and Breastfeeding

I'm glad that herbal remedies were a topic of discussion at the 2000 annual meeting of the American Academy of Pediatrics in Chicago. Herbs are an important part of health care and deserve serious consideration. But not all news on herbs is good news. Dr. Ruth Lawrence presented evidence at the conference that two popular herbal remedies for nursing mothers—fenugreek and comfrey—can pose a health risk to their infants. Many mothers take fenugreek to increase their milk supply (though it has never been proven to be effective). It has been shown, however, to occasionally cause hypoglycemia in the nursing mother, and it can raise blood pressure. It has also been associated with increased colic and diarrhea in babies. Comfrey, which has been banned in Canada, isn't just uncomfortable, but dangerous. It is rubbed on the nipples of nursing women to prevent dryness and cracking. When used in this way, it has been associated with serious liver disease and blood clots in infants.

what is best for babies? Unless the mother has an extreme exposure to toxins at home, at work, or in her diet, breast milk will remain safe.

I wish contamination of breast milk weren't even an issue. Ensuring uncontaminated air, water, food, workplaces, and homes would obviously be better. In the meantime, pregnant and nursing mothers would do best to minimize hazardous exposures to PCBs, mercury, and other toxins. I recommend you avoid eating fish from contaminated lakes and rivers; minimize your use of volatile solvents (such as those found in some cleaning products, paints, and hobby materials); have someone else pump your gasoline and pick up the dry cleaning; reduce the use of pesticides in your home and garden; and choose organic foods (or at least wash fruits and vegetables carefully). I also recommend you look into any medication or herb before taking it.

Nevertheless, even without any of these measures, breast milk is a safe food for infant health. It has tremendous protective qualities and benefits that outweigh the risks of low levels of most chemicals in the milk.

Allergies. Breastfeeding is a wonderful choice for babies with a family history of asthma, eczema, and allergies. And what you eat can further reduce allergies, as we saw in Chapter 6. When nursing mothers in one study were given either a placebo capsule or one containing probiotics (beneficial bacteria like those found in yogurt), the babies whose mothers got the probiotics had dramatically less eczema for at least the next four years. Look for a yogurt containing active cultures of *Lactobacillus reuteri* or of *Lactobacillus GG* (LGG) for the best proven effects.

Occasionally, exposure to some foods in Mom's diets can trigger an allergic reaction in kids. The most likely culprits are cow's milk protein, eggs, soy, nuts, and peanuts. If allergies are a particular concern, talk with your doctor about possibly eliminating some or all of these foods from your diet to help decrease the odds even further. This is not necessary for most families, but it is for some.

Learning the Ropes. By now you are getting the idea that breast milk is an amazing connection between two generations. Babies open their mouths and drink in your likes and dislikes, your joys, your problems, your strengths, and your weaknesses. It's a living connection more powerful and with a longer shadow than any of the bizarre elixirs Alice drank in Wonderland—although the effects are not flashy or obvious, but quiet, potent, and transformative.

Each meal is a living exchange, a graduate course in parental chemistry, and a hug inside and out. But it can take a bit of getting used to for both of you. And that's part of what the babymoon is about.

When my wife's milk came in and her nipples were sore, she remarked that this was harder than labor! She couldn't imagine that it would ever be anything other than awkward. But soon it was the most natural and joyful part of her day.

Proper latch-on and positioning are key to successful nursing. And to get it right, there is no substitute for having someone with experience watch a feeding session and give you feedback. In some countries, it would be common for village women to see you nursing and feel free to comment. For most women, however, it's worthwhile to engage a lactation consultant to support you as you learn. Hopefully, your doctor will know a great one. If not, groups such as La Leche League can steer you toward one nearby and provide answers to many common questions.

The first food your breast makes is called *colostrum*. It's a glorious appetizer meal. This small quantity of very rich fluid is also loaded with immune substances to get your baby ready for the world. Your baby will thrive on colostrum (and the fat you packed for him) for two to five days before your milk comes in. This a great time to get lots of help to be sure latch-on and positioning are ideal. Then when your milk comes in, you may want to connect with your lactation consultant again to talk about the changes.

Your baby can teach you as well. He will instruct you when it is time to feed. He'll let you know by crying or fussing, or smacking his lips, or sucking on his hand. Most new babies want to nurse 8 to 12 times every 24 hours. It was once common to teach mothers to nurse for a certain number of minutes on one side and then pull the baby off to switch sides. But by letting a baby nurse as long as he wants on the first side, he will get both foremilk and hindmilk which are satisfying in different ways. Foremilk is the thin milk he gets at the beginning of feeding. It provides most of the volume at each feed. Hindmilk is the high fat, low volume milk available toward the end of a feeding from the same breast. It acts like a rich, satisfying dessert. If he wants to nurse on the other side as well, great. But if not, that's fine too. You can start on that side next time.

If he seems interested in feeding again within two hours, consider whether he may be asking for something else, such as a diaper change or some interaction or something to suck on. I loved letting my kids suck on my little finger, soft-side up, as a way to connect. If he's happy with this, great. But maybe he really does want to eat.

Once nursing settles into a predictable rhythm, the pace or timing will likely change. But you'll be ready for it, because you and your baby are learning to dance to the beat of each other's cues.

Fantastic Formula

As you have gathered, I'm a strong advocate of breast milk for babies. All four of my children were breast-fed until . . . When my youngest son was nursing, his mother developed a serious medical condition and was forced to stop breastfeeding very suddenly. Even La Leche League said there was no choice. And for the first time in my life, I became immensely grateful for formula and for the years of research that formula companies had invested to make something healthy that my son could eat.

That experience changed me forever. I never again want to make a woman feel guilty for choosing to feed her baby formula. Today's formulas are the best available in history. And, as anyone can see, millions of bright healthy, happy, loving adults were raised on formula as babies. If women are given accurate information, I trust them to do what is best in their family situation.

If you use a formula, make the most of it. Use the feeding time as a bonding time. Consider skin-to-skin contact during feedings. Use feedings for gazing into each other's eyes. And take advantage of the bottle to allow both parents to be involved in the feedings.

Today there are many kinds of formula to meet many different needs. Which would be best for your child? For babies who are born healthy, on time, and without a strong family history of allergies or childhood diseases, I usually recommend a standard milk-based formula that's made by a reputable formula company and contains the fatty acids DHA and ARA at the appropriate levels. For my own son, who had no particular health problems, that is exactly what I wanted (but it wasn't available yet in the United States).

If allergies are a serious concern, I suggest considering a hydrolysate formula to start with. In these mixtures, the proteins are broken down into smaller pieces so they are less likely to trigger an allergic response. Most babies object to the strong taste of these formulas unless they have sampled them by four months of age. Some hydrolysate formulas are also available with supplemented DHA and ARA.

For strict vegetarian or vegan families, I might consider a soy-based formula to start. I tend to use other formulas for term babies only if a problem develops along the way.

Formula takes longer to digest than breast milk, so babies usually ask to eat only every three or four hours to start. Take advantage of these longer stretches between feedings for sleep, together time, or time alone.

If you're feeding with a bottle, the amount is easy to see and measure. Most healthy formula-fed newborns take 2 or 3 ounces of formula per feeding. By one month of age, most have increased on their own to about 4 ounces every four hours. By six months, the amount at each feeding will have increased to 6 or 8 ounces, but the frequency will have dropped to four or five times a day. If you time these larger feedings for when you are awake, your baby probably won't need to eat in the middle of the night.

Another way to express this rule of thumb is that the average baby takes 2 or 3 ounces of formula each day for every pound of body weight, up to a maximum of 32 ounces. A newborn weighing 7 pounds will take an average of 14 to 21 ounces of formula in a day. A four-month-old weighing 14 pounds needs 28 to 32 ounces.

Nevertheless, these are general guidelines. In real life, the amount may vary quite a bit from day to day and from baby to baby. It's best to remain flexible and to let your baby's appetite guide how much he eats. You don't need to coax him to finish a bottle or stop him if he still acts hungry. If he consistently chooses to take more or less than the expected amount, discuss this with your pediatrician.

Baby Bottle Beginnings

Many babies start feeding exclusively at the breast, but later switch to some or all of their feeds from bottles, either of pumped breast milk or of formula. This often coincides with maternity leave running out. If bottles are first introduced when mother returns to work or just before, it can make an already stressful time even tougher. It's easier on most families to start some bottles at least two weeks before returning to work. On the other hand, starting bottles too early can interfere with breastfeeding.

If you know that bottles are in your baby's future, I suggest beginning occasional bottle-feeding once breastfeeding has become easy and natural, and before the peak crying weeks begin. This usually means starting around 3 weeks, give or take a week. Most babies take to a bottle easily at this age. But some babies refuse the bottle at first, which can be both flattering and frustrating.

The transition is often easier if someone other than the mother offers the bottle. As a father, I found those opportunities to feed my children precious indeed. My children loved them, too. In addition, timing the feedings strategically can give the mother some much-needed rest.

Sometimes it's necessary for the mother to not even be close by for those first bottle feeds, because the baby would rather have the pleasure of nursing, if available. Babies are less likely to protest if the bottle is offered 20 to 30 minutes before a feeding would be expected, when there is room enough in the tummy to be tempted, but not enough hunger to demand what he knows works. Offer the bottle, but don't try to force it. You can keep re-offering it every 20 to 30 minutes—he may change his mind.

Running warm water on the nipple to bring it to body temperature can make the first bottles more appealing. While holding the baby lovingly, bring the bottle close to his mouth, but don't try to push it in. Bring it close, or brush it against his lips or cheek, to entice him to pull it in by himself. Some take bottles more readily if the person feeding them is rocking or swaying. You might try different positions or different shapes and textures of nipples to find what your baby prefers. Another alternative is to slip the bottle gently into his mouth when he is asleep. He may wake up already feeding happily.

Burpin' the Night Away

Some babies swallow air when they nurse, especially when they bottle-feed. You will usually want to try to get a burp out at least at the end of every feeding. Some babies also need it in the middle. You may want to feed until they pause, burp them, and then offer some more.

Different babies favor different burping positions. I like having the baby at least partially upright, so that gravity brings the air bubble to the top of the stomach. Then I like to put a little pressure on the stomach by leaning the baby forward slightly and/or gently pressing my hand against the tummy a bit to urge the bubble to escape. Then I'll gently pat or rub the baby's back with my other hand for three or four minutes.

I'm Melting!

What babymoon would be complete without enjoying a bath together? It might just be enough to make you melt with love.

A Splash of Water

I am 22 years old and a brand-new mom. Both our parents (my husband's and mine) live in different states and aren't able to come and help. We're new here so we don't have many friends, and the friends we do have aren't parents. There's so much I don't know! Like how do I give my little girl a bath? She's so tiny. Her birth weight was 7 pounds, 9 ounces, but that seems so small. What if I drop her? What kind of soap do I use? When does she need a bath? Today on the phone my mom asked me how bath time was going. She was shocked when I told her I hadn't given Emily a bath yet (she's four days old). Please help!

Jeanne

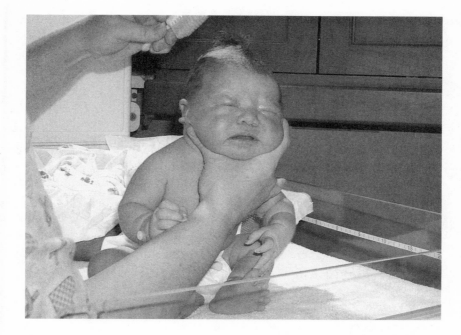

Most of us have some sort of a picture collection from our childhood—maybe a baby book, or a family scrapbook, or even a box of pictures and memorabilia from our first few years of life. In that collection, there are several common pictures. There's the wonderful shot of those tenuous first steps; the picture of the grinning baby covered ear to ear in green peas, yellow squash, and smashed banana; and the snapshot of the baby sitting in a bathtub, hair slathered with shampoo and piled on her head, complete with Kewpie doll curl. Bath time is an important part of childhood.

Your baby probably got her first minibath a short time after delivery. Perhaps a skilled nurse carefully laid her on a table or counter (not unlike a kitchen or bathroom sink countertop that is very, very clean) and cradled her head in one hand. With the other hand, the nurse gently washed her with a warm (not hot) washcloth. As soon as the bath was over, the nurse put a clean diaper on your baby and wrapped her in a warm blanket. Until the umbilical stump has fallen off and the belly button is dry, you can follow this pattern.

Here are some practical bathing tips:

- Plan a special time for your baby's first bath at home. It doesn't matter what time of day it is (babies adapt well to different times for baths, though many enjoy one right before bed), but you will want to select a time that works for the whole family.
- Get out the camera. It's not time for that Kewpie doll shot just yet, but you will want a picture to record this event.
- Select a convenient place. I mentioned using a kitchen or bathroom counter. You may also want to try a changing table or bed. I really like using a shallow, soft, contoured comfort tub on one of these surfaces. Or cover the area with a thick towel or waterproof pad, if needed.
- Get everything you will need ready before you start! The list includes water (of course), a washcloth, a bath towel (with a hood if you have one), a clean diaper, any items you routinely use during a diaper change (for little circumcised boys this would include Vaseline and gauze squares), and fresh clothes.

I do not recommend using soap or shampoo on babies this age. Newborns do not get sweaty or dirty except in the diaper area or if they spit up. Even these messes can be easily cleaned with water, which is much better for most babies' sensitive skin than soap.

Babies lose body heat very quickly; so make sure the room is warm.

Cradle your baby's head in one hand and use the other hand to remove her clothing. Gently wash her with a soft, warm washcloth and dry her off with a towel. Take time to admire her individual parts—all too often we bundle up our babies and never adore those precious feet. If you like, you can wash one area at a time and put a fresh item of clothing on as soon as an area is washed and dried. This is not necessary unless you are in a chilly room.

It is a good idea to start with the "less dirty" areas first, meaning leave the diaper area until last. As you go, be sure to wash gently behind her ears; in the crevices of her neck, elbows, and knees; and in between her fingers and toes. I had a friend who would make her one-year-old giggle while bathing her by saying, "Got to wash between those digits."

It's a good idea to wash a newborn's hair near the end of bath time. This will help prevent her from losing too much body heat. Most newborns don't have much hair, so it is easy to sponge it with water much the same way you do the rest of the body. Almost all babies dislike getting their eyes wet. If you tip her head back just a bit and work your way from the front to the back, you can avoid getting water in your baby's eyes.

When it's time to wash the diaper area, remove her diaper and sponge off the skin on her belly and bottom. Usually babies' genitals need only gentle cleansing. For little girls, wash from front to back. Don't be concerned if you see a white discharge or vaginal bleeding. These are both normal for newborn girls, and the discharge does not need to be wiped completely away. Leave whatever does not come off with one gentle pass. If you have a son, do not retract or pull back the foreskin on an uncircumcised penis. Do not wash the head of a circumcised penis before it is healed.

Now you can dress your fresh, clean, and oh-so-cuddly baby.

Some babies love bath time, though that is unusual at this age. Many babies are a bit frightened by the experience of having their clothes taken off and being exposed to the air. If yours falls into this category, you can comfort him by talking or singing to him during the bath. Your soothing voice will remind him that he is safe.

If he loves his bath, feel free to make it part of your daily routine. If he doesn't love it, it isn't necessary to bathe him daily. As long as you are changing his diaper regularly and cleaning his diaper area after poops (I usually don't recommend using prepared wipes that contain alcohol, soap, or perfumes), and spot cleaning after spit-ups, he shouldn't need to be bathed more often than every three or four days. Longer is OK for many babies—if he starts to smell, you will know it's time for a bath.

If your baby's skin seems to be drying out too much, you will want to cut back on the amount of time her skin is exposed to water. Apply an alcohol-free, unscented baby lotion daily, especially after each bath.

After the umbilical stump falls off and her belly button is dry, you will be ready to give her a tub bath. By that time you will feel like a pro, and you will be able to adapt the ideas I've already outlined to the tub. There are, however, a few additional things that I should point out.

Never, never leave your baby alone in a bath! Not even long enough to answer the phone or turn off the stove. If you remember that you left the stove on in the middle of bath time, take the baby out of the tub, wrap her in a towel, and take her with you into the kitchen to turn off the stove. On your way back, grab a dry towel to use when her bath is complete.

You only need to use a couple of inches of water in the tub, and make sure the water is warm—not hot. Babies' skin is very sensitive to heat. If you are unsure about a safe temperature, you can buy an inexpensive bath thermometer at a local baby store or drugstore. These simple devices change color to indicate safe and unsafe heat levels. (Note: If you haven't already done so, you need to turn down your hot water heater to no higher than 120°F.)

Use a tub that is the right size for your baby. Most baby tubs you purchase come with an insert for young babies. This makes it much easier for you to keep your child's head out of the water.

Gentle cleansers really are better for baby's skin during the first year or so. Use soap sparingly and avoid scrubbing. Don't use adult shampoo on your baby. The no-tears advertisements for baby shampoos are for real.

Make bath time fun. Use age-appropriate toys to engage your child in the whole experience. At first this might be something as simple as giving him a clean washcloth to suck on during the bath. Later, plastic cups and bowls make excellent pouring toys.

Right now your little one is so tiny. When you look at him, it's hard to picture that Kewpie doll shampoo hairdo. When I was a child, I remember hearing adults talk about how "having kids makes time fly." Now I have pictures of my kids with their own "shampoo-dos." Time does fly; it won't be long before you have a picture of your baby in the bath in that same time-honored pose.

Penis Confusion

My son was not circumcised at birth, at my husband's request. I am the one that gives him his bath and mostly change his diapers every day, but I never do anything specific to clean his penis. I've heard that I'm supposed to but have no idea what to do, and my husband tells me not to do anything specific. I just want to make sure I'm doing the right thing. Do you have any recommendations?

Texas

In the office, a wonderful mom asked me about her older son's newly acquired habit of licking garden snails. Little boys often have a very different sense of hygiene than their mothers. They delight in splashing in muddy water and think nothing of the trail of mucus running down their nose that prompts many mothers to action. Most little boys will not spontaneously wash their hands or clean their penises.

As if this conflict weren't enough, sources of child-care information have very different recommendations for the care of uncircumcised penises. Some advocate aggressive wiping using cotton swabs and alcohol to clean under the foreskin. At the other extreme, some authorities suggest doing nothing at all until puberty, proclaiming that the collection of cheesy material under the foreskin is natural and desirable.

I recommend a more moderate approach. Structurally, the penis consists of two main parts, the shaft and the head (which is called the *glans*). Urine and semen exit the body through the tiny opening at the tip of the glans. At birth, the shaft and the glans are covered by a single continuous layer of skin.

If circumcision is performed, the part of this skin that covers the glans is cut off. Immediately after circumcision the glans becomes swollen, tender, and a vivid red, since the foreskin was firmly attached to the glans before it was forcibly separated and then cut off.

In uncircumcised boys, the foreskin at first remains firmly attached to the glans, but gradually over time the attachments are broken (mostly by the stretching resulting from repeated normal erections). In 90 percent of boys, the foreskin is loose and mobile by age two, but the process can sometimes take five or more years. When the foreskin has separated from the glans, the foreskin can easily be retracted, or pulled back, to leave the glans exposed. Throughout life, a cheesy white material called *smegma*, consisting primarily of dead skin cells and secretions from sebaceous glands, will accumulate under the foreskin.

In uncircumcised boys, forcibly ripping the foreskin from the glans in the name of hygiene can lead to pain, scarring, and adhesions. I do not recommend trying to forcibly retract the foreskin or clean under an adherent foreskin with swabs, antiseptics, or even water.

On the other hand, even though doing nothing at all may be considered natural, similar reasoning would lead to not cutting your baby's hair, trimming his nails, washing his hands, or cleaning his bottom after a poop. Gentle hygiene enhances health.

Only the outside of the foreskin needs to be cleaned during the first year. It should be cleaned and bathed just like the rest of the diaper area. Sometime after your child takes his momentous first steps (not the second after!), you might want to very gently pull back on the skin of the shaft to see if the foreskin retracts.

If it doesn't, don't worry—and don't force it! There is certainly no rush. If urine can flow freely, the hole in the foreskin is big enough for now. As long as the foreskin doesn't retract easily (even in a 10-year-old), only the outside needs to be washed. If the foreskin retracts a little, it would be OK to gently clean the exposed part of the glans with water (but don't use soap while the foreskin is still partially attached to the glans, since it can irritate this tender area). After cleaning, always pull the foreskin forward to its usual position. This is important; otherwise it can get stuck and constrict bloodflow.

Once the foreskin has completely separated and retracts freely, begin to teach your son to retract his own foreskin and clean underneath it when he bathes, or at least once a week. For most little boys, this personal cleaning will not become a habit unless you encourage it. I recommend mentioning to him that you are cleaning his penis even when he is a baby. Mentioning it positively and frequently throughout the years can instill an important sense of responsibility, prevention, and hygiene that will benefit him for years to come.

The Yellow Mush Road

There is a yin and yang to parenting—a balance, a rhythm. Some parts are exhilarating, some exhausting. Just as you learn about your baby during meals and baths, you will also learn about him during diaper changes. It's not as romantic as nursing, but it is an important part of the parenting connection and a nice time for babies (and moms) to observe their fathers caring for them.

With every meal, and often with each bath, there may be a poop. As long as your child is in diapers, every single bowel movement will be right there for you to see when you change her diaper. During the diaper years, the stools undergo several changes. The first bowel movements are the thick, sticky, tarry meconium stools formed while the baby was still inside you. During the first week these give way—in breast-fed babies—to soft, yellow stools. They usually look like yellow mustard with little seeds. By the time a baby is one week old, she has an average of 8 to 10 of these pleasant (as stools go) stools each day. Formula-fed stools are often tan or yellow at this stage and a little firmer than breast milk stools. Either way, there are many dirty diapers!

For most breast-fed babies, the number of diapers will drop to about four per day by the time they're four weeks old (although many kids have a different pattern). Formula-fed babies usually poop less often at this age, and the stools do not change much with time until solid foods are introduced.

By eight weeks, the average will drop to one per day. Most formula-fed babies will not go less often than daily, but many breast-fed kids will poop even less often than this. I know many babies who only go every three days. If a happy, active, formula-fed baby goes four days or a breast-fed baby goes seven days without a stool, I recommend that he be checked by a pediatrician (sooner if the child seems to be in pain). Still, it can be completely normal for a breastfed baby to go only once every eight days—as long as the stool is soft when it comes out. Amazingly, breast milk leaves very little in the way of waste.

Enjoy this stage while it lasts. Before long, beginning solid food is likely to produce a noticeable change in the character of your child's stools. Most children's intestines are very responsive to the foods they eat. The poop may be either softer or firmer, but it will likely smell worse. Kids also smile and laugh more at this stage, which more than makes up for the unpleasantness.

17

Sunshine Smiles

When Your Baby Smiles (or Cries)

What a ray of sunshine it is when your baby smiles at you! And what visceral sadness and frustration when your baby cries. You can feel the desperation in parents' questions.

> **The New-Parent Hairstyle**
> My wife and I are pulling our hair out. Our daughter cries for hours every evening. What can we do about colic? We need help!!!
>
> **California**

Almost all babies develop a daily fussy period. The timing varies, but it usually begins at about three weeks of age and peaks somewhere between four and six weeks. For most infants, the most intense fussiness is in the evening. When the crying lasts for longer than three hours a day, it is called *colic*, but the phenomenon is present in almost all babies—only the degree is different.

Who Is This Screaming Monster?

Even though the temperament a baby displays in the first day of life correlates very well with the temperament you'll see in the years ahead, the rough fussy phase does not predict future problems. This is a temporary situation, even though it sometimes feels like it will last through eternity and beyond.

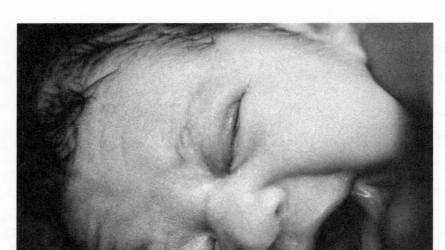

Because the crying epoch is such a common rite of passage for babies and their parents, I've pondered why nature may have designed this stage in a family's new life. Often, babies start as peaceful, curious miracles. Why would this give way to an evening screaming ritual that no one enjoys?

I believe that the fussy phase or screaming stage exists in order to change deeply ingrained relationship habits. Even after the miracle of a new birth, many parents and families would revert back to their previous schedules and activities within a few weeks if the new baby remained quiet and peaceful. It would be easy to continue reading what you want to read, going where you like to go, doing what you like to do, keeping everything as it was before if only the baby would happily comply.

Instead, the baby's exasperating fussy period forces families to leave their previous ruts and develop new dynamics, which include this new individual. Crying demands attention. As parents grope for solutions to their child's crying, they notice a new individual with new needs. They instinctively pay more attention, talk to her more, and hold her more—all because of the crying. Colic is a powerful rite of passage, a postnatal labor pain by which new patterns of family life are born.

The process of learning to soothe a crying baby can be a happy triumph for the new family.

For Crying Out Loud

This is the time to pull out the secret treasures you discovered during the babymoon. Helping a child with colic (or almost-colic) is primarily a matter of experimentation and observation. Different children are most comforted by different measures. Parents often expect that the solution that worked for their friends will work for them, but each person is an individual with individual tastes. True, most people prefer chocolate to Brussels sprouts. Nevertheless, my otherwise-normal college roommate, when it was time for him to propose marriage to his sweetheart, cooked her Brussels sprouts to propose because he knew she would love it! (They're still happily married). The soothing process involves trying many different things and paying attention to what seems to help your child, even a little bit—and then combining those things to multiply the effect.

Thankfully, you and your baby already have experience, during easier times, with many of the most powerful techniques—creating situations that are reminiscent of the time before birth. You may want to read through the suggestions in Chapter 16 again, if you haven't read them recently, to spark new ideas. I'll explain further practical ideas below, including Fifteen Minutes of Magic and feeding changes that can make a big difference in reducing crying.

Holding. Holding your child close is one of the most effective methods. The more hours they are held, even early in the day when they are not fussy, the less time babies will be fussy in the evening. Baby slings or snuglies can be a great way to do this without having to be "hands-on" every moment. And this practice will not spoil your child.

As babies cry, they swallow more air, creating more gas and more abdominal pain, which causes more crying. This vicious cycle can be difficult to break. Gentle rocking can be very calming (it is directly comforting and seems to help them pass gas). When you get tired, an infant swing is a good alternative for babies who are at least three weeks old with good head control.

Holding your baby in an upright position may help (this aids the movement of gas and decreases heartburn). Often a warm towel or water bottle on the abdomen can help. While awake, some babies prefer to lie on their tummies, while someone gives them a backrub. (To avoid the chance of sudden infant death syndrome [SIDS], do not put babies to sleep on their tum-

Fifteen Minutes of Magic

You might put on some of your favorite relaxing music. With your baby on his back, the feet are a great place to start a soothing massage. You can gently rub the top of the foot with your thumbs and the bottom with your fingers. Then separate his toes, and roll each one lightly between your thumb and forefinger, perhaps tugging slightly. Next, make a circle around the foot with one hand, and pull his foot through, hand-over-hand, and again with the other hand. You may want to lay his leg on one palm and knead the calves and hamstrings. End with gently pulling his whole leg through the partial circle of your hand, from foot to thigh, over and over, working toward the heart. Now it's the other leg's turn.

You can do the same for each hand and arm. Open his hands and gently knead and rub the palm and the back of the hand with your thumbs and fingers. Separate the fingers, and one by one pull each through your thumb and forefinger. And then his whole arm through the circle of your hand, working toward the heart.

You can turn him on his tummy, and let your hands glide down his back in gentle, firm strokes, with thumbs just to either side of his spine.

There is no one magic method. Be an artist with your hands to gently massage your baby, paying attention to his cues and your own. I'm a fan of relaxing music, warm towels, and perhaps a little baby oil or infant massage gel. Candles, a safe distance from your baby, can be a mesmerizing treat. There is something primal about a flickering flame.

mies.) The gentle pressure on the abdomen may help. Another great position is being carried, tummy down, along your forearm, perhaps rhythmically patting the back with the other hand.

Baby Massage. If you've ever had a massage, you know how soothing and wonderful touch can be. Infant massage has been the subject of recent studies and shown remarkable benefits. Dr. Marshall Klaus reported that in one study of premature babies, those who received three 15-minute massages a day had nearly 50 percent better weight gain, scored better on developmental tests, and went home from the neonatal intensive care unit an average of six days earlier! For full-term babies, a daily massage during the screaming stage can reduce crying and improve sleep for all concerned. Your instincts on how to give a soothing massage to your baby are probably all that you need. But if you are hesitant, a number of good instruction books are available.

Massage can be particularly powerful if Mom is depressed. Not only does the baby's crying decrease, but the brain wave patterns of distress and depression measurably decrease as well. In my experience, Mom benefits directly from giving the massage (the reduced crying) and also benefits from getting a massage of her own.

Soothing Sounds. Singing lullabies to your baby can be equally soothing. It is no accident that lullabies have developed in almost every culture. The noise of a vacuum or a hairdryer is also soothing to many babies.

Go for a Drive. Some children seem to do best when they are going for a ride in the car. If your baby is one but you can't always hop in the car, you might try the Sleep Tight Infant Soother, a device originally developed by a pediatrician father to imitate car vibrations and sounds. Research has shown remarkable success, with babies responding in an average of four minutes. Today, similar devices are available from several manufacturers. Or you might try placing (and watching) your baby, carefully swaddled, on top of a gently vibrating clothes dryer.

Sucking. Some babies need to suck on something in order to calm themselves. We know that some babies suck their tiny thumbs even before they are born. Infants are hardwired to need and enjoy sucking as a separate experience from feeding. This need is more pronounced in some babies. This sucking behavior is most obvious when these babies are tired, bored, or in need of comfort. The breast can be a wonderful way to meet this need, even when the baby is not hungry.

Children who suck their thumbs are able to begin at an early age to meet their own need for extra sucking. These children fall asleep more easily, are able to put themselves back to sleep at night more easily, and sleep through the night much earlier than infants who do not suck their thumbs.

Many parents are worried that their children won't stop thumb sucking at the appropriate age. The great majority of children stop thumb sucking spontaneously as they get caught up in learning new skills and no longer need to be stimulated or comforted by sucking, usually before their first steps (unless they have been engaged in thumb-sucking battles with the parents). If your child has not spontaneously stopped thumb sucking by the time he is walking, there are gentle ways to encourage him to stop. Right now, however, you do not need to be concerned about your child's natural way of getting the stimulation and comfort he needs in an independent and healthy way. According to the American Dental Association, thumb sucking does not cause permanent problems with the teeth or jaw line, unless continued beyond four or five years of age.

Pacifiers are another popular alternative to comfort babies who delight in non-nutritive sucking and they may slightly reduce the risk of SIDS. However, clear evidence suggests an association between pacifier use and breastfeeding problems—though it is not always clear which causes which. Trouble nursing can lead to increased pacifier use, and vice versa. If you want to nurse and to offer a pacifier, I recommend waiting on the pacifier for at least a few weeks until nursing is flowing easily for both Mom and baby. I recommend the same for helping a baby find his thumb. This still leaves plenty of time before the peak crying period begins.

Besides the possible breastfeeding problems (including nipple confusion, early weaning, breast infections, and early return of fertility—all tied to not nursing as much), children in day care who use pacifiers tend to get more ear infections later in the first year. And in the early months, pacifiers can fall out at inopportune moments. Babies are still ill equipped to pick up an object and maneuver it to the mouth. Unable to manage the mini-crisis themselves, young babies cry to summon their adults to do this work.

The American Academy of Pediatric Dentistry solidly prefers pacifiers to thumbs for meeting children's sucking needs (because pacifiers are easier for parents to control). I think pacifiers and thumbs are both fine for most babies. But bottles should never be used as pacifiers (this can cause terrible tooth decay). Nor should pacifiers be used to say, "Quiet down!" without words, or as replacements for noticing babies or their needs.

When babies suck on breasts, fingers, thumbs, or pacifiers between feedings, they are able to create their own mini-vacations that are reminiscent of some of their favorite moments—feeding in mother's arms or the quiet stillness before they were even born. What a nice gift to allow them to make this magic for themselves!

Comfort Food

What we feed and how we feed can make a true difference. For a while, formula roulette was a common treatment for colic, switching to one brand after another until the crying was over. But the results were rather disap-

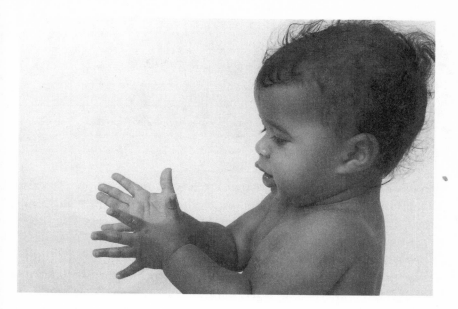

pointing. This led to the myth that feeding changes don't help. More recently, we've learned better.

How We Feed. If a bottle-feeding takes less than 20 minutes, the hole in the nipple may be too large. Feeding too quickly and increased air swallowing can lead to more crying. Try a different brand nipple or a different model in the same line.

For breast-fed babies, the concentration of breast milk changes during a feeding. The *foremilk* at the beginning is plentiful but low in calories and fat. The *hindmilk* at the end of emptying each breast is far richer and may be more soothing. Sometimes you can reduce colic by allowing the baby to finish draining the first breast before offering the second. If the baby still seems to be uncomfortable or eating too much, then offering only one breast (as often as desired) over a two- to three-hour period might give the baby more hindmilk.

What We Feed. According to a study published in the December 2000 issue of *Pediatrics*, babies who had been diagnosed with colic cried for about an hour less per day than expected when they were switched from a cow's milk formula to a hypoallergenic formula in which the protein had been

Preventing Eczema

Eczema that starts in the early weeks of life is often due to a reaction to cow's milk protein. Switching from a cow's milk formula to a hydrolysate formula or removing cow's milk from a nursing mom's diet can often reverse the condition. You might switch back when the baby's gut is a bit more mature. Most babies outgrow milk allergies, especially if you catch symptoms early and give them a break.

hydrolyzed (cut into little pieces that are less allergenic). Forty percent of the babies no longer had colic after one week on the hypoallergenic formula (28 percent of those who didn't switch formulas also outgrew the problem after a week, as expected). Some babies need time to grow to be able to digest some proteins.

If breast-fed babies have colic, sometimes they outgrow the colic more quickly if the mother temporarily removes nuts, peanuts, cow's milk, and perhaps eggs or fish from her diet until the colicky baby's system has had a chance to mature.

There are a lot of stories about foods that breastfeeding moms should avoid. Most often I hear about abstaining from broccoli, cabbage, beans, and other gas-producing foods. I've found no studies of consumption of these foods that have convinced me of any increase in gas or crying in the babies. This makes sense to me. The gas we get from beans comes from the undigested part that remains in our intestines. The portion that enters a mother's bloodstream and then makes its way into the breast milk is not the part that causes gas.

Stimulants such as caffeine or caffeine-related compounds (like those found in chocolate, I'm sorry to say) may contribute to crying, though. Even if they didn't seem like a problem before the crying period started, this might be a good time to try eliminating such foods for a few weeks.

Other foods in your diet may also irritate the baby. Again, experimentation and observation will guide you. Even so, the babies who have a tough time with a certain food in Mom's diet are likely to be the ones who would have an even tougher time with formula.

Even though I believe the fussy phase exists partly to bind us closer together as a family unit, taking a break is a good idea. Each of you can take charge and spell the other. Perhaps you can find someone else to give you a break together. Time for oneself is an important part of the new family dynamic. You will be able to pay more loving attention to your baby when you are refreshed.

Even full-blown colic will not last forever! After about six weeks of age, it begins improving slowly but surely, and it is generally gone by 12 weeks. If it is not improving at this rate, consider other reasons for crying such as gastric reflux—the tummy contents sloshing up and burning the lining of the esophagus.

Babyhood is a time of spitting up. Since the sphincter at the top of the stomach is often loose, many babies spit up milk out of their mouths or noses. In otherwise healthy, happy babies who are growing well, the spit-up is mostly milk rather than stomach acid, and nothing needs to be done (except a lot of laundry).

In some babies, though, the acid makes the lining of the esophagus tender, red, and swollen. They might arch their backs in pain. The acid can also be inhaled into the lungs, irritating their sensitive linings. These children might not gain weight well or might cry and cry from discomfort. Some might develop a chronic cough, wheezing, or recurrent pneumonia. A few even stop breathing (apnea) to try to protect their lungs. All of these children need treatment and relief from their reflux.

During the screaming stage, whatever the cause, lasting new depths of relationships will be forged as you pay attention to your baby's subtle responses and work together to support each other.

Am I Adequate?

Many parents are worried that their babies are not getting enough to eat. It's one of the most common reasons that mothers stop nursing at this stage.

Moms who breastfeed are often worried because they can't see or measure how much their babies are eating. It requires trust. Babies are born with a sophisticated mechanism that prompts them to nurse until they are full and to stop when their nutritional needs are satisfied. Moms are built with a sophisticated mechanism to make the amount of milk their babies need.

Concerns arise because there is often a growth spurt around the same time the crying period starts. The baby's hunger increases first, triggering the mother to make more milk, but there is often a brief lag. It's not unusual for supply and demand to be out of balance for two or three days. And mothers instinctively sense that their babies want more than they are providing. As the growth spurt progresses, babies get stronger and more efficient at nursing. They are able to drink more in a shorter time. But from a mother's perspective, her instinct tells her that her baby wants more, the baby is spending less time at her breast, and is crying more often. No wonder a sense of inadequacy can develop if she is not warned to expect this possibility.

Pumping breast milk can be a great solution for some families, especially if a mother and baby will need to spend time apart. Pumping can help to increase the milk supply. Also, having extra breast milk on hand can take some of the pressure off. And watching the amount of pumped milk increase is reassuring to some mothers. But for others, who are only able to pump a few drops, the meager amounts they see may increase anxiety. Small pumped amounts do *not* mean that the baby isn't getting enough. Healthy babies are more efficient than any pump at getting milk from the breast.

You and your baby are designed to thrive during this breast milk dance. It's normal for babies to lose some weight shortly after birth, before Mom's milk comes in. Losing up to 10 percent of the birth weight may be OK. Although this may cause some alarm at first, if your baby has returned to her birth weight with two weeks of breastfeeding, you are likely making a good supply of milk. It's also very reassuring if your baby becomes content soon after starting to nurse and seems content after you have finished nursing (except for maybe a two- to three-day adjustment period for growth spurts). Making six or more wet diapers a day is physical evidence of a good milk supply. If you are still concerned, it's a good time to get in touch with a lactation consultant to learn how you can increase your supply—or learn that there is no need.

It can be very nice for families to wake up the baby for one last feeding before the parents go to bed, especially if the parents' bedtime is fairly consistent. This little bit of scheduling can help babies establish eating and sleeping rhythms that work with those of the rest of the family. It gives an anchor to start getting some longer stretches of sleep at night. If you prefer that she learn to sleep on her own, lay her down sometimes when she is sleepy but not quite asleep.

Whatever else is happening with the feedings, anyone who is eating needs to have appropriate physical activity to make the best use of that food.

Baby Cardiokickboxing

Television, videos, video games, computers, and school priorities have combined to make the present generation of children the most sedentary in history. Helping your child develop a habit of daily, fun, active play is one of the best gifts you can give. And it's never too early to start!

The youngest exercise program I have ever seen had powerful results. The babies involved were tiny premies, averaging about two and a half pounds in weight, and still three months before their due dates. Typically these babies would spend the day lying still, and they would lose bone strength week by week until they were big enough to start moving about on their own. In this remarkable study, published in the July 2003 issue of *Pediatrics*, half of the babies were put on an exercise program: for five minutes a day, five days a week, someone moved their limbs through a gentle, passive workout. These babies were compared to another group who just got contact and stroking for the same amount of time (might personal touch influence bone strength?). In just four weeks, the babies in the exercise group had significantly stronger bones than their inactive peers.

Further research is needed to learn more about the best amount and kind of exercise for babies, but even for the youngest of us a little physical activity can make a big difference. It's never too soon to make exercise a daily habit for our children.

Tummy Time

I know tummy time is important for infants, but my daughter gets very frustrated when on her tummy for more than about 10 minutes. What can I do?

Help

Think back to the water aerobics that went on inside you when you were pregnant. Your baby still needs active periods with something to press against. The latest recommendations are for kids to get at least 30 minutes of age-appropriate physical activity per day throughout childhood, and once the umbilical cord has fallen off, one of the best ways to do this is "tummy time." Episodes of 10 minutes each should be fine.

There are ways to make it fun. For example, putting your hand behind her feet so she has something to push against can give her a sense of power. Or rolling up a small towel and placing it under her chest can get her head up higher so she can see and do more. Also, try getting on your tummy in front of her, so you can look at each other and giggle. Or use a mirror, just like at the gym. Music often helps as well, and tummy time on a bed is sometimes more fun than on the floor, assuming you're careful. Her favorite might be tummy time lying on top of you so she can push and kick against you, just like in the good old days.

Is That a Real Smile or Gas?

Around the same time as the peak of the fussy period, most babies start to have a real, joyful, social smile. Again, we see the balance of parenting.

By now, babies are clearly tuned in socially. They have started to become fascinated with their own hands, staring at them as they slowly turn them over. But the human face remains more fascinating than anything else. This is especially true of their parents' faces.

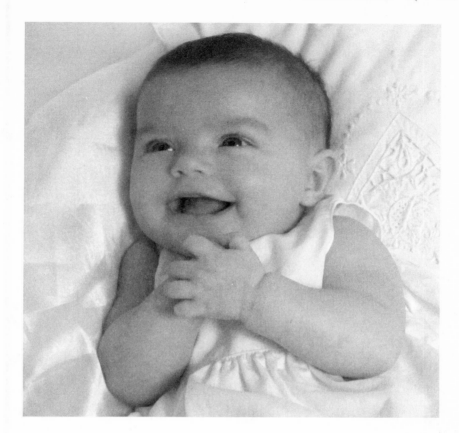

Babies can already recognize their parents on videotape and determine if the voice and video are out of synch. They also tend to respond differently when they see their mothers (comforted and calm) and when they see their fathers (perky and playful). (When they see strangers, they go from bright-eyed to bored.) They react differently if you are smiling or frowning.

Your baby has learned to try to get your attention with gurgles, coos, and body movements. Now she is able to reward you with a genuine smile when you delight her. You can recognize these smiles because the cheeks rise (called a Duchenne smile) or the mouth opens (an open-mouth smile); in moments of sheer joy, the mouth opens *and* the cheeks rise.

Smiles may not be frequent yet, but once you've experienced your baby smiling at you, you will be motivated to learn all the ways you can make her do it again. And she will be busy learning how to make you smile.

Yes, this is the fussy phase, but it is also the dawning of days of delight.

18

Holding a Rattle, Holding a Conversation, Holding Your Heart

The First Developmental Milestones

The days of just looking and listening are over. Not content to be a spectator, your baby begins to reach out to handle the world. Still unable to move from place to place, she delights in you as the source of objects to grasp and explore. This is a great time for toys and activity centers. But even though you may feel you need a break, make the most of your opportunities rather than leaving this entirely to stand-alone types of entertainment.

A Question of Timing

The lack of an age range for this chapter may be disconcerting to some parents. But from here on, we'll be looking at activities and issues, not ages. Before birth, in a limited environment with limited options, development proceeds at a fairly consistent pace, with most pregnancies lasting 266 days, give or take a few. But once a baby is born into this world of possibilities, his genetic makeup, his interactions with his parents, and the slice of the world that he sees all give him options about where to focus.

One baby may be more interested in rolling over and another in manipulating toys. One may roll at two months and play with rattles at four months; another may roll at four months and play with rattles at two. Neither is necessarily "better." You'll find a few dates in this and subsequent chapters as reference points to help orient you, but take them with a grain of salt. Far more important than comparing your child to any chart or calendar is noticing what she is working on and observing what makes

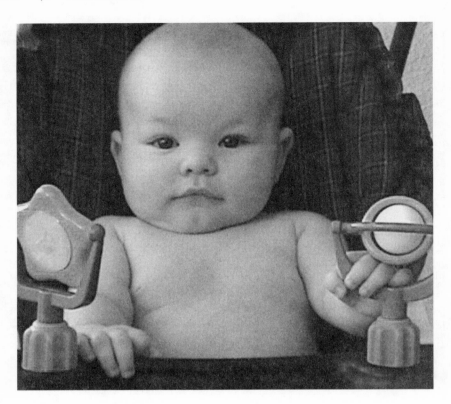

her light up with joy. Connect with each other on the cutting edge of her development.

Play is a child's work. Her joy in playing encourages her to engage in those activities that stimulate her growth and development—provided that this mechanism isn't short-circuited by a steady stream of passive entertainment (something that has become likely only in the past 50 years). Activities such as watching television or fancy toys that perform while she watches can artificially satisfy her inborn desires for both play and adult attention, thus robbing her of joy-filled opportunities for growth (in much the same way that processed, partially hydrogenated snack foods can replace the magic of a ripe peach).

To find clues as to the best toys or games at any age, turn off the TV, put away the passive-play toys, and watch your child. Many kids will begin to play or interact spontaneously, using whatever is at hand; take note of how your baby chooses to play. If he becomes directionless or frustrated, interact with him playfully and his choices will begin to emerge. Spontaneous' play gives us important clues to the cutting edge of a child's development.

Children put the most energy into newly emerging skills. Activities of moderate novelty tend to be the most interesting and the most fun. Once a child has mastered something, he will want to repeat it to wallow in his success, but eventually he will begin to grow bored, either changing the activity slightly to keep it interesting or moving on to something else. Activities that are too new, too difficult, or too overwhelming will frustrate him and fail to hold his interest.

One of the joys of parenting is finding that zone of moderate challenge for your child and setting up fun opportunities for him to teach himself through exploration and play.

Even though the timing of individual achievements varies from child to child, and even though all areas of development are related, each milestone is part of a unique unfolding story. We'll look at two story arcs in this chapter: grasping a toy and communicating by making noise.

Grasping at Life

As you saw in the gorgeous photo on page 121, taken by Kevin Kelly, a baby can grasp an adult finger on her very first day in the world. And thanks to the window of ultrasound, we know that babies can grab on to things in the uterus months before that. We also know that some of the reaching out young babies do is triggered by reflex, some is haphazard, and some is intentional—even if not precisely controlled or coordinated.

When a newborn fixes her eyes on something intriguing, especially in the quiet alert state, she is likely to become animated. Her hands (and her mouth) may begin to open and close. Eventually, she is likely to swipe toward the object with her arms and/or legs. This reaching is a choice, triggered by something she sees. Her swipe at the object may not even come close, but it is one step toward the incredible hand-eye coordination she will develop over the coming years that will enable her to master tying shoes, winning at Mario Brothers, playing the piano, or performing neurosurgery.

Because there is a time lag between the eye contact and the swipe, and because the hand movement may be so far from the object, some researchers have thought that this movement is random or a simple reflex to move when the baby sees something. But researchers at Ithaca College found that babies will not swipe at something if they have already tasted it and it is bitter; they will swipe at it if they have tasted it and it's sweet. A baby knows when he wants what he sees, and he wants to have it in his hands. Sometimes the swipe will connect, and sometimes someone will give him something interesting.

When a newborn takes hold of your finger, the tight grab is mostly the result of a beautiful reflex. A reflex is an action that has been hardwired to occur in certain situations and that doesn't require conscious choice to bring it about. Newborns come with a rich array of early reflexes.

If something is pressed into the sole of your baby's foot, her toes will curl down and try to hold on (the plantar grasp reflex). If something presses on her chin, her hands will try to grasp whatever is in reach (the mental grasp reflex). And when something is pressed into her palm, her fingers will close around it (the palmar grasp reflex) and she will hold on. Her sense of touch will give her lots of information about the object. She will learn how it feels in her hand and what happens when her arm moves. It will become familiar, recognizable to her—even among other similar objects. She will respond differently to items she is familiar with.

By around four weeks of age, babies develop at least two different streams of visual processing in the brain. One is for objects that are small, familiar, and close by (the "how," or action, stream). The other is for objects that are larger and stationary (the "what," or perception, stream). By this time, a baby is much more likely to swipe at something only if it might be reachable and graspable.

It's not until the automatic grasp starts to fade that babies can learn to consciously take hold of the world around them. As happens so often in life, reflex gives way to choice. And choice opens the door to deeper delight. Babies become increasingly fascinated by their own hands and then by objects they can handle. Playing with them is such a delight at this stage.

I like to introduce them to one toy at a time so they can savor the joy of discovery. A lightweight rattle with a handle can be a multisensory extravaganza. A soft doll with a simple face can enchant and amuse. Whimsical faces, interesting sights, sounds, and textures are ripe for exploring. A board book with pictures—especially one you have just read to your baby—can make a great toy. You'll learn which are most captivating to your child and how this changes over time.

The objects need not be toys. Common household objects can be even better to explore (if they are safe, with no sharp edges or small parts to

Over the Rainbow

Around the same time your baby is consciously reaching and grasping, he undergoes a gradual transformation that is as remarkable as the scene in *The Wizard of Oz* when Dorothy leaves the black-and-white world of Kansas for the brilliant colors of Oz. The red, blue, and green cones in his retina come online. All the rainbow of colors we see are a combination of these three primary colors of light. There is nothing inherent about the primary colors that makes them primary—it is only that we have these three types of cones, and that the entire spectrum of visible light can be coded for by using only these three reference points. Another species could use a different number or group of colors as primaries.

More than five million cones line the postage-stamp of tissue at the back of the eye we call the retina. More than five megapixels. The result is that the eye is able to pick out a pinpoint of color. As quick as a glance, the patterns change, and the eye is able to seamlessly generate another precision picture of the world around us.

As the world of color emerges, this palette will color your baby's choices of where to gaze, what to reach for, and what to play with. For about 1 in 25 people (including one of my children), some or all of the cones do not come in, resulting in some degree of color blindness. By far the most common type is red-green color blindness. Color blindness is usually tested for at children's four-year physicals, but it may be suspected earlier since color blindness is almost always a hereditary condition.

Red-green color blindness is a recessive condition passed on the X chromosome. Only one healthy color vision gene is necessary to provide color vision. Since boys have only one X chromosome, it is much easier for them to be color-blind. If their mothers are carriers (having one normal X chromosome and one color-blind X chromosome), the sons have a 50 percent chance of having the condition. Red-green color blindness occurs in about 8 percent of American males. These men cannot pass the condition on to their sons (since they give their sons a Y, not an X, chromosome), but they will pass the gene to their daughters.

All girls whose fathers are color-blind will at least carry the gene for color blindness. In order for a girl to actually be red-green color-blind, she must have a mother who is a carrier AND a father who is color-blind. This happens in only about 0.64 percent of American girls (although these numbers vary considerably in other population groups).

By being aware of their condition, we can help our children learn other ways to distinguish between red and green—the position of traffic lights, for instance. And we can decorate their worlds and wrap their presents in the millions of nuances of color that are still available to them.

choke on). I love handing babies an empty paper towel roll, a measuring spoon, a kiwi, or a smooth wooden chess king they've seen me using.

Reaching Forward

Over time, their grasping behavior will become more sophisticated and precise. From nondirected movements when seeing objects to aimed swings. From lying on their tummy and stretching with a whole arm to rake or corral a nearby toy, to picking up a block in their hand. Usually, kids grasp first with the little-finger half of the hand and move to the thumb-side with practice, accompanied by irrepressible giggles. Then they'll demonstrate their emerging mastery by passing toys from hand to hand with obvious glee. And on to holding two toys at once! Then, with sheer delight, they will bang them together. Soon they start peering at smaller objects, captivated by objects the size of a raisin as they are about to develop a precise finger-thumb grasp. By the time they are taking their first steps, they are ready not just to hold objects, but to build with them, to stack, to nest, and to display their power by toppling the whole construction over.

One study from France tracked the changes of reaching. Young babies tried to reach with both arms and both legs. As they matured, they tended to reach for objects with both hands. Then they began to discriminate. They would reach for large objects with both hands and small ones with only one hand (not necessarily the hand that would become dominant in the second year). By the time they were ready to walk, they were reaching with one hand already opened to just the size of the object.

Joining Your Baby's Journey

As you join your baby on this journey of the hands, you will gain skill at noticing what kinds of objects and what kinds of play are most fun for him. You might observe that he likes being on his tummy with a toy just out of reach: too close and it's no challenge, too far and it's frustrating, but make him stretch a little and watch his smile of satisfaction and achievement. You might find he likes to be on his back while you dangle colorful toys over him, just within his reach. You'll know you're on track as he giggles when he successfully reaches up, grabs the toy, and pulls it to his chest in triumph.

I'm a huge fan of toys, but I'm suspicious of some developmental toys on the market, either because they put pressure on parents or children or because they seem to me to short-circuit babies' inborn desires for exploration and mastery. The baby walkers that infants can sit in to push themselves around the room are a good example of this. They were once very popular because babies enjoyed them, and parents could use the opportunity to get other things done. Then we learned that children who used the walkers easily satisfied their urgent desire to move across the floor, becoming less likely to struggle to crawl and thus hindering their development. In contrast, walking toys that children lean on and push, like some great toy trucks with handles, help support kids to work toward their goal to move across the room and can aid development.

An idea called "sticky mittens" may be healthy fun for kids trying to learn how to grasp. These mittens have Velcro palms that stick to the edges of toys, allowing babies to pick things up and shake them before they would be able to otherwise. Clearly these are great fun. Amy Needham and her colleagues at the Department of Psychological and Brain Sciences at Duke University looked at what would happen if pre-reaching babies (aged two to three months) got to play with these mittens for daily 10-minute sessions over a week or two. Did this take the edge off the desire to explore? On the contrary, once the gloves were off, the kids who had this "enrichment time" were more interested in the objects around them than their peers were. The "mittened" babies were more eager and more accomplished explorers who began using increasingly sophisticated styles of handling objects. They also dropped objects less often than their peers when the mittens were off.

Perhaps it was because the supermittens tapped into the babies' strong desires before they had the motor skills to do what they really wanted. Perhaps the successful Velcro swipes gave babies confidence and information about how to move successfully. Perhaps it was just the extra 10 minutes of attention from their parents. But at least in the short run, the mittens seem to be a real "pick-me-up" for babies learning applied physics at home.

Babies become increasingly fascinated by the shapes of objects as their ability to grab them grows. They are curious about (and aware of) how the world around them fits together. In an earlier study at Duke University, Amy Needham found that four-month-olds were more interested in shape differences than in differing colors or patterns. And work at the Université René Descartes in France has established that by three or four months babies are able to make sense of three-dimensional shapes, even in a two-dimensional drawing. If something is out of proportion or perspective, they will notice.

In your baby's quest to handle the world, she is watching you to see how you do it. In a fascinating study at the University of Chicago, researcher Amanda Woodward had an actor casually drop a hand onto one of two toys while five-month-old babies watched. Once they had seen this several times, she would casually drop her hand on the other toy or along a different path. The babies were uninterested. But when the actor reached for a toy and grasped it, the babies became alert and paid attention. They cared about which toy she reached for and how. Even at that tender age, they were tuning in to purposeful versus random movements, especially movements they were trying to learn about. (In the next chapter, we'll talk about the intriguing implications of this if you reach for french fries or fruit.)

And this can happen even earlier! In an interesting collaboration, Amanda Woodward and Jessica Sommerville at the University of Chicago are now working with Amy Needham at Duke to see how sticky mittens might change how babies view the world around them. Preliminary results suggest that just one session with the mittens gives babies a sense of possibilities that awakens a fascination with the things you purposefully grasp and handle long before they might otherwise notice.

Junior Detectives

Your baby is a detective on a mission—and a detective who doesn't need a notebook to record the clues he discovers. He is paying attention to try to learn the causes and effects related to his movements. Researchers at the University of Michigan took three-month-old babies and placed them one at a time under an interesting mobile. If a baby happened to flex his right knee by more than 85 degrees, the scientists would reward the baby by moving the mobile. Babies were able to figure out exactly what it took to keep the mobile moving. When they were brought back 24 and then 72 hours later, they had memorized how to move in order to get the result they wanted.

Babies are paying attention to clues beyond just what they see and feel. Sometimes it takes them a while to learn which clues are relevant. Researchers at St. John's University did a similar study in which three-month-olds learned to kick-control a mobile while in the presence of a noticeable aroma in the room. When the babies tried again a day later, they remembered what they had learned—if the same aroma was present. If no aroma was present, they weren't sure if the same rules applied, so they experimented again and were soon able to move the mobile. But if a different aroma was present in the room, the babies were confused; it was as if they had never seen the mobile before. Baby detectives are learning which clues are important and which are not as they try to make sense of the world.

As parents, you get to be detectives as well, solving the ever-changing mystery of what will make your baby smile. And the clues you unearth are also the best clues to the developmental tasks that are important for your baby to learn next. Children tend to be most excited about skills they are on the brink of mastering. If you try to engage your baby in an activity that is beneath her developmental level, she will quickly get bored. If you try to interest her in something that she is not yet ready for, she will become upset. Remember that babies don't tend to cry when they fail, but rather when the activity isn't at the right developmental level. Your fun task is to find that zone of moderate challenge—*the fun zone*. Provide fun situations in which she can teach herself through playful exploration.

There is no need to try to force kids to learn in order to achieve their maximum potential. Forced teaching hinders development. These principles apply equally to "gifted," "average," and "special needs" children. You don't create an Einstein by pushing a child. Relax. Enjoy him. We provide a loving, nurturing, gently stimulating environment, and his own development unfolds like an acorn becoming an oak—just as it was doing before he was born. Marvel as the inner drive to grow propels him forward. Have fun!

Grasping at Language

There are two sides of the language coin: understanding and speech. The two develop in tandem, but understanding, or receptive language, leads the way at each stage. Receptive language begins to develop even before birth as babies begin to respond to and remember words, voices, and music, as well as the steady sound of their mothers' heart. Every little bit of expressive language you hear is the visible tip of a huge subterranean wealth of language your baby has heard, learned, and remembered.

We'll leave aside the baby's cries for the moment—vocalizations that may begin as early as the first breath and may become complex tools for communication, with different cries conveying different requests. Here, we'll consider not the shouts of infancy, but the whispers, the quiet growth of a spoken language.

The Voice of a Dove

Babies begin by making cooing sounds—beautiful, soft vowel sounds—unbroken by syllables. As the weeks go by, they begin to experiment with varying the volume of their cooing. Within several months, they practice varying the pitch. This happens even in children who are completely deaf. And you can bet your baby is paying attention to your vowels, learning from you when you are just being yourself. Researchers at the University of British Columbia showed 4½-month-old babies videos of the faces of two women surrounded by black drapes. One woman lip-synched the short vowel /i/, while the other simultaneously lip-synched the short vowel /a/. A speaker halfway between them played one of the two vowel sounds at the same moments. Babies turned to watch the face whose lips were forming the vowel heard on the speaker. They would also imitate that vowel back to the screen.

Coded Messages

Sometime in the second half of the first year, babbling begins. This is the sweet sound of consonants and vowels mixed together. The amount and quality of babbling vary, depending on how well babies hear and how much people speak to them.

Conventional wisdom teaches that babies' babbling is just the happy accident of their opening and closing their mouths and jaws and learning how to use their lips and tongues. The latest research suggests instead that babies are enthusiastic code breakers pursuing a high-level mission: deciphering the secret code by which their parents communicate. They do this the way professionals do, breaking down the code into small chunks. A study published in the September 6, 2001, issue of *Nature* provides fascinating evidence of this. Dr. Laura-Ann Petitto studied children with normal hearing who were born to deaf parents who communicated primarily with sign language. These babies babbled—with their hands! They produced bite-sized bits of sign language. I believe babies' early "mamama" and "bababa" are not random noises but part of a very sophisticated process of imitation, experimentation, and understanding that enables them to break the secret of a foreign language more quickly than I could.

> ⭐ **He Adores You Both**
> ⭐ OK, this is embarrassing. My baby says Dada but not Mama. I know
> ⭐ I shouldn't care, but it hurts. I'm there for him. I'm trying to teach
> ⭐ him. What does this mean?
>
> **Anonymous**

The "dadada" sound is easier to say than the "mamama" sound. I wonder if, in ages past, moms heard this sound and told the dads that this sound meant "father" (to get the dads involved and make them feel better). Or maybe babies are trying to draw their dads in.

Baby Talk

Soon babbling gives way to jargon, when kids begin to imitate the sounds and tones of adult speech. They jabber on and on, and if you didn't know better, you would swear it must be some real language. Around this time, kids begin to point at objects around them. Pointing is a key step in language development.

Kids' jargon begins to coalesce into a few words, using the same sound for the same object over and over again. This might be "ba" for *ball* or "dah" for *dog*. The first words are usually nouns—names of people, animals, or objects that are important to the child.

Symbolic gestures begin during this period. A child will pick up an object, perhaps a remote control, and point it at the television to indicate that she knows its use. Putting a hat on her head and the telephone to her ear are all symbolic gestures.

The time period for gaining the first 50 or so words is often very slow. Babies may or may not say their first words before taking their first steps, but the first words are understood long before then. And babies are already working toward saying them.

Which words do babies learn first? Not the words they hear most often, but the words they hear most often as single-word communications, according to research by Michael Brent, Ph.D., who presented findings at the 2001 American Association for the Advancement of Science meeting in San Francisco. Parents instinctively speak to babies using single words, and this instinct pays off. About 9 percent of everything mothers say to their babies consists of isolated words. It doesn't matter whether these words are nouns, verbs, adjectives, or adverbs—the ones that are used most often in isolation form the foundation of language.

The early words are usually very simple and useful for getting the children's needs met. Most kids at this stage either overgeneralize (all men are "Daddy," all animals are "doggy") or overrestrict (only my cat is "kitty"). Words appear and disappear in kids' vocabularies. This slow ebb and flow causes many parents to worry, especially if they know other kids of the same age who appear to be talking up a storm. But during this slow wait for single words, a rich, complex comprehension is developing almost unseen.

A New Language

Eventually, in another year, an explosion of language will follow. This is when children rapidly learn to use hundreds of words and begin combining them in unique ways ("spoon comb" for fork, or "me puter TV now" for wanting their turn at the computer monitor—you've been surfing long enough). Most kids come out with delightful, original utterances during this stage, making great fodder for baby book memoirs. Verbs, adjectives, and pronouns are incorporated into their repertoires: "Her goed to the store."

After another plateau, most children will go through another language explosion, this time of sentence complexity. At first, all past tenses end with -ed ("Boy falled down.") and all plurals end in -s ("I like mouses and gooses."). Rules of grammar will begin to find their places, and at the same time, intelligibility improves greatly. People outside the family will be able to understand whatever the child is saying.

Before you know it, language will become sophisticated enough to give rise to wordplay. Puns, jokes, and poetry will mark the flowering of this remarkable growth period. ("Daddy, you can't take a shower. Mom already took it!") But the exuberance of four-year-old speech all starts with baby coos—and even before that with hearing your voice in the womb.

A Shared Journey

It's never too soon to get in the habit of reading to your baby. Books with simple rhymes can be great (the memories of Dr. Seuss books have echoed through my head since childhood). So can picture books, where you point to pictures of what you are naming (babies do understand pictures). Reading is a habit to enjoy together throughout the childhood years and even beyond (I love listening to my parents read to my kids or my kids read to my parents, a time of real family togetherness). Reading together deepens and accelerates language growth, closeness, and understanding the world.

Say Cheese. Researchers at the University of Georgia, the University of Utah, and the University of Miami found an interesting correlation between smiling and learning language. They observed mothers and babies in face-to-face interactions. The babies were 4 to 24 weeks old. When Mom was smiling and gazing at her baby, or when the baby was smiling and gazing at Mom, both the quantity and the quality (speech-likeness) of babies cooing or babbling increased significantly. Furthermore, the amount of speechlike sounds was highest when Mom was Duchenne smiling (with cheeks raised), especially if the babies were gazing at their mothers and smiling back.

Verbal Ping Pong. Your baby learned a long time ago, from listening to you, that spoken language comes in bursts. She may coo or babble for a bit and then pause, waiting to see what you will say. Ping. It's your turn. Talk and coo and babble back to your baby, using her language and mixing in some of yours. Pong. Act like you both understand exactly what each of you is saying. Ping. Your baby will learn hundreds of words from these conversations, even though she will not be able to say any of them for a long time. Pong. Meanwhile, you will learn to understand what your baby is trying to communicate. Game, set, match. You both win.

High Sign. Many of the emotional meltdowns children will experience between about 9 and 30 months will bubble up from the frustration of not being able to communicate. Their ideas far outstrip their developing language skills. The "terrible twos" will be less terrible the more children learn how to get across their intense and conflicting thoughts.

> **Thumbs Up**
> I've heard of using "baby sign language"—even with hearing kids.
> Does it work? Does it help? Thanks so much for your input.
> **California**

Baby signs are like sticky mittens for the mind. Shaking your head or moving your hand is far easier to learn than the intricate manipulation of lips, jaw, and tongue necessary for each new word. Large muscle coordination is learned before small muscle coordination—at about the same time kids want to express themselves.

Before their first birthdays, most babies are interested in learning important high-impact words: "no," "bye-bye," and the names of the people and animals in their lives. Parents waving with each "good-bye," shaking their heads with each "no," and petting the back of their hand when talking about the kitty will make this much easier. You may also want to pick out signs to indicate each of the other family members.

The signs used by your family don't need to match anyone else's. Each sign is most effective if it is natural and simple to perform and if everyone in the family uses both the word and the sign consistently. In other words, try not to say "kitty" without petting the hand, and try not to pet the hand without saying "kitty."

If you want to select new signs over the next several months, it will be important to watch and observe what your child seems to want to communicate about. Most children like simple ways to express basic requests such as "I'm hungry," "I'm thirsty," "Change me," "Pick me up," "Put me down," or "Take me outside." They might simply begin to touch their hand to their mouth whenever they say, "eat"; tilt their head back when they say, "drink"; and pat their bottom when they say, "diaper." Transitions can also be tough for children at this age, so a simple sign for "all done" can be very useful (perhaps outstretched palms or tapping the wristwatch).

These very simple maneuvers create rewarding ways for parents to connect with their children. They make an already magical time even richer, deepening family bonds. As other family members get involved, not only can baby signs lessen temper tantrums and frustration in little ones, but they can ease sibling rivalry as well.

The book *Baby Signs*, by Linda Acredolo and Susan Goodwyn, is a terrific resource for parents with children under three years. For families or day care staff who use American Sign Language (ASL), ASL can afford the same benefits as baby signs—as long as the signs are simple.

Give It Here. One way to practice both grasp and language is the back-and-forth game. Offer your baby an interesting object to hold. Then put out your hand to ask for it back. You can keep this back-and-forth going for as long as this early precursor to backyard catch charms you both.

The Nature of Vaccines

Needles loom nearby almost every time a baby visits the doctor for a checkup. The vaccines they contain are a way to teach babies a different sort of language. Viruses are bits of genetic code, strings of machine language that communicate to cells what they should do. Vaccines help children to recognize this biochemical language, and to form a response of their own, rather than letting viruses or bacteria order them around.

Today's children routinely receive 23 immunizations (not counting a flu shot) before they even enter kindergarten, more than double what children received even a decade ago. Immunization fears are at an all-time high, intensified by the recent concern over mercury-containing vaccines. The debate has reached Congress. Like antibiotics, vaccines have prevented unfathomable suffering, but they also have a cost. Just because we can make a vaccine doesn't mean that we should give it. Instead, we need a sober, ongoing reevaluation of the risks and benefits of each vaccine in the ever-changing world in which we live.

> ### Vexing Vaccines
>
> Many of the ingredients in vaccinations concern my husband and me. I would like to know if any studies have been done on how vaccinations affect the developing brain of an infant. . . . Would there be any harm then in postponing her immunizations, say, until she's two?
>
> **Modaja**

My hope is that our public conversation, rather than being sidetracked by fear, strengthens this rational reevaluation process. Check the Centers for Disease Control and Prevention (CDC) website for the latest information before each immunization. All of the current vaccines in the routine schedule are available without added mercury (thimerosal). The current recommendations represent the best information we have and are updated at least once a year. In most situations, it is safer to get the vaccines than to miss them. I chose to vaccinate my children not because I had to, but because I wanted to protect them by helping their bodies learn about important infectious diseases—sticky mittens for the immune system.

The Sun, the Moon, and the Stars

Your baby is so excited about handling and seeing the surrounding world, that feeding times can get distracted. Babies get so excited with each new discovery that catches their attention they try to turn and squirm while eating, pulling the bottle or breast along with them.

Often nursing mothers feel as if they are no longer making enough milk or as if the baby wants to wean. Many have told me they feel heartbroken that they can no longer satisfy their babies. But it's because babies feel so secure in their mother's presence and love—and because they are confident in a plentiful food supply—that they have the luxury of indulging their engrossing new hobby of discovering uncharted worlds. You are still your baby's greatest love. But at this stage their minds are going so fast that some babies can't just think about one thing at a time. They may need an activity center when they ride in a car seat or a stroller to keep up with their insatiable need to handle, to play, to experiment, to joyfully explore. Some babies even feed better if they can hold a toy while they eat.

You may miss those quiet, intimate feeds, gazing into each other's eyes, but these fast-food, bumpy-road, drive-through nursing sessions usually only last for a few weeks before the novelty of every stray sight and sound isn't as interesting as the deep satisfaction of nursing. In the meantime, it's usually nice to get in at least one feeding in the early morning and one in the evening in a darkened room with minimal distractions. Your supply may be out of synch with your baby's erratic demands for a day or two, but you are both amazing at getting back in rhythm.

What About Bottle-Fed Babies?

Bottle-fed babies go through the same stage. You may have heard a solution from friends, parents, or in-laws. You may have seen it in Internet chat rooms and discussion boards:

> "Add some cereal to the bottle. He'll nap better."
> "You're so tired! You should put some cereal in your daughter's bottle, then she'll sleep through the night."
> "Your son looks too skinny. You're not feeding him enough. Put some cereal in his bottle."
> "He still acts hungry? Try putting some cereal in the bottle. He'll be much less fussy."
> "Spoon feeding is a hassle. Put it off as long as you can. Cereal in the bottle is quick, convenient, and makes them sleep longer and cry less. What more could you want?"

Your pediatrician says this is not wise (except as a treatment for reflux). Dietitians and nutritionists concur. Introducing solids before four months might cause food allergies. Your well-wishers discount these recommendations because cereal in the bottle worked wonders for their children.

Throughout most of history, children were breast-fed exclusively during these early months. During the previous generation or two, when bottle-feeding became very popular, rice cereal was often put into the bottle at a very early age. What were the results?

Most children seemed to thrive. But a small number of babies did not tolerate the addition because their sucking and swallowing actions were not yet fully coordinated. They inhaled small amounts of the cereal into their lungs, which led to pulmonary problems.

I'm much more concerned about a subtler issue. Babies are born with a wonderful mechanism for knowing how much food they need. During the early months, they take their cues from the volume of what they drink. Adding cereal derails this mechanism. It forces them to take in deceptively large amounts of calories. It teaches them to overeat.

By starting with a spoon, resting between bites, and stopping when your child lets you know he's full, you will be laying an excellent foundation for good eating habits throughout his life. A major study looking for the causes of obesity found that short-circuiting young children's self-regulation of how much they eat is a major cause of later obesity. Cereal in the bottle does just that.

Babies who are fed this way may appear to be unaffected, but those few weeks of added convenience may result in a lifetime of struggles with weight. This common practice may have contributed to our being the most obese generation in history. And it doesn't even work. Scientists at the Cleveland Clinic studied the effect of cereal on sleep and found that adding the cereal did nothing at all to speed up the age of sleeping through the night. That first uninterrupted six-hour stretch of sleep came no earlier in babies who took cereal early.

People swear otherwise. I suspect the reason is that kids do fall asleep a bit more quickly, and some babies may even go a bit longer between feedings. There is no scientific evidence, though, to support the claim that cereal in the bottle will help an infant increase total sleep time or decrease crying.

Drawing on the wisdom of experience and the latest scientific knowledge, the American Academy of Pediatrics recommends against adding cereal to the bottle. It may be tempting after your 16th straight sleep-deprived night to cut a bigger hole in the feeding nipple to add rice cereal. But it won't offer lasting help, and it may be giving your baby a lasting gift that both of you will regret.

Instead, I recommend that you do an early-morning and a late-night feeding, gazing into each other's eyes in a darkened room with few distractions—preferably with skin-to-skin contact—just like I recommend for nursing moms. Healthy babies will get plenty to eat, and the quiet connection will feed their soul.

Look at Me

Babies at this stage are more consciously in love with their parents than ever before. Contrary to earlier thought, babies are clearly self-aware before they are two months old. One of their first explorations is a systematic attempt to discover their own bodies (during which ear tugging often leads to unfounded suspicions that there is an ear infection). As they also turn their attention outward to the objects filling the world around them, they may look every which way and find new glee in toys, but their greatest smiles and giggles are reserved for their parents.

Your eyes are your baby's mirrors. If you happen to gaze at her face just a few degrees beside her eyes, her happiness will fade, and she will turn her gaze elsewhere or work harder to get you to look into her eyes.

Your smile lights up her world, like hers does yours. And your expressions are the captions of her world. When a baby is playing with a jack-in-the-box and out pops a surprise, the mother learns from her baby's body language whether the baby felt surprise, pleasure, fear, or boredom. Gauging the baby's response, Mom will react without thinking. The baby will then notice Mom's response and react accordingly. A mother can consciously change her mirror reaction, and the baby will still respond to her reaction. If Mom laughs, the baby may laugh, even if he was startled at first. If Mom reacts with a scared face, the baby may cry, even if he was initially delighted.

Our natural reactions help interpret the world for our babies. We effortlessly teach them who we are, and beyond this, we help teach them what they are themselves feeling. Even as they branch out to handle and comment on the world, we remain the sun, the moon, and the stars to our little treasures, as they are to us.

19

Sitting, Sampling, Separation, and Strangers

Milestones—Round Two

Sitting up expands your baby's horizons and begins a wonderful season of parenting. Feeding is often a central issue, and sampling solids is a source of great pleasure. At around the same time that these advances create a sense of growing triumph and possibility, your baby's mind is also able to sense new fears, especially fears of strangers and separation from you.

The Sitting Story

In some traditions, from the ancient mystics of the East to the Beatles' guru Maharishi Mahesh Yogi to the Jedi knights of *Star Wars*, the aspired-to grail is to sit in a lotus position deep in such peaceful meditation that the constraints of gravity are overcome and you are able to levitate off the ground. But babies start the sitting story cross-legged, gently hovering, suspended upside down in the watery world of the uterus. When the big day comes, they land in a world where gravity tethers them in place. They can flail their arms and legs about, but moving their torso very far happens at the pleasure of others. And they see the world from lying on their back or from the limited horizon of tummy time.

When your baby is propped in a sitting position, on your lap or in a car seat or swing, he revels in this right-side-up view of the world. From his supported sitting experiences, I suspect he starts paying attention to you sitting—in the car, at the table, on a couch. His aspired-to grail is the everyday miracle of sitting that the rest of us usually take for granted. To be in a comfortable, upright position with hands free to play or work or (someday) eat.

Sitting alone is a major childhood milestone, an accomplishment your baby will celebrate with pride. Spending a little time in assisted sitting can stoke his desire for this achievement and give him spine strength and balance training. And it's fun. I've used swings, exercise saucers, and Johnny-jump-ups to let my own kids practice sitting, bouncing, twisting, and rocking with an upright view—often to the beat of music playing in the background. What delight! The jump-up was more fun than a waterslide, and the exercise saucer better than a theme park. These devices can be like sticky mittens (see Chapter 18) for the spine. Still, parking kids in any device like this (or in a theme park) for too long may be a disservice to them. Balance is important for them in sitting; it is also important for us as parents.

Tripods of Triumph

With practice, babies are able to maintain a sitting position with less and less external support. They do this by planting their own hands in front of them to create a human tripod. They can't use their hands to play. If they are tempted to pick one up to touch a toy, they topple over. And they would topple soon anyway.

You will see your baby's growing adeptness at sitting as her hands come closer to her body as she sits. Soon she will be able to (briefly) manage the trick of forward-backward balance, but she will keep her hands planted beside her diaper to keep her from tumbling sideways. If she dares to reach for a toy, over she goes on that side.

Until one day when lifting up her arms and sitting works for a few seconds. Then she tumbles again. It doesn't work the next time, but it does the time after that. Perhaps for a bit longer.

You start to see that training for the everyday sitting we take for granted is like training for an Olympic sport for your baby. *But it's a team sport.* With each of those tumbles, she is not able to get back to a sitting position to try again without you. She is a persistent athlete with great potential. You are her valuable partner on this quest.

Look, Mom, No Hands!

Your baby is deeply happy when he is able to sit without using his hands, but he may be concentrating so much on balancing that the glee doesn't show on his face. At first he may not risk playing with a toy because he knows he still can't get back to sitting if he falls over. But before long, he tries and learns to play gingerly with toys directly in front of him.

Behind the scenes, he is gaining not just strength and coordination, but a huge step forward in his innate knowledge of the physics of the world around him—how gravity and balance work. Just before babies learn to sit, they blink when an object approaching them takes up enough of their field of vision. This works well if the object is approaching at a steady rate. But researchers at the Norwegian University of Science and Technology have found that more mature sitters are able to intuitively judge the speed of an approaching object, factor in its acceleration or deceleration, instinctively calculate the correct time to collision, and blink at the perfect moment. Sitting is not just a physical skill. It is a mental chess match, a physics course, and a rewiring of the reflexes on an unconscious level.

And in just a few more weeks, your baby will be a natural sitting master—twisting, turning, reaching for objects with easy confidence, ready to play with abandon. If he should take a header, no matter, he can right himself and make it look like the topple was done on purpose. An early sitter sits like someone learning to dance or paint by numbers. Now your baby sits like Picasso painting or Astaire dancing. I'm not sure sitting gets any better than this.

What a sense of freedom, of achievement! This mastery represents at least two months of sustained, directed effort. And the hard work is all your baby's. He is responsible for learning the physics, the kinesiology, the strength training, the determination, the failure, and the internal motivation. But your part in the process is vital. Your role is to draw on your own instincts to provide him with a nurturing, safe environment. And to give him loving attention. To respond to his requests and needs. To provide his training meals, to clean his uniform (his diaper), to be his coach and partner. And to be a role model. In short, you get to be on the winning Babies' Olympic Pairs Figure Sitting team by doing the same things you did before he was even born.

Congratulations!

A Tangible Sign

For some parents, the achievement of sitting may seem removed from the unfolding choreography of development that went on before birth. That was physical. This is something their baby learned.

The first tooth, however, is a tangible sign that this physical cascade of development continues. Inside, your baby's organs are changing; the lining of her gut is becoming a stronger barrier (preparing her to eat new foods); cartilage is turning to bone; and connections in her brain are being made at a dizzying rate. But these, you must imagine. A tooth you can see. As it pops through, you are glimpsing a tiny bit of the sequence that began and continued inside the womb, what now seems like a lifetime ago.

Baby Teeth

For a baby, the mouth is an exquisitely sensitive portal connecting the world around him to his developing mind and body. He uses his mouth to meet his mother, to sate his constant hunger, to comfort himself between feedings, and to explore objects in the widening world around him. When hard teeth begin protruding into this soft, sensitive orifice, it is a major event in the life of an infant.

> **Teeth Timing**
>
> My child has no teeth; he is nine months old. Is there a problem that I should get checked out? I worry about this because he has been so early at all the other developmental stages.
>
> **Dana, Indiana**

Many parents worry about the timing of the appearance of their children's teeth. While the average time for the first teeth to push through is between five and seven months of age, there is a wide range of normal variation. The teeth might come in as early as one month of age, or they might wait until a child is almost 18 months old. Anywhere in this range can be normal. Some babies are even born with teeth.

Generally, lower teeth come in before upper teeth, and girls' teeth usually erupt earlier than boys' (much like with everything else). On average, the bottom two middle teeth appear at between 5 and 7 months, the top two middle teeth between 6 and 8 months, the bottom two side teeth (or canines) between 7 and 10 months, and the top two side teeth between 8 and 11 months. Any different order is fine too (if picturesque). And it is OK for the first steps to occur before the first teeth.

A Healthy Smile

The breast milk or formula that comforts and nourishes your baby can also cause severe tooth decay. Most parents I talk to don't know how to care for their babies' teeth.

Unlike adult cavities, which are usually hidden from view, baby tooth decay strikes the most visible portion of the front teeth. But parents are lulled into complacency because during the months the teeth are gradually

weakening, the damage is invisible. Once the protective tooth enamel has been breached, the ugly process of decay accelerates. Thankfully, this problem can be prevented easily.

What nourishes your baby also nourishes the normal bacteria that live in her mouth. These bacteria turn the sugars found in formulas, milks, and juices into acids strong enough to etch the enamel of the teeth if there is prolonged contact.

Tooth decay can be prevented by a combination of strengthening the enamel and reducing prolonged exposure to the acids. Fluoride is the most effective way to strengthen teeth. The optimum concentration of fluoride in water is 0.7 to 1.2 parts per million. Check with your pediatrician by the time your baby is six months old about fluoride levels in your area.

The clear saliva you see from time to time drooling from your baby's mouth helps to prevent lengthy exposure to tooth-damaging acids. Enzymes in the saliva digest the sugars in milks and juices into safe forms that your baby can use. Also, the swishing of the saliva in the mouth actively washes the teeth.

The problem comes at that wonderful moment when a baby falls asleep. Saliva production plummets. Swallowing decreases. And any liquids that are still in her mouth will pool next to her teeth, slowly dissolving the enamel.

Moving feeding time forward so that your baby is awake for even 15 minutes after finishing can significantly protect her teeth. This is easy advice to give, but in some families it can be very difficult to follow. Some babies enjoy the comfort of sucking to soothe themselves to sleep. In such cases, an orthodontic pacifier or a bottle of water may quiet them immediately before they drift off.

But for many babies, the act of feeding is the only way they become drowsy enough to fall asleep. Gently brushing the teeth becomes extremely important for these children. If the cleaning is done during deep sleep (when the baby is limp and not moving), she is unlikely to awaken, and her teeth are rescued from hours of decay. This should be done whenever a child falls asleep within 15 minutes of feeding.

Baby-bottle tooth decay can also occur during waking hours if a child is allowed to walk around with a bottle. The American Academy of Pediatrics wisely recommends that parents only give bottles during feedings or when administering medications, and that bottles not be used as pacifiers.

Tooth decay may not seem like a big deal, but these are the only teeth your baby will have during the years when much of her personality and self-image are formed. And a feisty two-year-old is much likelier to cooperate with good burshing (and other) habits begun as a baby.

I applaud the American Academy of Pediatric Dentistry's recommendation to start cleaning babies' teeth at least once a day as soon as they come in, if not before. Gently cleaning your baby's gums can help prevent gum disease later on and help soothe her gums while she's teething. Once the teeth come in, use a tiny dab of baby tooth cleanser (generally without extra fluoride) on a soft infant toothbrush or some soft gauze.

Cleaning your baby's teeth is a practical expression of your love. Children with healthy teeth can chew food easily, learn to speak clearly, and smile with confidence at you and the world.

Teething

No topic has gone through wider swings in medical opinion than teething. A century ago, teething was considered to be the leading cause of infant mortality. Most serious symptoms of the applicable age group (including seizures and infantile paralysis) were blamed on teething. At the turn of the 21st century, the prevailing medical opinion has swung in the opposite direction, maintaining that teething probably does not produce any symptoms at all—not even pain, crying, or problems sleeping. I'm glad that teething is no longer the wastebasket diagnosis it used to be, but I strongly believe that it can be an uncomfortable process for some children and can cause low-grade fevers, increased mucus and saliva, and related symptoms.

There is some good scientific evidence to support this position, but high-quality information is scarce. Young teethers can't talk. We don't know the moment teething pain starts and stops. The pain and its remedies are very difficult to evaluate scientifically. Therefore, we must rely on observation—general observations by many parents and care providers, as well as specific observations of our own children.

Babies experience great pleasure and satisfaction through their mouths. Eating brings them delight. Even when not feeding, sucking on a finger or pacifier can change crying to contentment. When babies grow enough to move about and explore the world, they do it by placing objects in their mouths.

When their mouth becomes a source of pain, it is quite unsettling for some kids. If you've ever bitten the inside of your cheek, you know how distracting a bit of newly irregular flesh can be. For a baby, the intrusion of a hard, sharp tooth through tender, swollen gums can be quite an adjustment. Some get used to it quickly, but at first it can be more uncomfortable than a pebble in your shoe.

Ouch!

What can I do for the real bad teething times? My little girl did really well with some of her teeth, but she is in a lot of pain now. Wakes up every two hours and cannot eat much. Is there any magic solution?

Theresa, Durango, Colorado

The teeth (or tooth) that cause the most pain varies from child to child. It is often the first tooth that causes the most discomfort—or those big molars, when they arrive. For many babies, working on several teeth at once is the worst. Like sitting, each tooth coming in may be a two-month achievement; teething pain (and drooling) may appear months before the tooth.

When they are teething, babies bring their hands to their mouths because pressure on their gums brings relief. Massage tends to be more soothing when it comes from someone else, and teething is no exception. A great way to comfort a teething baby is to rub his gums firmly and gently with a clean finger. The first few passes are sometimes a bit uncomfortable, but he'll get more and more relaxed as the massage continues.

Providing cool things to chew on is another effective way to treat teething. Wet washcloths or terrycloth toys fresh from the fridge or freezer have been the most popular with babies and toddlers in my practice. Some are delighted with smooth, hard objects, like the handle of a hairbrush. I've not met many babies, though, who prefer soft plastic teething rings. Whatever you select, be careful that the object is not something your child might choke on.

When he's still uncomfortable, he might benefit from homeopathic teething tablets or a natural teething gel. Many parents report that these gentle remedies have been lifesavers. Infant acetaminophen or ibuprofen can provide stronger pain relief on occasion, if necessary. All of these can also help with sleep.

Benzocaine teething gels are a mixed blessing. They do reduce pain, but they can also leave a baby's mouth feeling as if he has just been to the dentist. Some babies object to the swollen, numb sensation as much as they do to the pain. Either way, the effect of these gels is very short-lived. And they do carry a small risk of allergic reactions and decreased gag reflexes.

As your baby's teeth come in one by one (or two by two), the brief discomfort the family experiences now is preparing him for a lot of truly delicious family meals ahead. All too soon he'll be saying, "Please pass the corn on the cob."

But first—mush.

A New Era

The first spoonful of baby cereal can be a bittersweet experience for a mother who has exclusively breast-fed her baby. Until now, every ounce of nourishment that has been added to her baby's growing body after that very first single cell has come from her own body. The brain, the heart, the mus-

cles are all built from nutrients that were once part of her. The baby is quite literally her flesh-and-blood offspring. With the first spoonful of solids, the baby begins partaking of the world alongside his mother, not through her.

Starting solids is a major milestone regardless of what your baby was eating before. Holding a newborn in your arms is incomparable magic, but a wonderful new stage of smiling, laughing, and interaction comes now, signaled by the introduction of solid foods.

Looking at a baby's development is far more important than looking at a calendar to decide when is the right time to start feeding him solids. It was once popular to do this according to a rigid timeline of set serving sizes at certain intervals, but we now know that each baby develops uniquely.

Your baby may know it is time before you do! The most obvious sign is a baby who still seems hungry after getting enough milk (8 to 10 breast feedings or 32 ounces of formula in a day). Your darling may lean forward eagerly or act fussy when you are eating.

Babies who are ready for solids can lift and support their own heads. They usually weigh at least 13 pounds and have often doubled their birth weights.

They display curiosity about the world around them, following objects with their eyes and smiling at what they see. They have set off on the journey of trying to sit up, even if they have not reached mastery yet.

Newborns are built for liquid nutrition. They instinctively push their tongues against anything inserted into their mouths. To succeed with solids, babies will need to overcome the strong tongue-thrust reflex they are born with.

For most babies, this readiness happens at between four and six months. Not coincidentally, this is the same period when most babies have increased caloric needs and are starting to deplete the iron stores they are born with. Iron-fortified infant cereals can help supply these needs. But again, don't look at the calendar: watch for the developmental cues instead.

For the first several days, more food is likely to end up on the baby's face than in his mouth. Pictures and videos taken during these historic days will be treasures for a lifetime.

If your baby gets upset at solids or doesn't seem interested at all, go back to nursing or bottle-feeding exclusively for a week or two, and then try again. There's certainly no rush before he's at least six months.

I do recommend at least trying solids by the time babies are rolling easily and sitting independently, even if they haven't yet seemed interested. This will give them a good opportunity to learn the process of eating and swallowing while their brains are primed for it.

When the first spoonful is accepted and swallowed, at whatever age, you and your baby enter a new era in your relationship, a rich time of deepening new interactions. You are becoming friends.

Something's Gone Terribly Wrong

The beginning of the 21st century brought a tidal wave of childhood obesity that was finally too serious to ignore. When the Centers for Disease Control and Prevention (CDC) released its latest round of figures on October 8, 2002, it marked a 20-year period in which the percentage of obese children had increased steadily, reaching the status of a dangerous epidemic. Clearly the way we have been feeding our children isn't working.

Different cultures have different staple foods. Some Eastern cultures are built around rice. Some Northern cultures are built around seafood. The culture of the American child is built around french fries. Hot dogs, chips, cheeseburgers, fried chicken nuggets, soda, and candy are among the most commonly eaten foods. Children's meals in many restaurants contain no fruits, no vegetables, no whole grains, and no lean protein sources.

Startling evidence suggests that the dietary habits that lead to obesity are already established before age two. This offers tremendous hope to parents of babies. There is time to help them build the lasting habit of deeply enjoying eating healthy foods in healthy amounts.

The Feeding Infants and Toddler Study (FITS), published in the January 2004 *Journal of the American Dietetic Association*, followed the eating habits of more than 3,000 children aged 4 to 24 months. Researchers found that soda is being given to children as young as seven months. Nearly 25 percent of older toddlers are not eating a single serving of fruit or vegetable on a typical day. French fries are far and away the most commonly eaten vegetable after the first year. Almost 30 percent of babies start solids before they are 4 months old; almost 20 percent start juice before 6 months and cow's milk before 12 months. And 30 to 40 percent are having sugary fruit drinks every day by 15 months. Most babies are getting daily desserts before they take their first steps. By age two, children's diets mirrored the typical adult diet in the United States to an amazing degree.

But these unhealthy habits are not inevitable. Before 1980, we enjoyed 20 years during which the percentage of overweight children remained steady. Children are built to enjoy the treat of eating delicious foods that strengthen their minds and bodies, satisfy their appetites, and fuel their unbridled exploration of the world.

Most children start out by eating grains, fruits, and vegetables. But we lose them when they switch to empty-calorie table foods later in the first year. In this chapter, we'll look at a powerful, achievable way to start solids that will give your baby strong momentum toward a lifelong habit of taking pleasure in the healthiest foods. In the next chapter, we'll look at making the transition to table foods as a step forward, not as a step off a cliff.

The Way You Want to Feed Your Baby

We've seen that your baby has been learning from you since before she was born. When she was learning about your face in the first days of life, she tried to imitate your expressions. When she learned about grasping objects, her attention was riveted on the objects you grasped and handled. When she starts to eat solids, she will be paying very close attention to what you eat.

Most of us would recoil from putting soda in a seven-month-old's bottle or handing her a french fry as her first table food. But if we drink soda or eat fries in front of her, *we are doing almost the same thing*. Later, when she makes the switch to table foods, she will find ways to get the foods she's been watching you enjoy.

The First Step

The first step toward starting solids in a healthy way is to be sure that the foods she sees you eating are the foods you want her to enjoy next year. This is the time to eat the way you really want to and the way you want to pass along.

Many of us have unhealthy habits that we've accumulated over the years. The miracle of having a child is often our best opportunity to shed those habits that don't serve us and to develop new ones that do. Our parenting instincts make it easier to do something for our children that we would not do for ourselves alone. These changes, of course, directly benefit our children as they follow our examples. They also benefit our children by giving them healthy, energetic parents, both now and in the years to come. They add freshness to our marriages or adult relationships. And of course, they are what our own bodies are crying out for.

The Second Step

Along the same lines, the second step to starting healthy foods is to take charge of the food advertisements to which your baby is exposed. In the womb, you provided a safe environment for her. Part of providing a safe environment now is shielding her from advertisements that are aimed at leading her down an unhealthy path. Children are greatly influenced by what they see on screens. Before their first steps, babies tend to see television as a kind of reality. If they are close enough, they may try to grab and eat the things they see on the screen. If your baby will be in the room with you when you're watching something, try to choose entertainment without fun commercials for empty foods.

Starter Cereal

In most cultures, the first solid food is a mushy cereal. Rice cereal has the advantage that very, very few children have an allergy or intolerance to it.

The best way to tell the right time to start cereal is when your child seems to be asking for it. He is not going to say, "Dad, excuse me, can I please have solid foods?" It is more likely that when you are eating, he will look at you as if to say, "How come you aren't giving me some of what you're having?" This communication will likely be in the form of fussiness or intense interest when you are eating. This is a good time to begin solid foods, or you can begin anytime you want, using the guidelines stated earlier in this chapter. Here are a few tips for easing into the solid-food period:

- Try to make this meal, and as many meals as practical, an unrushed family event. Be sure to have a camera ready for the first one.
- If you choose rice cereal, it can be purchased in jars or as a dry mix, or you can prepare your own by cooking rice without salt or seasoning and pureeing it in a food processor or blender. Commercial baby cereals are fortified with iron and perhaps zinc, minerals that are very important for babies. If you choose the dry mix, the rice cereal box will have directions for mixing it in the correct proportions with either breast milk or formula for baby's first meal, which is quite diluted. As your baby gets older, the cereal can be mixed to a thicker consistency.
- Use a spoon to feed your baby. I like soft ones.
- With the rice cereal mixed, place your child in a propped-up position and move the spoon toward his mouth. The first few days, he will tend to push the cereal right back out with his tongue. This is because babies have a thrust reflex that causes their tongue to push anything that is put in their mouths back out.
- Within several days, your child will begin to get the idea of closing his lips around the spoon and swallowing. Once he does, you can begin to monitor the amount of food he needs (which is not a predetermined amount, but varies from child to child). In order to find what's right, keep moving the spoon toward his mouth and look for signs that he is losing interest. If he turns his head away, clamps his lips shut, or appears bored, it is time to stop. Otherwise, keep moving the spoon to his mouth as long as he keeps opening it and looking happy.
- Babies who start solids at between four and six months usually do best to get solids in this way once or twice a day, with breast milk or formula at the same meal.
- I prefer allowing most breast-fed babies to nurse first when their vigorous suck will keep up their mother's milk supply. Then they can eat as much cereal as they want. You may want to offer your baby your

breast again at the end, in case he's interested. You want him to leave the meal feeling satisfied.

- For most formula-fed babies, I recommend starting with the cereal first. Because these children have more limited taste experience, I want them to get some of the solids when they are hungriest. They can then drink as much as they want when they lose interest.
- There is no need to coax healthy babies to try "one more bite" or to make airplane noises to trick them into eating more.
- By starting with a spoon, resting between bites, and stopping when your child is full, you will be laying an excellent foundation for good eating habits throughout his life.

After your child has done well with rice cereal, you can begin feeding him oatmeal and barley if you wish. Other solids can be introduced once he has been eating cereal for at least a week or two and is tolerating it well. I am slow to broaden the variety of foods before six months, unless kids seem to demand it. The earlier a food is introduced, the more likely it is to cause an allergy. For many children, the gut is still quite immature before six months, allowing whole proteins to slip into the bloodstream and perhaps trigger food allergies.

Food Allergies

True allergies to foods are more common in babies than many people suspect. About 6 percent of children have food allergies, and up to half of these allergies are to cow's milk protein. Most children who are allergic to one food are not allergic to others, although many who are allergic to cow's milk are also allergic to soy.

People can be allergic to any food, but in children, 90 percent of all food allergies are to one of five foods: cow's milk, eggs, peanuts, soy, and wheat. Symptoms might include eczema or another skin rash, loose stools, bloody stools, constipation, poor weight gain, ear infections, fussiness, or poor sleep. Exclusively breast-fed kids can still react to these foods in their mothers' diets, especially to cow's milk.

Thankfully, babies outgrow most food allergies. More than half the time they are gone by the first birthday. Allergies to peanuts, nuts, fish, or shellfish, however, are usually lifelong.

The grains, vegetables, and fruits introduced as first foods are selected because they are among the least likely to trigger allergies.

What's Next?

I have not found convincing scientific evidence about the best order for the next foods to introduce. One common rule of thumb is to choose vegetables and then fruits. The reasoning is that it is harder to go back and develop a taste for vegetables after enjoying the sweeter fruits. This may be true for some kids, but for most, it's not too tough to get them to like a variety of both fruits and vegetables beginning in any order.

I usually like starting vegetables first, because I want kids to have many long memories of enjoying a wide variety of vegetables before they enter the picky time later in childhood. Most children do not keep formed conscious memories from before the age of two-and-a-half or three years. Instead, they use their early daily experiences to form lasting, deep, instinctive emotional responses to help guide them through life.

Positive memories of both vegetables and fruits are a valuable gift. Drs. Melvin Heyman and Susan Roberts describe this in their excellent book on metabolic imprinting. If a baby comes to enjoy a vegetable as part of every lunch and dinner, and comes to think of fruit as the perfect dessert, this will become the unconscious blueprint in her mind of what a proper meal should be. This both tastes yummy and also feels right.

Many of us have unconscious blueprints, formed during our early years that draw us back to unhealthy foods to make us feel loved and secure. Cookies for comfort, fries to feel good. You have the opportunity now to give your baby a wonderful gift. The foods that satisfy her soul in the future can be foods that also invigorate and nourish her body.

Popular choices for the first veggies include peas, green beans, squash, sweet potatoes, potatoes, and carrots. Give your baby only one new food at a time. Talk to your baby about what he is eating. Be sure to wait three to five days before starting another one to determine if he has any reaction to a food (perhaps a rash, a tummy ache, vomiting, or diarrhea). Most reactions to foods at this age are soon outgrown. Changes in stool color, smell, or consistency are to be expected. And it is normal to see bits of undigested food in the stool while his body is learning to process the new foods.

The Source of Your Baby Food

Convenient jar baby foods are available. The early foods usually come without additives or fillers. Check the ingredients—peas and water, carrots and water, and so on.

You can also make your own baby foods. This has the advantage of providing nutritionally rich foods with fresh taste, smell, and color. You can increase the variety of your baby's diet at a lower cost than that of jar foods. Another advantage is that your baby can start to make a connection between the whole food and what she is eating. She can watch you peel a banana and mash half of it, then she eats half while you eat half. Or pop half the banana in a blender with a little breast milk or formula. The food connection can extend even further if she goes with you to a farmer's market and sees you pick out foods, bring them home, and prepare them for all of you. Our local farmer's market has been one of the biggest boons to my children's nutrition. Our weekly expedition is a fun family ritual that they will continue with their kids.

Of course, making your own baby foods can take time. Cheryl Tallman and Joan Ahlers, a pair of moms, created Fresh Baby, a time-saving kit with dozens of simple, healthy recipes for quick, tasty homemade meals for babies. They joke about their friends calling them supermoms, because their secret was that they found a way to cook all their meals for their babies in only about 30 extra minutes per week.

If you wish, you can easily make your own food without buying any kit or extra equipment. Steam and puree. You can find many free recipes online.

Fresh Peas

Steam peas over low heat until tender. Do not overcook. Fresh or frozen peas (not canned) are fine. If you prefer, you can microwave or boil the peas, although boiling makes them lose some of the nutrients. Put some of the peas on your plate with your baby watching. Put some of the peas through a food mill, baby food grinder, blender, or sieve. Add a little of the cooking liquid, breast milk, or formula to make a puree of the desired consistency. Serves the whole family.

Deciding between jars and homemade is another opportunity for bi-empathy (as is the whole process of starting solids). Look at your needs, budget, and schedule and at your baby's perspective. His taste buds are quite different from your own. But you may want to try jar peas once and fresh peas once to see what you can learn about both of you. Serve yourself and your baby some of each. Compare color, taste, and smell. I picked peas because it is one of the toughest to prepare at home. Many foods don't need to be strained (like apricots, yum—just steam some fresh apricots and maybe some fresh ripe pears, put them in a blender, and enjoy).

You might choose homemade foods, you might choose commercial foods, or you might choose to do a combination, depending on your schedule. Whichever you choose, most babies eat a healthy diet with their first foods.

As you know, I'm a fan of organic foods, especially for pregnant women, nursing moms, and young babies. We still know too little about the effects of persistent chemicals on early development for me to feel confident about feeding lots of chemically grown foods to children at such a critical stage of development. Organic baby foods are available commercially. Also, the conventional baby foods are often tested and found to have very low levels of pesticides.

If you choose fresh produce for your baby (or toddler), some foods tend to be higher in pesticide residues than others. Stonyfield Farm Yogurt commissioned the Environmental Working Group to do a shopper's guide to pesticides in produce by analyzing more than 100,000 tests for pesticides on produce collected by the U.S. Department of Agriculture and the Food and Drug Administration. The tests were performed after the produce had been washed or peeled. Among the foods highest in pesticides were apples, cherries, peaches, pears, and potatoes. These would be good foods to buy organic or to get through commercial baby foods. Among the foods that consistently had the lowest levels of pesticides when grown "conventionally" were avocados, bananas, and peas.

But My Baby Hates Peas

If you drink coffee, you may remember the first time you took a taste. It was horrible! How could anyone like that disgusting stuff? But we humans have an amazing ability to acquire a taste for almost anything.

Many baby foods that we consider very bland have a strong impact on children. Babies have extremely sensitive taste buds. Their vision may have slightly soft focus, but their senses of taste and smell are much sharper than ours. Some new tastes seem revolting, but even these new tastes can be acquired.

"My baby hates peas!" I hear this about peas more than any of the other first foods. Perhaps this is a good reason to start with peas if your baby seems eager for new flavors. For a reluctant or late eater, you might start with sweet potatoes or even fruit.

In an exciting study of babies with a demonstrated dislike for peas (perhaps you can picture the expressive faces of those enrolled in the study), each was fed peas as the first bite of solid food for the day. If the baby made a disgusted face or spewed the peas, they were discontinued that day in favor of other foods the baby liked. The babies were not force-fed the peas. By the end of only 10 days, 85 percent of the pea-haters had become pea-lovers! They literally giggled at the sight of peas.

The best way to get your infant to eat any new food is to desensitize her to the taste. You can often accomplish this by using the new food for the first bite of solids each day for 10 days. Some studies suggest it may take up to 15 days for some children. The FITS study found that many parents give up after only several tries. A small minority persists long enough, and these are richly rewarded. Whatever it takes, invest the time early on to give your bundle of joy a delight in peas, green beans, carrots, squash, and sweet potatoes.

Building a Bridge of Carrots

Often you can build a bridge to a new flavor by mixing it with one kids already enjoy. If your baby likes carrots or potatoes, you might try offering potatoes with a few peas or a carrot-and-pea combo. Go light on the new taste at first, but you can gradually increase the amount until the new flavor is also a popular part of the repertoire.

Never force or coax your child to eat more of a new food than she is ready for, but always be ready to scoop up more if your child is still interested. Some new tastes take longer to acquire than others, but continuing to expose your baby to small amounts of healthy foods (that the adults in your family eat) will pave the way for excellent eating habits in the years to come.

The Grafruvegi Family Balancing Act

As you introduce new foods into your baby's diet, your eventual goal is to balance between grains, vegetables, and fruits (meats are also OK, especially to provide iron and zinc, but your baby already has a good protein/calcium source in breast milk or formula). It's also nice to balance between the various colors of fruits and vegetables. Different colors represent different nutrients in the foods. Among the early veggies, balance between yellow/orange and green. Among the fruits, avocados and kiwis are green, bananas and pears are white, peaches are orange, and plums are purple. As an older toddler told me recently when he bit me, "Dr. Greene, eat all the colors!" He was right, it's a great idea to teach kids to "eat the rainbow."

Different foods can change the color of the stools as well (peas can turn them green, beets can turn them red), but there is no need to use your child's diet to control stool color. You might, however, use different foods to balance stool consistency. After starting solids, some babies tend to get constipated, while others get diarrhea. Bananas and rice cereal tend to make the stools firmer. Pears, peaches, plums, peas, apricots, and especially prunes tend to loosen them up.

Yellow Light, Red Light

It's best to avoid some foods for babies, especially when they are just starting out. Some of these are common sense. Others may surprise you.

The biggest red light is to foods that are choking hazards. First foods should all be foods that your baby doesn't have to chew. Even when he gets pretty good at chewing, there are a number of choking hazards to avoid during the first year: nuts, peanut butter, popcorn, whole grapes, chunks of meat, and hunks of raw vegetables. Most raw vegetables are best delayed until some molars are in and then introduced as thin shavings. Also, babies should not eat alone.

Another red light throughout the first year is honey, because it can cause a serious disease called *infant botulism*.

Teas are wonderful beverages later in life but are usually unwise during the first year because of the ways they change how the body handles iron, calcium, and other functions (depending on the type of tea).

There is *no* reason for babies to get products made with partially hydrogenated oils, trans fats, or high-fructose corn syrup. These foods do not help to build strong bodies, and it is much easier never to develop a craving for them. Check the labels on prepared foods, especially all crackers and drinks.

Also try to minimize added sugars, salt, and starchy fillers. Babies can usually enjoy foods happily without these—until they develop a taste for them.

Whole milk, nuts, peanuts, fish, and other seafood are all best avoided throughout the first year because of the possibility of allergies (and other reasons). The best timing for starting egg whites, citrus fruits, tomatoes, strawberries, and chocolate remains unclear. Most experts agree that starting before nine months is unwise. If you are considering starting any of these foods before your child's first birthday, talk with your pediatrician about your baby and your family first. A history of asthma, eczema, allergies, or frequent ear infections would make me more inclined to wait.

It is usually best to avoid egg yolks, cheese, yogurt, and wheat before eight months to reduce the risk of allergies. But these can be wonderful transition foods as babies start to want to eat what is on the table.

If you are going to home prepare vegetables for your child, you might want to minimize homemade carrots, beets, turnips, spinach, or collard greens before eight months. In many parts of the country, these vegetables contain large amounts of nitrates, which can cause anemia in infants. The vegetables used in prepared baby foods are selected for their low nitrate levels.

Juices should not be started before six months of age (unless needed as a gentle medicine for constipation). And fruit juice should never be given in a bottle or at bedtime at any age. After six months, 100 percent fruit juice can be a healthy part of the diet but should be limited to no more than 4 to 6 ounces a day—all the way until kindergarten. Higher amounts are associated with poor nutrition and a number of other health problems. One study suggests that children who get too much juice may have a risk of ending up shorter and fatter than their peers. Vegetable juices or juice blends can be a great way to get veggies in or to help kids learn to like the taste (I like orange-carrot juice for toddlers). Diluting juice with water or using juice to flavor water can be a healthy beverage choice. But the extremely popular fruit juice drinks and juice cocktails loaded with added sweeteners are not healthy beverages for kids.

This may sound like a lot of cautions, but it actually leaves a huge variety of wonderful foods to explore together. Bon appétit!

The Safety Net

In our modern culture, I recommend a good multivitamin as an important safety net, especially during the ages of peak development. Clearly this starts before the baby is born. Your child thanks you for swallowing her prenatal vitamin for her. This continues during the time she gets a liquid-only diet. Formula has a multivitamin blended in. For bottle-fed babies, another supplement is unnecessary before the first year. If your child is nursing, your vitamins should supply her needs, with the possible exception of vitamin D.

Vitamin D is the vitamin we make from being outside in the sunlight. Breast milk contained an ideal amount for the lifestyles of the recent past. But with more time indoors, more use of sunscreen (a good thing), and a more mobile society (people living in latitudes different from where their skin melanin content lets in the ideal amount of the sun's rays), sometimes the balance is off. Unless you're sure you're getting enough, a supplement containing vitamin D is wise.

Once breast-fed babies start solids, I also like to give them a multivitamin/mineral supplement with iron. Breast milk remains an ideal food for babies. The concentration and amount of nutrients they get through the breast milk changes significantly to allow them to make up the rest from their solids. Just in case they don't get what they need from the solids, I like the safety net. If they don't get enough zinc, for instance, it can affect their developing immune system. If they don't get enough iron, it can affect their ability to learn.

Millions of children in the United States are low enough in iron to affect their developing brains. They may feel tired, weak, or cranky. They tend to get sick more often. But they might be deficient even without noticeable symptoms.

Just as in the circus, a safety net lets you relax while you soar. Eating should be fun and relaxing. Let fly!

Memories

Babies have a deep body memory. Your baby remembers the foods you ate when you were pregnant. She remembers the foods you ate while nursing her. She will remember the foods she sees you eat now.

She will also remember interactions. An interesting study from St. Francis Xavier University and Yale University introduced babies (at the starting-solids age) to two different strangers on video screens. One stranger on the screen could see and hear the baby and interacted directly (what we call a contingent interaction). The other stranger was a tape replay of that person interacting with another baby (a warm, but noncontingent interaction). Babies were much more interested in the one interacting with them personally. No surprise. But a week later, they *still* preferred that person, even if both strangers were now responsive. Babies prefer and remember interactions in which someone is paying attention to their cues.

The same is true with babies' toys. Select toys where the play value is in response to your baby's actions, rather than the toys just acting on their own. We call these "contingent toys." These are more fun, last longer, and support your baby's development.

Around the time that babies are sitting up to see the world and starting to eat some of the world around them, they start thinking of people, toys, and foods that are not right in front of them. Your baby has been able to tell the difference between you and strangers from the earliest days of his life. Young babies prefer their mothers and fathers (and others who are frequently involved in their care) but will usually respond happily to others as well. Until . . .

They begin to get upset when others come too close—even regular babysitters, grandparents (who may be heartbroken), or one of their parents (who may feel very unsettled by this). At about the same time, most babies begin to fuss and cry whenever you leave their sight, sometimes even to step into the next room.

What's Going On?

Separation anxiety and stranger anxiety both coincide with a new intellectual skill called *object permanence*. Your baby now remembers objects and specific people who are not present. He will search for toys that have dropped out of sight. He is able to call up a mental image of what (or who) he is missing. He doesn't want a stranger, because the stranger is not *you*.

Babies understand about people leaving before they learn about people returning. They can tell from your actions that you are about to leave. Anxiety begins to build even before you go.

Babies can't tell from your actions that you are about to return. They have no idea when—or even if—you will come back. And they miss you intensely. For them, each separation seems endless.

Dropping a screaming child at day care tugs at parents' hearts. And much nighttime screaming is an expression of separation anxiety. Sleep is a scary separation. To us, peek-a-boo and bye-bye are fun ways for us to interact with kids. For babies, these are issues of great concern.

Will This Ever End?

Most healthy babies and toddlers exhibit at least one phase of stranger/ separation anxiety as part of normal development. The first peak of separation anxiety usually takes place in the second half of the first year and lasts for about two to four months, although there is great variability in this.

There is often a second peak in the second half of the next year. At this time, toddlers have emerging language skills and a strong desire to communicate. They have developed a rich, multimedia array of ways to communicate with you that strangers just don't understand. The second peak of separation anxiety usually fades as language skills improve.

In some children, the two peaks run together, resulting in separation anxiety for up to eight months or so at a stretch. Either way, separation is usually a dominant issue from about six months until language is understood by strangers.

What Can We Do in the Meantime?

Once children have learned about leaving, you want them to learn about returning. Separation/return games, and short practice separations are quite helpful. The classic separation/return games are peek-a-boo and Where's the Baby?

I like playing peek-a-boo with the feet. With the baby lying on his back, lift his legs "up, up, up" to hide your face, and then "Peek-a-boo!" as you open his legs wide. Often babies love to open their legs themselves to find you.

In Where's the Baby?, you drop a lightweight cloth over your baby's head and ask, "Where's the baby?" Now pull the cloth off again, grinning and saying, "There you are!" Soon your baby will delight at pulling the cloth off and laughing. The cloth can also be placed over your own head, or you can partially hide behind a chair or around a corner where you will be discovered easily.

Hiding and finding objects is another fun form of separation/return play. Place them under clothes or buckets, anywhere the baby can delight in finding them.

With practice separations, tell your baby that you will be going to another room and that you'll be back soon (even though the baby will not understand the words yet). If there's crying, repeat the reassurance that you'll be back soon. Then, pop back in smiling and say, "Hello." "Bye-bye" is one of the first words most babies learn. You want to teach them to understand "hello" as soon as you can. Gradually make these practice separations longer and longer. The baby will learn that you'll come back and that it's OK when you are gone for a bit.

How Do I Leave?

When you really leave, do not make a big fuss over going and do not sneak out. Children need a simple, affectionate, direct "Bye-bye, I'll be back." Be sure to tell them when you'll be back. Anxiety can be contagious. The more anxious you are about leaving or about others caring for your baby, the more anxious your baby will be. If the caregiver can engage your child with a toy or mirror, it can make your leaving easier. If you are leaving your child at day care or someplace other than home, the separation will be easier if you spend a few minutes there with your child (and also with the new caregiver). Regular routines make the "returning" lesson easier to learn. Transitional objects, such as blankets or stuffed animals, are healthy ways to minimize separation anxiety.

Separation anxiety is more pronounced when children are tired, hungry, or sick. When your timing is optional, try to arrange separations for when your baby is happy and satisfied or to have a transitional lovey for cuddling.

Changes

Your baby is growing away from you and growing closer to you at the same time. You are getting to know each other better than ever before. Shared meals can become a touchstone in the swirl of changes that will remain steady throughout the life of your family, unlike the baby teeth and clinging, which your child will shed more quickly than you think.

20

Great Explorations

Baby Discovers the World,
and the World Discovers Baby

Soon your intrepid explorer sets off across the floor in search of new discoveries. Of course, like all explorations, this journey is built on earlier journeys and is only the beginning of many more.

The first thing your baby did after sperm and egg joined was to embark on an emblematic journey down the fallopian tubes. The climax of the astonishing marvels of fetal development was an even more amazing journey through the birth canal—or perhaps through the abdominal wall. The distance was short, but it's hard to imagine a longer journey. Worlds were traversed in a few inches. And your baby was radically transformed in transit (as were you!).

Soon after the grand arrival, your baby was on the move again. But this time he recruited you to carry him where he wanted to go, a little king in his snugli litter. He charmed you with smiles and tugged at your heartstrings with his cries. Sometimes carrying him about was the only way to calm him, the only way any of you could rest.

This was a wonderful transportation solution for your baby, because his top priority was getting to know you. But soon he began working on alternate travel arrangements—locomotion where he could be in control. Stretches and wiggles gave way to "Look! He rolled over!" And he was on the move again. The urge to propel oneself across the floor grows increasingly strong in the second half of the first year.

Crawling is one of the classic behaviors most associated with babies. I hear crawling questions from parents every week. The truth is, many babies never crawl! They do need to find some way to move across the floor. Each will do so at unpredictable times and in distinctive ways. Your baby may be

a scooter (one who likes to stay upright and scoot across the floor on his bottom). Some roll over and over to get where they want. Many babies prefer creeping, or wriggling forward on their stomach. Many children will crab-crawl, moving backward. And of course, many children will get up on all fours and crawl forward in the traditional way. Each child is unique.

A Mind-Body Thing

As with other parts of development, getting mobile changes the way babies think. And thinking changes the way babies move. One of the first things we notice is that babies become aware of three-dimensional space in a new way. *Where* things are starts to matter as much as *what* things are.

Canadian researchers introduced a toy to babies, along with an accompanying soundtrack. Young babies clearly made the link between the toy and the sound, regardless of where the sound was coming from. Babies just eight weeks older, who were now starting to move across the floor, noticed and cared *where* the sound was coming from. Their ability to locate sounds in space had matured, but so had their sense of the world. They didn't link the toy and the sound together anymore unless both were coming from the same place.

At about the same developmental time, *what* babies look at changes. Your baby was fascinated by her parents' eyes in the first moments after birth. She is still fascinated by your eyes, but increasingly now in *where* your eyes are looking. She is less likely to gaze at you than to gaze at whatever you are (and gaze at you when you are looking at her, partly to learn about herself in the mirror of your face). She is learning about space and how you relate to where things are.

Soon your baby is able to hold an image in her own mind of where things in the room are located, even without being able to see or hear them. Rachel Clifton and researchers at the University of Massachusetts—Amherst demonstrated this by first showing babies an object that made a sound while they were in a lit room. When the lights were turned out and the sound turned off, seven-month-old babies were still able to accurately reach right for the object. They were aware of *where* it was located in space and had created a mental map so they could find it with no sensory clues. In another study, Dr. Clifton found that 8½-month-old babies were able to perform complicated, multiple-step locations in the dark; their knowledge of space continued to grow as their mobility increased.

A remarkable perceptual change happens at about the same time. Before this, your baby is learning where things are located in the room in relation to her. As she gets more mobile, though, she develops an increasing sense of where things are located in relation to each other. Researchers at the University of Wales demonstrated this by using colorful beacon objects to help babies locate toys. Six-month-olds were not aided in their searches by these beacons. But 8½-month-olds were able to use the beacons to quickly find what they were looking for. They had a much better feel for how objects in the room related to each other.

The developing body and mind work together to prepare your baby to explore the world beyond her fingertips with increasing mobility and sophistication over a very short period of time.

Treasure Hunting

At the same time, her increasing skill with her fingers and thumbs leads her not just to handle objects, but to do things with them. She is eager to change and rearrange the world. She would rather crumple paper than just touch it. She wants to put small objects in others, to move things around, to knock things over. She may push a car along the floor and then pick it up to peer at the wheels, pondering what makes it go. And then, of course, almost everything goes into her mouth.

The Great Mouth Detective

On their journeys, most babies will evaluate the treasures they discover by placing them in their mouths. This phase provides rich opportunities for playing with your baby. The indiscriminate desire to put things in the mouth is also one of the great feeding opportunities of childhood, sadly squandered by many parents. And mouthing teaches your baby's immune system about his world. But mouthing behavior is also a vital time to address safety issues.

Babyproofing

Anytime your child makes a surge in development—from crawling to dating to driving a car—it's an important time to take a fresh look at providing a *safe*, nurturing environment for your child. Once again, a powerful way to do this is to put yourself in his socks. Look at the world from his point of view.

Get down on the floor. You'll see how tempting it would be to use your new finger dexterity to put that paper clip you found into the electric outlet, to eat the remnants of a colorful balloon, to sample that bit of dog food

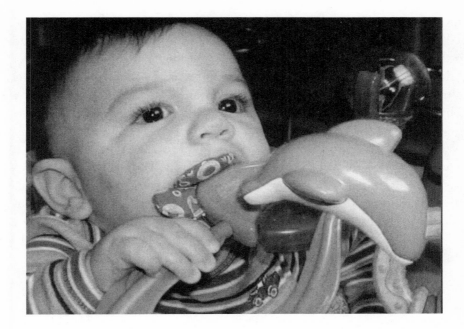

(or dog whatever). And what lurks behind that cabinet door? You've got to find out! And what does that cord lead up to? You've got to pull on it!

Even for parents skilled at bi-empathy, it can be tough to see everyday dangers in your own home. You might want to ask a friend (especially an experienced dad or mom) or a babyproofing service to come take a look. The services in my area are convenient and surprisingly inexpensive.

 You Can't

My five-month-old baby tries to put everything into his mouth. If this is normal behavior, when and how can we wean him from it?

Cedric

The Number One Cause of Childhood Injury. "Rock-a-Bye Baby," the lullaby about a baby toppling from a poorly placed cradle, warns of a very real danger. Falls from open windows, down stairs, and from other heights injure more children than any other cause. Sometimes these injuries are minor cuts and scrapes; sometimes they are life-threatening traumas. Children love to climb, so furniture is best kept away from windowsills and balcony railings. Window guards, window stops, or safety screens can let "the wind blow" but keep a child from falling out. In addition, placing shrubbery or something soft under danger areas can lessen the injury if a child does fall. When kids get mobile, it is very important to block stairs.

Where and When Children Drown. Many drowning tragedies are preventable; understanding where drowning happens makes it easier to prevent. According to a major study in the July 2001 issue of *Pediatrics*, infants are most likely to drown inside the home (in bathtubs or buckets) and toddlers in swimming pools or hot tubs.

Balloons as a Cause of Childhood Deaths. That's right. Balloons bring about more deaths than any other toy! Objects that pass the Small Parts Test Fixture (the cylinder with a diameter of 3.17 cm that is used to gauge the safety of small toys) can cause choking. The biggest culprits in this category are spherical objects such as balls and marbles or objects that have spherical parts such as dolls with spherical heads. Far more dangerous, however, are objects that have the ability to conform to the shape of a child's airway such as balloons and disposable diaper stuffing.

The Power of No. Teaching your baby the meaning of the word *no* is an important part of babyproofing, as well as an important life lesson. To be effective, you don't want his world to be dominated by *noes* but by *yeses* and appreciative narrations of his exploits ("That's a lemon. You found a lemon. You picked up a lemon. Good job! What does it smell like?").

When his exploration gets into areas you would rather it didn't, you can resolve most situations by whisking away the object of concern or by distracting him with something else. You can minimize these occurrences by intentionally seeding the room with safe, fun objects for him to discover and play with—as well as by proactively removing those that he shouldn't.

But he needs a few clear limits so he can begin to learn his place in the world.

The first time your baby goes to touch something inappropriate, pauses, and then looks back at you, he is asking for your help in setting limits to his exploring. This is the time to begin teaching children not to act in ways that will hurt themselves, hurt others, or damage objects. It's time to lay the foundations for teaching your baby about constructive behavior.

You can respond with a firm "No" by naming the problem ("No touching the stairgate" or "No biting the cat") and, if appropriate, by providing a brief break in his freedom to explore. If the same behavior persists more than seems reasonable, it may be worth asking yourself why. One family in my practice had an intrepid crawler who kept crawling into the fireplace. It didn't seem to matter how many times the parents said no, gave time-outs, slapped his hand, or erected increasingly strong barriers—the little guy found a way in and a way to spread cold ashes around the family room.

When they came to me about the problem, we considered what may have been motivating him. He didn't seem like he was trying to be bad or defiant. He didn't seem to be trying to get a reaction out of his parents. He just seemed to crave being in the fireplace. So I suggested he might be feeling a need to explore an enclosed space. I suggested getting a dark cardboard box about the same size as the fireplace (with plenty of ventilation, of course). They got one and put it in their family room. Soon he approached it and glanced back at his parents. To his surprise and delight, they nodded in encouragement.

He opened the box "door" and slipped inside to play the way he needed to play. Later he maneuvered back over to the fireplace. He looked back at his parents to see if anything had changed. They shook their heads. "No. The fireplace is a no." He turned away cheerfully and never went back to the fireplace again.

All kids need limits. But different babies respond in different ways at different times. The same solutions will not always work. This is the time for the bi-empathy you started practicing before your baby was born. As you see the world from both adult and baby perspectives, new insights will occur to you. You know more than you think you do. And if you get stuck from time to time, invite someone to brainstorm with you. Parenting is a team event.

No Matter What. This is a stage in your child's development to be sure you are ready for an emergency, just in case. Most babies navigate this age of exploration happily, but it is important for you to know infant cardiopulmonary resuscitation (CPR) and to have the poison control number easily at hand.

School for the Immune System

While children are learning about how to behave in the world, their bodies are learning about how to defend against invaders. The immunity they inherited from their mothers is waning; their own immunity is building slowly; and during the brief trough in between, the rate of new infections is at its highest for most children.

Infections can be minimized both by decreasing the exposure to germs and by optimizing your child's immunity. Here are five powerful ways to decrease germ exposure:

- **Day-care decisions.** Decreasing the number of kids around your baby decreases her exposure to germs. Regular contact with six or fewer children dramatically decreases germ exposure (and illness), especially in the winter months. Unfortunately, this is often not the most practical option.

- **Washing up.** We all know that hand washing is a good idea but may be unconvinced that it makes a big difference, especially in a busy day-care center where there are so many germs. But when staff in a busy facility actually do wash children's (and their own) hands at key moments, the results are spectacular. Key moments? The most important times are after nose wiping, after diapering or toileting, before meals, and before food preparation. Before a child picks his nose would be nice but not really practical.

- **Instant hand sanitizers.** Talk about convenient! A little dab will kill 99.99% of germs without any water or towels. This type of product uses alcohols to destroy germs physically. It is an antiseptic, not an antibiotic, so you can't develop a resistance to it. And here's the cool part—it's fun. Many kids think it's a treat to get to use it. We asked our local day-care center to try it, and they began washing all those times they knew they should. I'd love to see a bottle in every diaper bag and a dispenser at every changing table.

- **Paper towels.** Using paper towels means you can dispose of possible germs before they spread, which isn't an option with shared cloth towels.

- **Air filters.** HEPA (high-efficiency particulate air) filters can remove 99.97 percent or more of the pollen, dust, animal dander, and even bacteria from the air. Plants can also be excellent air purifiers (if no one in the house is allergic to them).

Echinacea

In the United States, more than $300 million is spent each year on echinacea, mostly in an attempt to treat and prevent the common cold. Parents want something natural and gentle that works. But does echinacea work in children? Researchers from the University of Washington and Bastyr University (an alternative medicine institution) decided to find out.

A total of 524 healthy children were included in the study. When they got colds, half of them were given echinacea and half were given an inactive placebo. It was kept a secret which was which. The findings were published in the December 3, 2003, issue of the *Journal of the American Medical Association*. There were no differences between the two groups in the duration or severity of cold symptoms. Colds lasted an average of nine days, with peak symptoms lasting a day and a half, whether or not the children got the herbal remedy. But more than 7 percent of the children taking echinacea developed a rash. Echinacea appears to do nothing to help treat colds in children. It doesn't help them feel better or get better quicker. But it does cost money and can have side effects. It is possible that echinacea may help to prevent colds, but this has not been proven. I hope someone will look into the possibility as carefully as this team looked into echinacea as a treatment.

Supporting the Immune System

Here is an ABC and XYZ of the kinds of things you might think about for maintaining and promoting immune function:

- **Avoidance of unnecessary antibiotics.** The more kids use antibiotics, the more likely they are to get sick more often, with longer, more stubborn infections caused by more resistant organisms.
- **Breastfeeding.** Breast milk is known to protect against gastrointestinal tract infections, otitis media (ear inflammation), invasive *Haemophilus influenzae* type b infection (flu), respiratory syncytial virus (RSV) infection, and other types of upper and lower respiratory tract infections—even years after the breastfeeding is done. Kids who don't breastfeed average five times more ear infections.
- **Cigarette smoke.** Keep your child as far away from smoke as possible! It disrupts normal immune function. Exposure to secondhand smoke is responsible for many health problems, including more than 2 million unnecessary ear infections each year in the United States.

- **Xylitol.** This is a natural, nonsugar sweetener (found in raspberries and plums) that has been proven to make it harder for bacteria to stick to kids. Studies suggest that it is a gentle way to prevent ear infections, sinus infections, and tooth decay. I use this as just one example of looking at prevention options rather than just treatment. Identifying and managing allergies in order to prevent ear infections would be another great example, but it doesn't start with X.
- **Yogurt.** The beneficial bacteria in some active-culture yogurts can help to gently prevent tummy aches, diarrhea, food poisoning, food allergies, eczema, sinus infections, bronchitis, pneumonia, and colds, among other things. The American Academy of Pediatrics suggests starting babies on yogurt as early as eight months of age.
- **Zinc.** A healthy diet is necessary to build a healthy immune system; it all works together. Zinc is one example of a nutrient that's directly linked to early illnesses. Children who are zinc deficient get more infections and stay sick longer. Iron is another good example.

Celebrate Stuffy Noses

Young kids average three to eight colds a year, each lasting about a week. It's nice for your baby to be on the lower end of the range, but you wouldn't want to eliminate colds entirely. If children miss out on these infections, their immune systems are more likely to overreact later to nonharmful particles, leading to asthma or eczema, according to research published in the February 17, 2001, issue of the *British Medical Journal*. The body is built to fight off and learn from these infections. Children do not benefit from antibiotics for colds, even when there is green or yellow mucus from a runny nose (a normal stage in a cold).

Allergies

This may be a good age for your baby to be exposed to pets. With food allergies, delaying exposure until the gut is mature reduces allergies. But what about with airborne allergies? Because allergies to animal dander are common, people long assumed that early exposure to pets made allergies more likely. A number of studies have turned this assumption completely upside down. The August 2003 *Pediatrics Synopsis Book* summarizes the current understanding. For a child who has not developed allergies, exposure to a dog or multiple pets appears to *decrease* the risk of allergies, eczema, and (in one study) even asthma. Babies' learning immune systems came to see pet dander as normal and were less likely to react to it when they encountered it later.

In the studies summarized, as the numbers of cats and dogs went up, hay fever, eczema, and other allergies decreased. For a child who already has allergies but not to pets, getting pets does not appear to help or hurt. For a child who is already allergic to pets, there is no allergic benefit to keeping the pets, and exposure will make symptoms worse. If a child has asthma and is pet-allergic, then it may be wise to remove the pet from the home.

Fevers

Not very long ago, when my parents were children, a high fever in a child could easily mean the end. High fevers resulting in death were common. Today, most of the devastating illnesses causing these high fevers are either treatable (thanks largely to antibiotics) or better yet preventable (thanks largely to vaccines). Nevertheless, for generation after generation on our planet, a high fever in a child was a chilling terror to her parents—their dream, their darling might slip away from them despite everything they could do. Seeing fever as the enemy is deeply ingrained in our cultural memory.

Fever, far from being an enemy, is an important part of the body's defense against infection. While a fever in a child signals to us that a battle might be going on in her body, the fever is fighting *for* your child, not against her.

Most bacteria and viruses that cause infections in humans thrive best at normal body temperature. Raising the temperature a few degrees can give the body the winning edge. In addition, a fever activates the body's immune system, accelerating the production of white blood cells, antibodies, and many other infection-fighting agents.

Many parents fear that fevers will cause brain damage. Brain damage from a fever usually will not occur unless the fever is higher than 107.6°F. Many parents also fear that untreated fevers will keep going higher and higher, up to 107°F or even more. Untreated fevers caused by infection will seldom go over 105°F unless the child is overdressed or trapped in a hot place. The brain's thermostat will stop the fever from climbing above 106°F.

Some parents fear that fevers will cause seizures. For the great majority of children, this is not the case. About 4 percent of children will occasionally have seizures with fever. Once a child already has a high fever, a febrile seizure (one caused by the fever) is unlikely with the current illness. In any event, febrile seizures are over in moments with no lasting consequences (except one study suggests that, on average, babies who have had febrile seizures are smarter!).

What Constitutes a Fever? While 98.6°F is the normal body temperature most of us hear about, the real normal value varies among individuals and throughout the day. The daily variation is minimal in children younger than six months of age, about 1°F in children from six months to two years, and gradually increases to 2°F per day by age six.

A person's baseline temperature is usually highest in the evening. Body temperature, especially in children, is normally raised by physical activity, strong emotion, eating, heavy clothing, elevated room temperature, and elevated humidity. A temperature up to 100.4°F may be entirely normal (no fever). A temperature of 100.5°F or above should be considered a fever. Lower values also might be a fever, depending on the child.

How Do I Treat a Fever? A fever does not necessarily need to be treated. If your child is playful and comfortable, drinking plenty of fluids, and able to sleep, fever treatment is not likely to be helpful. Steps should be taken to lower a fever if your child is uncomfortable, vomiting, dehydrated, or having difficulty sleeping. The goal is to bring the temperature between about 100° and 102°F, not to eliminate the fever.

When trying to reduce a fever, first remove excess clothing or blankets. Don't bundle your baby, even if he has chills (contrary to what was once a widely held theory). The environment should be comfortably cool (one layer of lightweight clothing and one lightweight blanket to sleep). Two medicines are useful for reducing fever in children: acetaminophen and ibuprofen. Acetaminophen is given every four to six hours and works by turning down the brain's thermostat. Don't use it before your baby is three months of age without first having him examined by a physician. Ibuprofen is given every six to eight hours and helps fight the inflammation at the source of the fever. It is not approved for children under six months.

A lukewarm bath or sponge bath may help cool a febrile child after medication is given; if it's before, the temperature might bounce right back up. Cold baths or alcohol rubs cool the skin but often make the situation worse by causing shivering, which raises the baby's core body temperature.

When Do I Need to Call the Doctor? Fever is a signal that something is going on in your child. Usually this is a minor illness, but it can be a serious infection such as meningitis. Any child younger than two months with a fever should be examined by a physician right away to rule out a serious infection. Children of any age who have a fever higher than 105°F should also be seen, unless the fever comes down readily with treatment and the child is comfortable. Any child who has a fever and is very irritable or confused, has difficulty breathing, has a stiff neck, won't move an arm or leg, or has a seizure should also be seen right away.

Even without such symptoms, it's wise to at least call your doctor if a fever lasts longer than 24 hours. And babies should certainly be seen if a fever lasts longer than 48 hours (or 72 hours if they are acting like they have a minor cold).

While caring for your baby's fever, remember the shadows of the many generations before ours when a fever would break a mother's heart. The fever was the body's desperate attempt to save the child. Remember now that fever is a friend—alerting you to potential problems, activating the baby's immune system, and directly fighting bacteria and viruses.

Antibiotics and Probiotics

About 40 percent of the time kids see a doctor, they leave with a prescription for antibiotics. This astounding figure includes sick visits as well as routine wellness checkups. Antibiotics were one of the most wonderful discoveries of the 20th century. Since their introduction in 1941, they have relieved and prevented incalculable suffering. In the right setting, antibiotics are a powerful, lifesaving tool against bacterial infections.

Microbe Confusion

Most people vaguely lump viruses and bacteria together in their minds. Let's take a closer look at the teeming microscopic world. Viruses are tiny geometric structures that can only reproduce inside a living cell. They range in size from 20 to 250 nanometers (one nanometer is one billionth of a meter). Outside of a living cell, a virus is dormant, but once inside, it takes over the resources of the host cell and begins the production of more virus particles. Viruses are more similar to mechanized bits of information, or robots, than to animal life.

Bacteria are one-celled living organisms. All bacteria are surrounded by their own cell walls. They can reproduce independently, and inhabit virtually every environment on earth, including soil, water, hot springs, ice packs, and the bodies of plants and animals.

The average bacterium is 1,000 nanometers long. If a bacterium were my size, a typical virus particle would look like a tiny mouse-robot. If an average virus were my size, a bacterium would be the size of a dinosaur over ten stories tall. Bacteria and viruses are not peers! Antibiotics designed to kill bacteria do *not* kill viruses.

Thankfully, most bacteria are harmless to humans. In fact, many are quite beneficial. Some, though, cause serious diseases.

Oops!

Because antibiotics were such a revolutionary advance in the treatment of infectious diseases, doctors slipped into the habit of prescribing them for minor illnesses, even those known to be viral, just to "be on the safe side." They also thought this might help the child get better a bit faster.

Now we know that the opposite is true. This practice is harmful to children and to the environment by selectively breeding ever-more frightening bacteria. Children may get better a bit quicker at first, but then they are likely to get sick more often, with longer, more stubborn infections. This short-circuits the learning that the immune system is designed to do at this stage.

The routine use of antibiotics makes life worse for children and parents—even apart from the side effects and allergic reactions many children have. To be on the safe side, antibiotics should be withheld unless they are clearly needed.

I will teach you *one sentence* that can greatly improve your child's health. Use this tool before the doctor even examines your child. When you are explaining why you came in, add the sentence, "If there is any way to safely help her feel better without antibiotics, that's what I would prefer."

If antibiotics are needed, by all means use them—with gratitude and confidence. I can't overstate what wonderful medicines they are when used appropriately.

Probiotics

I do recommend that whenever a child needs antibiotics that probiotics be given as well. These are active cultures of beneficial bacteria given to reduce side effects and to replenish the beneficial bacteria in the gut that are destroyed by the medicine. Probiotics are found in supplements and in some active-culture yogurts. When giving yogurt to kids under two or three, full-fat yogurt is best to support brain growth.

Ear Infections: A New Era

When DrGreene.com opened, we received more questions on ear infections than on any other single topic. Children are more likely to get antibiotics or have surgery because of ear infections than any other single cause.

About one-third of children get no ear infections. About one-third have one or two. But about one-third have a lot. If your baby falls into this third group, don't settle for round after round of antibiotics. Look into why your child might be susceptible and what steps you might take to prevent them. Although there remains a big gap between what we know about ear infections and what happens day to day across the country, newly released guidelines may revolutionize how ear infections are handled.

Contrary to common practice, most children with ear infections should *not* be treated with antibiotics, according to powerful evidence-based guidelines released in March 2004 by the American Academy of Pediatrics and the American Academy of Family Physicians. While some of us have been following this approach for years, currently in the United States there are more than 10 million ear infection antibiotic prescriptions for the 5 million ear infections diagnosed in children each year—about half of all the antibiotic prescriptions in young children are for ear infections. Some kids really need them, but most do not. Each time a child takes a course of antibiotics, future infections become harder to treat. A typical healthy child carries a pound or two of rapidly evolving microscopic bacteria in his or her body. Antibiotics cause the selective breeding of the more resistant strains, which leads to the use of newer, harsher, more expensive antibiotics, with more side effects. For decades, this cycle has been getting worse. But with these new guidelines, it's all about to change.

Focus on Pain

I've long said that doctors should be giving more pain medicines than antibiotics to children with ear infections—because every child with an ear that is inflamed enough to need antibiotics clearly deserves pain relief. In addition, many children who don't need antibiotics also deserve relief for their sore ears. The March 2004 AAP/AAFP guidelines strongly recommend that we pay attention to children's ear pain. Children should not suffer in silence. Actually, they are far from silent—but we doctors haven't adequately listened.

Every examination for an ear infection should include an assessment of a child's ear pain. And pain relief should be part of the treatment plan. Parents often want to start antibiotics for the ear infection because their child has woken up screaming in pain. They mistakenly think that starting antibiotics will reduce a child's pain. Stunningly, in the first 24 hours, there is no difference in pain level whether or not the child gets antibiotics. The children deserve relief.

Oral acetaminophen and ibuprofen are available over-the-counter and do help. Topical drops specifically for earache relief are also now available over-the-counter in the eye/ear care section of retail stores throughout the U.S. These relatively new products have a long history of use in other countries.

The Antibiotic Mistake

Most parents are taught to think that if an antibiotic is given to their child for an ear infection, the medicine will help the child to recover. Not necessarily! Of the more than 10 million annual antibiotic prescriptions for ear infections, somewhere between 8.5 million and 9.5 million prescriptions didn't actually help the children, according to the best medical research (and according to the American Academy of Pediatrics). Put another way, we have to treat between 7 and 20 children with antibiotics for ear infections before one child benefits from the medicine. About 80 percent of ear infections will clear up easily without antibiotics. For those that don't, often the antibiotic won't help either. Sometimes it does. In 5 to 14 percent of children, the antibiotics will take one day off the length of the ear infection. But by comparison, up to 15 percent of children who take antibiotics will develop vomiting or diarrhea and up to 5 percent will have allergic reactions, some of which may be quite serious. Wouldn't it be great to limit antibiotic use to the children who really need it?

The 2004 AAP/AAFP guidelines aim to do this by improving the accuracy of ear infection diagnosis; by targeting antibiotic use for a select group of children with ear infections; by paying attention to pain relief for *all* children (especially during the first 24 hours of an infection); by improving our selection and timing of antibiotics; and by taking steps to prevent ear infections in the first place. A welcome change indeed!

The Diagnosis Secret

If your little girl has a stuffy nose, a slight fever, and wakes up crying, tugging on her ear, and saying, 'My ear hurts!'—then she may have an acute ear infection. But it is almost as likely that she has a cold virus, with ear pain from pressure in the ear, and no acute bacterial infection at all. She may need earache relief, not ear infection treatment. Ear infections cannot be accurately diagnosed just based on the story, either by good doctors or by good parents. Physical evidence is needed to confirm the diagnosis.

So when was the last time you heard your doctor say, after looking into your child's ears, "I think your child has an acute ear infection, but I'm not sure either way"? If you've heard this, you may have a great doctor! As parents, we want our doctors to be accurate diagnosticians, certain of their findings. The secret truth is that the diagnosis of ear infections is often uncertain. An eardrum might be red just from crying. Even in the best of hands, uncertain diagnoses happen every day—and we would all be better served if we respected doctors' honesty in this regard. An uncertain ear infection should be handled differently than one that is clear-cut. I applaud the 2004 AAP/AAFP guidelines for creating a treatment category for uncertain ear infections.

One Thing Is Certain. Fluid must be present in the ear, behind the eardrum, for there to be an ear infection (what doctors call otitis media). The tiny eardrum is a sensitive structure, and can hurt for many reasons including stretching, trauma, irritants, changes in pressure, changes in temperature, viruses, allergies, and ear infections. Many supposed ear infections aren't infections at all, just earaches. Far too often people get antibiotics for earaches, when these are the last thing they need. By definition, ear infections have fluid. Sometimes doctors can see this fluid through the eardrum by looking in the ear. Sometimes the view is obscured by wax, by a thickened eardrum, by a narrow canal, or by a screaming child. Sometimes the otoscope device the doctor uses doesn't fit the child's ear canal well enough to seal when she squeezes a little puff of air to try to flutter the eardrum to reveal fluid. Tympanometry is a test the doctor can use to measure fluid.

An EarCheck is an inexpensive home device that parents can pick up at the drugstore to easily detect fluid behind the ear, using sonar-like technology. This device can take some of the guesswork out of ear conditions in half a second, at the touch of a button. One thing is certain: no fluid means no ear infection. This can save many an unnecessary doctor visit, with over-the-counter treatment at home. If fluid is present, there are still important questions to be answered.

Vanilla Ear Infections Versus Red-Hot Ear Infections

With garden-variety ear infections (what doctors call otitis media with effusion, or OME), germ-filled fluid is present in the middle ear. Most ear infections in children are OME. We've known for about a decade that antibiotics are not necessary for these vanilla ear infections (as I like to call them). In fact, it is perhaps even more important for these children to avoid antibiotics than it is for their peers, to avoid selectively breeding their most virulent bacteria.

An acute ear infection (what doctors call acute otitis media, or AOM) can hurt like hell! These acute infections start abruptly, with the normally delicate eardrum becoming suddenly tender, red, hot, swollen, and painful— like an inflamed appendix. The ear may be filled with pus. The revolutionary 2004 AAP/AAFP ear infection guidelines teach us that even these red-hot ear infections (as I like to call them) are often better treated without antibiotics! The body is usually able to kill and drain the infection on its own. But no wonder that soothing relief for the inflamed eardrum is such a priority in these guidelines. Something that is too often neglected.

Who Should Get Antibiotics for Ear Infections?

The consensus, evidence-based 2004 guidelines recommend that babies under six months of age with red-hot ear infections should be treated with antibiotics for 10 days and pain relief for at least the first 24 hours, whether or not the diagnosis of an acute infection is certain. Remember, antibiotics do not help pain during the most painful first 24 hours, and help pain only minimally after that. Kids six months to two years old should receive 10 days of antibiotics and at least 24 hours of pain relief for a red-hot ear if the diagnosis of an acute ear infection is certain (it must be an abrupt onset, with physical certainty of fluid in the ears, *and* clear evidence of an inflamed eardrum—all three). If the diagnosis of an acute infection is uncertain in these kids, they can be treated with pain relief and observed without antibiotics, unless they've had a fever of 102.2 or higher in the last 24 hours, or severe symptoms.

What Does Observe Mean?

Ask your doctor if the *observation option* is appropriate for your child. It's the best option for many children, even many of those with red-hot ear infections. In the absence of antibiotics, the child receives treatment tailored to her symptoms—especially toward relieving her pain.

Pain relief is part of the observation option, especially for the first 24 hours. In addition, a responsible, available adult is needed to be able to take action if the child is getting worse or has not improved within 48 to 72 hours. The doctor may ask the adult to call if there is a problem. Or a visit may be scheduled in 48 to 72 hours, in case the child isn't improving. Or the doctor may call in 48 to 72 hours to check in over the phone. Or the doctor may give the child a SNAP at the initial visit—a Safety Net Antibiotic Prescription—to be filled if the child is getting worse or has not improved within 48 to 72 hours. The observation option doesn't leave the child to suffer. It just gives the body a chance to work at fighting off the infection before intervening with antibiotics, if necessary. I recommend choosing this option whenever it is appropriate.

The Bottom Line: How Well Does Observation Work? Investigators have compared matched children with acute, red-hot ear infections who were treated initially with observation (including earache relief) and those who were treated initially with antibiotics. How did the two groups fare? I'd rather be treated with observation! The two groups felt the same as each other after 24 hours, and again after 2–3 days, and 4–7 days. The same percentage in both groups were over their ear infections after 7–14 days. Persistent fluid in the ear was the same in both groups. Pain duration was the same in both groups, although those in the observation group were more likely to get pain medicine. Fevers lasted, on average, a day less in those who started with antibiotics. The risk of spreading bacterial infection or bacterial complications was statistically the same in both groups, although the numbers were too small to see a real difference. The trend, though, was more than three times as many spreading or complicated infections in those who got antibiotics. And, of course, those who got antibiotics were also far more likely to develop nausea, vomiting, diarrhea, skin rashes, and other antibiotic side effects—all the while selectively breeding more resistant bacteria in that particular child, and in the environment. Whenever it's appropriate to treat with pain relief rather than antibiotics, the choice is clear. No contest.

Growing Independence and Food Choices

Babies' development of an independent immune system parallels the independence afforded by their newfound mobility and increased dexterity with their fingers and thumbs. Exploration of small objects takes on new sophistication. Now she picks up, turns over, inspects, passes from hand to hand, bangs, mouths, drops, and picks up all over again. The urge strengthens, not just to explore the world, but also to manipulate it—to create changes in her environment. A new sense of autonomy begins to develop. Your baby may begin to turn away from the spoon when someone tries to feed her, insisting on holding it herself or self-feeding with finger foods. This may be a sudden change, or it may be gradual. It may be something she wants all the time or something she wants in addition to being fed by you. Either way, your baby is growing up!

Cheerios and similar cereals are a popular first finger food. You only want to offer one or two at a time in the beginning, while your baby gets used to the new experience. They quickly turn to mush in the mouth. If a baby accidentally inhales one, the hole in the center helps prevent choking. (When hard ball candies were replaced by Life Savers, it really did save lives—but I'm still a fan of taking candy from a baby.)

Small pieces of soft banana or soft-cooked carrots can be other nice early finger foods. I especially like the idea of there being one fruit, one veggie, and one grain choice. But babies may go on strike, not wanting Mom to select their foods and wanting to select them for themselves.

A Fantastic Opportunity

This is the moment when we lost the last generation to healthy nutrition. Parents found their children rejecting baby foods. And they didn't know what or how to feed the babies they loved. They didn't want their kids to go hungry. So the finger foods that many kids sampled were salty, partially hydrogenated, artificially colored, white-flour crackers, sugary sweets, and sippy cups of flavored high-fructose corn syrup drinks. The babies would take these without protest! By mainlining these artificially concentrated flavors to their taste buds, we took away kids' ability to exult in the gentler rainbow of flavors in fruits, vegetables, and healthy grain products. Fruits and vegetables dropped from their diets. Many parents thought it would be easier to get them to eat veggies when they were older. Not so. The habits were ingrained for the short run and the long haul. We gave them a blueprint for failure, both for the foods they would want and for how their bodies would store and use those foods.

When your baby is in the stage of exploring by carelessly putting almost anything from bits of fuzzy lint to slow-moving spiders in his mouth, that's the moment to supply him with a variety of healthy food options—not things you try to coax him to eat, but things he can discover, mouth, and enjoy. He is primed for variety more than at any other time in life. But variety on his terms.

This is a great age to turn the high chair into a treasure map. For many kids, the best way to do this is with a muffin or ice cube tray. Each slot can hold a few tasty, bite-sized treasures. You might want to cover some or all of the treasures with a napkin or a cloth. Or hide the peaches under a layer of pears. I like using one or two of the cups for a dipping sauce. Applesauce, yogurt, or pureed baby fruits and vegetables are all good choices.

Other cups might contain sweet potato cubes (easy to steam or microwave), diced pears, small half-slices of bananas, soft-cooked carrots (either half medallions or shredded), diced soft-cooked green beans, shredded apple, diced kiwi, small pieces of cheese, diced avocado, quartered grapes, diced peaches, bite-sized pieces of wheat toast, or oat cereal. Imagine all of the possible combinations!

You might want to share one (or more) treasure-map meal with your baby to demonstrate how dipping is done. He might like cheese in applesauce, carrots in smushed peas, or peaches in yogurt. He might just put his fingers in the applesauce and make a mess. He might try combinations you would reject. That's OK.

Some babies love it if you name the things they are eating. You will want to use portions that you are comfortable tossing, storing, or reusing in another way.

Let him set the amount he eats. As long as he and the options are healthy, don't try to get him to eat more or less. And let him select from among the options which he prefers right now. Be sure to provide at least some veggie, fruit, and grain options. If he is going only for the grains and not the veggies, increase the number and variety of veggie cups in the future, and decrease the number and variety of grain choices.

The foods you offer should dissolve easily in the mouth (like cereals) or be soft (like bananas), cooked (like carrots, peas, or spinach), or shredded (like apples) to make them easy to swallow. Apples can also be cooked. Cut them into cubes or strips and pop them in a microwave for three minutes or so. You may want to dust them with cinnamon first. When they cool, they are a delicious finger food. They don't need any added sugar. Even without it, they are sweet enough to be a yummy dessert.

When babies are ready to try grapes, they should be sliced to reduce any choking hazard. The skin is the toughest part for a baby to manage. At first, you might need to peel them for your little emperor.

The Food off Your Plate

When we give children good nutrition, we are giving them the building blocks that literally become the eyes we look into, the knees that get scraped, the bones that support their growing bodies, their inquisitive brains, and their hearts that pump quietly night and day down through the years. But, we can't give something we don't have.

Sometime during this process, often around nine months of age, most babies develop an intense desire to eat whatever it is their parents (or others) are eating. This is a critical part of child development because your child will strongly imprint your health patterns. Eating junk food while offering our children vegetables just doesn't work.

I can remember the brave little face of my son. Daddy was drinking a cup of coffee. My little boy kept asking for a sip. I declined by saying that it tastes yucky to kids and making a face. He persisted, and I gave him a little sip. His face combined shock, disgust, and disappointment. His eyes got big and watered. Then he smiled and said, "More."

It reminded me of the time I smoked a cigar offered to me by an older boy on a scouting trip. Kids' desire to imitate at this early stage is a deep, powerful force. Tap into it.

Of course, your baby is a new individual who will want some foods that you don't eat. She won't take all the ones that you do. Still, don't miss out on the power of imitation to make healthy eating habits natural for your child. Many times I've seen kids accept a new food just because it was literally on Dad's or Mom's plate first and then casually (or even reluctantly) transferred to theirs.

It's important, though, not to appear to be trying to convince her to try it. If you seem eager to get her to eat it, the unconscious message is that it isn't good, but it's good for her. Kids are often very sensitive to any pressure in this regard, even if it's subtle.

When your child begins wanting food from your plate, it can be totally natural to let it be fresh fruits, vegetables, grains, and lean protein and calcium sources. When she wants to taste what you are drinking, let it be something you would be happy for her to drink (soon, if not right now—drinking milk in front of her might make her eager to try it at 12 months). Don't waste this opportunity by letting your baby's foray into the world of adult foods be potato chips, french fries, or sugary treats.

Your Baby's Personal Gourmet Chef

When you are serving meals, whether from your plate or on her high chair, from a spoon you hold or from his own fingers, take advantage of creative flavor combinations designed just for your baby.

A baby more easily acquires a love for new foods if they're combined with other flavors he already enjoys. It's also a way to keep the foods you want in his repertoire. Babies need variety and consistency. This is especially useful for finding a way to add fruits and/or vegetables to every meal. And you'll need this to meet the eventual (conservative) goal of five servings of fruits or vegetables each day.

If your baby likes oat cereal, try serving the little Os mixed with diced apricots, cherry chunks, or another fruit. If your baby likes pasta, try pasta topped with baby food peas or carrots. Mashed potatoes can be delicious with embedded peas or diced carrots or green beans. Or make mashed potatoes with half regular potatoes and half pumpkin (mmm!). If graham crackers are his favorite treat, try spreading smashed bananas or (yes) avocados on them. Or baby food apricots or plums. Or applesauce. Graham crackers can be a nice produce vehicle. So can macaroni and cheese. Try macaroni and peas or carrots.

Whether the meals are treasure tray offerings, baby-inspired meals, or baby-tailored versions of your meals, it is wonderful when you can share the same yummy foods. Often, it doesn't take much work to make them delicious for all of you. If you are going to make sweet potato cubes for your baby, you might try dusting them with nutmeg before cooking to make a tempting treat. The moms who created Fresh Baby suggest dusting them with ginger or cinnamon if you want something exotic. They've also got a recipe for pumpkin sauce (like applesauce) as a tasty way to get orange nutrients.

Only you can find the combinations that work for your baby and your family. But delicious possibilities abound. You might want to make a list of the foods your baby does like to help spark your creativity for making "bridge" meals. And online parenting communities can be great sources of recipe ideas.

Even earlier, bringing your baby to a farmer's market and letting her watch you cook can make the whole process even more fun (and more powerful). And she is so eager to learn about the world of foods.

This window will not last forever. Sometime during toddlerhood, usually during the second half of the second year, tastes usually constrict drastically. I believe that one reason for this is that, generations ago, parents might be distracted (perhaps with a new child) and toddlers often wandered off to explore on their own. Curious toddlers might encounter dangerous stuff out there. They developed a suspicion of new plants or meats that they discovered. Maybe toddlers today still carry a bit of that suspicion. As with pet allergies, babies' bodies learn what is safe when they are younger. They are designed to reject tastes they are not very familiar with. Before this happens, it's nice to at least introduce any adult tastes you would like your baby to learn to love (of course, some of these will have to wait at least until her first birthday).

But now is the time to get your baby familiar with good food—when she is built to yearn for both variety and repetition, and when everything goes into her mouth of her own free will (unless, of course, you appear to be trying to get it there).

21

First Steps

The World of Walking

No milestone of development is the focus of more attention than learning to walk. Parents talk about it beforehand and remember it long afterward. If it seems late, they worry. When I see families at a baby's first birthday, parents are often concerned something is wrong with themselves or their child if walking hasn't started yet. That's a lot of families, because more than half of the babies in the United States start to walk after their first birthday! The normal age for first steps has a broad range. About 95 percent of babies will take this giant step sometime between 9 and 17 months. When babies start to walk, they and their parents feel happier.

Walking will forever change your baby's perspective of the world and your view of your baby. In fact, at the moment of that first step, your baby becomes a toddler.

Getting Upright

The desire to walk independently, just like Mom and Dad do, is quite intense. Not surprisingly then, babies often take great joy in being upright. One of my magic tricks in an examining room is to take a screaming baby lying on the table and to pull him to a standing position as we hold each other's hands. Often, he forgets what he was crying about as soon as he is upright.

The desire to be upright is internal; it's built in, like the choreography he performed before he was born. With learning to get upright, your role as parents is not to enforce workouts or practice schedules, but to provide a safe, loving environment in which your baby can experiment. And, of course, to provide nourishment, take away waste, talk with your budding

star, and enjoy his progress. It can also be nice to have suitable objects in the environment for him to use to pull himself up. Research at the University of Illinois at Urbana-Champaign, demonstrated that babies' awareness changes as their physical skills do. Babies who are working on pulling themselves upright learn that some objects in the room are what we call pillars—objects that are stable when pulled. Before this age, babies tend to expect all objects to move if pulled.

It's when babies need pillars for support that they learn at another level what chairs and couches and tables really are. Before this, they may just be large, uninteresting objects, not good toys at all. Now they are treasured gateways to another dimension.

When babies are able to pull themselves to standing, there is a sense of triumph and glee. But there is also a renewed sense of urgency to walk. Sleep is often more difficult at this stage than at any time previously. Parents and children are exhausted.

The Sleep Recession

It is not at all unusual when a child who has been sleeping through the night without any problems, suddenly finds the nights of blissful rest are over when she learns to get upright. If the baby is sleeping in another room, parents may hear their child crying and get up to check on the problem, only to find that their baby is standing up in the crib holding on for dear life and screaming in what seems to be complete terror.

All of us emerge from sleep several times during the night. We usually fall back asleep without even remembering it. Now, the baby is so excited about pulling herself up that she doesn't sleep as soundly as she once did. When she does wake up, she wants to use this most exciting of new skills. And the crib slats are the most perfect pillars she might see all day. These pillars stare down at her no matter which way she faces. And after all, tonight might be the night. Maybe she will be able to take a step! So as tired as she is, she expectantly pulls herself up.

But then she's stuck; she wants (craves?) to stay upright. But she also wants to fall back to sleep. She's caught in an insoluble dilemma, one of many "loops" you will help your child sort out over the years. She can't let go and lie back down. But she's so exhausted, she's miserable. Already upset, she misses her parents and may feel afraid and alone (separation anxiety is often at its peak at this stage). When she cries, she is calling to you for help.

How Do You Want to Respond?

There is no one right answer for every family. Again, this is a good opportunity to consider the situation from both adult and child perspectives.

Many parents try to hold out for a while each night, then give up and bring their baby to bed just so they can get some rest. This solution often doesn't feel great to anyone involved. Everyone suffers for a while, and then the baby learns that prolonged crying will get her what she wants. The pattern turns into an ingrained habit.

One solution is to scoop up your baby right away and take her back to your bed to sleep with you to help her forget her dilemma (no pillars in sight!). This will also build a habit she expects. It may or may not be one the whole family enjoys, but it is the very best option for some.

You might pick her up, rock her to sleep, and hope she stays asleep when you lay her back down. The downside of this approach is that the next time she wakes up, she is likely to face the same dilemma all over again—sometimes several times a night. If rocking to sleep is your plan, I recommend doing it quickly, because she will want this every night, and you both need your rest.

A popular response is to leave babies to work out the problem for themselves, sometimes with reassurance after progressively longer intervals. Although I'm not usually a fan of leaving babies alone to cry it out, especially during the separation anxiety stage, I know a great many families who have had fabulous results with this approach. It can be the best option for some.

Another solution that has worked wonders for many families (including my own) is to gently help her learn to get out of her dilemma by getting her hands free from the crib rails and laying her back down in her sleep position. With one hand, gently hold her hips down on the mattress while you help a bit to soothe her back to sleep. You might sing to her, pat her, and tell her you love her. You may even want to make a recording of your voice reading her a story or singing lullabies so your middle-of-the-night ministrations aren't as taxing. Eventually she will fall asleep. She will likely cry for a while first to alert you to how she's feeling.

If you are there, what still feels negative to her? Does she still want to stand up and is upset that she can't have it both ways? Does she want to be in your arms, so she can be upright and fall asleep? Is she asking to go to your bed? You know she doesn't feel abandoned or scared. What do you do from here?

You might scoop her up. You might leave her there. Or you might just stay with her, gently holding her down until she eventually figures out nighttime is not for standing. Babies usually protest this approach for the first few nights, sometimes for hours. But soon thereafter, most will learn to fall back asleep quickly on their own.

Cruising

Once your baby has pulled himself upright, the next task is to start cruising—walking while holding on. Cruising is a little like riding a bike with training wheels. They are both fun in their own right, but they remain in the shadow of the next step of development. They confer new mobility but not the unrestrained freedom of traveling on one's own.

As your baby gains skill at cruising, the force of his hands on the support objects becomes less and less. Meanwhile, invisibly, inside, development continues to unfold. His cerebellum, the balancing part of the brain, grows rapidly. The long nerves down to his feet gain their myelin insulation. The long bones of his legs start to remodel in preparation. The hinge joints of his knees, the ball-and-socket joints of his hips, and the sliding joints of his ankles all mature just in time. The involuntary stepping reflex that propelled your baby on Day 1 has long since disappeared, making way for calculated steps he makes by choice.

At about the same time, a new depth of self-awareness emerges. Australian researchers have demonstrated that this is the time when babies become fascinated with video images of themselves, as opposed to those of similar-looking babies. Mirrors hold new fascination for them as well.

There's no benefit to coaxing a baby to walk, any more than there is to coaxing him to take one more bite or to eat bananas. You set the table and offer him the opportunity, but he decides what to do and when.

Everything a healthy baby needs in order to walk will develop together with remarkable grace within the supportive environment you create, again reminiscent of his growing brain and nerves and bones in the womb before he was born. You can't—and you don't need to—make this next archetypal rite of passage happen.

Baby's First Steps: A New Beginning

This journey began just months ago, and yet now it is hard to imagine life before your baby. Together you've been on the journey of a lifetime. What

Dr. Greene takes his first steps.

started as a single-cell remarkable DNA combination is now getting ready to take a step without holding on. You've come so far!

When your baby does take that step, in some ways it is a step away from you. Even if it is a step into your loving arms, it's a giant step toward independence. It will change her view of herself and of you forever.

It's an ending and a beginning.

The sparkle you see in your child's eyes will be delight at her own achievement. Her feat of balancing on two tiny feet while moving forward changes everything. She'll be free to roam and play where her heart takes her (or so it seems to her).

She will be so deeply happy with herself! All will be right with the world. In this moment, she will not be performing for anyone else but fulfilling a long-sought-after goal of her own. She will be a separate individual in a new way.

And it's time for you to take a small step away from her. Let this achievement belong to your child. You don't want to overpower her accomplishment with excessive praise; she doesn't need excessive praise. Let the motivation to grow remain hers. Just sparkle back at her with deep respect for what she's done.

Celebrate together an amazing journey. From the moment your baby was conceived, you've nurtured, loved, protected, and taught her—whether you both were awake or asleep. Your baby has sprouted and grown and changed almost beyond recognition. She has imitated you in visible and invisible ways.

Finally, after sleepless nights; countless diaper changes; watchful illnesses; moments of fear, confusion, laughter, and exhaustion—the time has come. Your baby lifts her arms. Her foot comes up. Congratulations! You are the parent of a toddler.

You have the journey of a lifetime ahead of you. Together. Thankfully, a map for this journey is written into the core of your being. But how you travel, only time will tell. And your child toddles into the future.

The world will never be the same.

References

Chapter 1

BBC News World Edition. Lemon Juice Could Stop AIDS. October 2002.
news.bbc.co.uk/2/hi/asia-pacific/2318519.stm 11.

Carson, B. M. *Human Embryology and Developmental Biology*. 2nd ed. St. Louis: Mosby,
1999.

Department of Energy Genomics Research Programs. Oak Ridge National Laboratory.
Human Genome Project information. ornl.gov/TechResources
/Human_Genome/home.html.

Gilliam, M. L., and R. J. Derman. 2000. Barrier methods of contraception. *Obstet Gynecol
Clin North Am* 27, no. 4 (December): 841–58.

Hoffman, R. *Hematology: Basic Principles and Practice*. 3rd ed. New York: Churchill
Livingstone, 2000.

Judson, O. *Dr. Tatiana's Sex Advice to All Creation: The Definitive Guide to the
Evolutionary Biology of Sex*. New York: Metropolitan Books, 2002.

Lander, E. S. "Readings from the Book of Life." Commencement speech, Williams College,
June 8, 2003. williams.edu/admin/news/commencement2003/lander.html.

Larsen, W. J. *Human Embryology*. 2nd ed. New York: Churchill Livingstone, 1997.

National Center for Biotechnology Information, The International RH Mapping
Consortium. A new map of the human genome. ncbi.nlm.nih.gov/genemap.

National Human Genome Research Institute. Advancing human health through genetic
research. www.nhgri.nih.gov.

———. Online Mendelian inheritance in man. ncbi.nlm.nih.gov/Omim.

Ridley, M. *Genome: The Autobiography of a Species in 23 Chapters*. New York: Perennial,
2000.

———. *Nature Via Nurture*. New York: HarperCollins, 2003.

———. *The Red Queen: Sex and the Evolution of Human Nature*. New York: Perennial,
1993.

Sadler, T. W. *Langman's Medical Embryology*. 7th ed. Baltimore: Williams & Wilkins,
1995.

Tsiaras, A., and B. Werth. *From Conception to Birth*. New York: Doubleday, 2002.

Chapter 2

American Museum of Natural History. The genomic revolution. amnh.org/
exhibitions/genomics/o_home/index.html.

Carson, B. M. *Human Embryology and Developmental Biology*. 2nd ed. St. Louis: Mosby,
1999.

FertilityPlus [a nonprofit website for patient information on trying to conceive].
fertilityplusamnh.org/exhibitions/genomics/o_home/index.html.

How do I know if I'm pregnant? 2001. *JAMA* 286, no. 14 (October 10): 1794.

Larsen, W. J. *Human Embryology*. 2nd ed. New York: Churchill Livingstone, 1997.

Sadler, T. W. *Langman's Medical Embryology*. 7th ed. Baltimore: Williams & Wilkins, 1995.

Tsiaras, A., and B. Werth. *From Conception to Birth*. New York: Doubleday, 2002.

Wilcox, A. J., D. D. Baird, D. Dunson, R. McChesney, and C. R. Weinberg. 2001. Natural limits of pregnancy testing in relation to the expected menstrual period. *JAMA* 286, no. 14 (October 10): 1759–61.

Chapter 3

Carson, B. M. *Human Embryology and Developmental Biology*. 2nd ed. St. Louis: Mosby, 1999.

Gabbe, S. G., J. R. Niebyl, and J. L. Simpson. *Obstetrics: Normal and Problem Pregnancies*. 4th ed. New York: Churchill Livingstone, 2002.

Larsen, W. J. *Human Embryology*. 2nd ed. New York: Churchill Livingstone, 1997.

Sadler, T. W. *Langman's Medical Embryology*. 7th ed. Baltimore: Williams & Wilkins, 1995.

Tsiaras, A., and B. Werth. *From Conception to Birth*. New York: Doubleday, 2002.

Chapter 4

Anderson, R. R. 2001. Rest azured? *J Am Acad Dermatol* 44, no. 5 (May): 874–75.

Carson, B. M. *Human Embryology and Developmental Biology*. 2nd ed. St. Louis: Mosby, 1999.

Cullington, H. E. 2001. Light eye colour linked to deafness after meningitis. *Br Med J* 322, no. 7286 (March 10): 587.

Cumming, R. G. 2000. Iris color and cataract: The Blue Mountains Eye Study. *Am J Ophthalmol* 130, no. 2 (August): 237–38.

Gerrish, C. J. 2001. Flavor variety enhances food acceptance in formula-fed infants. *Am J Clin Nutr* 73, no. 6 (June): 1080–85.

Goel, N. 2002. Depressive symptomatology differentiates subgroups of patients with seasonal affective disorder. *Depress Anxiety* 15, no. 1 (January): 34–41.

Hammond, B. R., Jr. 2000. Iris color and age-related changes in lens optical density. *Ophthalmic Physiol Opt* 20, no. 5 (September): 381–86.

Jeffcoat, M. K., J. C. Hauth, N. C. Geurs, M. S. Reddy, S. P. Cliver, P. M. Hodgkins, and R. L. Goldenberg. 2003. Periodontal disease and preterm birth: results of a pilot intervention study. *J Periodontol* 74, no. 8 (August 1): 1214–18.

Kobayashi, H. 2001. Unique morphology of the human eye and its adaptive meaning: Comparative studies on external morphology of the primate eye. *J Hum Evol* 40, no. 5 (May): 419–35.

Larsen, W. J. *Human Embryology*, 2nd ed. New York: Churchill Livingstone, 1997.

Mennella, J. A. 2002. Flavor experiences during formula feeding are related to preferences during childhood. *Early Hum Dev* 68, no. 2 (July): 71–82.

Mennella, J. A., C. P. Jagnow, and G. K. Beauchamp. 2001. Prenatal and postnatal flavor learning by human infants. *Pediatrics* 107, no. 6 (June): E88.

Rebbeck, T. R. 2002. P gene as an inherited biomarker of human eye color. *Cancer Epidemiol Biomarkers Prev* 11, no. 8 (August): 782–84.

Sadler, T. W. *Langman's Medical Embryology*. 7th ed. Baltimore: Williams & Wilkins, 1995.

Tsiaras, A., and B. Werth. *From Conception to Birth*. New York: Doubleday, 2002.

Yanoff, M., J. S. Duker, J. J. Augsburger, D. T. Azar, G. R. Diamond, D. Miller, N. A. Rao, E. S. Rosen, A. A. Sadun, M. Sherwood, J. Sugar, and J. L. Wiggs. *Ophthalmology*, 2nd ed., St. Louis: Mosby, 2004.

Chapter 5

Bayley, T. M., L. Dye, S. Jones, M. DeBono, and A. J. Hill. Food cravings and aversions during pregnancy: relationships with nausea and vomiting. *Appetite* 38, no. 1 (February 1, 2002.): 45–51.

BBC News. Madonna reveals pregnancy cravings. June 7, 2000. news.bbc.co.uk /1/hi/entertainment/780483.stm.

Carson, B. M. *Human Embryology and Developmental Biology*. 2nd ed. St. Louis: Mosby, 1999.

Duffy, V. B., L. M. Bartoshuk, R. Striegel-Moore, and J. Rodin. 1998. Taste changes across pregnancy. *Ann N Y Acad Sci* 855 (November 30): 805–09.

Gabbe, S. G., J. R. Niebyl, and J. L. Simpson. *Obstetrics: Normal and Problem Pregnancies*. 4th ed. New York: Churchill Livingstone, 2002.

Larsen, W. J. *Human Embryology*. 2nd ed. New York: Churchill Livingstone, 1997.

Pope, J. F., J. D. Skinner, and B. R. Carruth. 1992. Cravings and aversions of pregnant adolescents. *J Am Diet Assoc* 92, no. 12 (December): 1479–82.

Sadler, T. W. *Langman's Medical Embryology*. 7th ed. Baltimore: Williams & Wilkins, 1995.

Tsiaras, A., and B. Werth. *From Conception to Birth*. New York: Doubleday, 2002.

Wijewardene, K. P. Fonseka, and C. Goonaratne. 1994. Dietary cravings and aversions during pregnancy. *Indian J Public Health* 28, no. 3 (July 1): 95–98.

Chapter 6

Carson, B. M. *Human Embryology and Developmental Biology*. 2nd ed. St. Louis: Mosby, 1999.

Christian, M. S., and R. L. Brent. 2001. Teratogen update: evaluation of the reproductive and developmental risks of caffeine. *Teratology* 64, no. 1 (July):51–78.

Cook, D. G., J. L. Peacock, C. Feyerabend, I. M. Carey, M. J. Jarvis, H. R. Anderson, and J. M. Bland. 1996. *Br Med J* 313 (November 30): 1358–62.

Food and Nutrition Board. *Dietary Reference Intakes for Calcium, Phosphorus, Magnesium, Vitamin D, and Fluoride*. Washington, D.C.: National Academies Press, 1999.

———. *Dietary Reference Intakes for Energy, Carbohydrate, Fiber, Fat, Fatty Acids, Cholesterol, Protein, and Amino Acids (Macronutrients)*. Washington, D.C.: National Academies Press, 2002.

———. *Dietary Reference Intakes for Thiamin, Riboflavin, Niacin, Vitamin B_6, Folate, Vitamin B_{12}, Pantothenic Acid, Biotin, and Choline*. Washington, D.C.: National Academies Press, 1999.

———. *Dietary Reference Intakes for Vitamin A, Vitamin K, Arsenic, Boron, Chromium, Copper, Iodine, Iron, Manganese, Molybdenum, Nickel, Silicon, Vanadium, and Zinc.* Washington, D.C.: National Academies Press, 2001.

———. *Dietary Reference Intakes for Vitamin C, Vitamin E, Selenium, and Carotenoids.* Washington, D.C.: National Academies Press, 2000.

———. *Dietary Reference Intakes: Proposed Definition of Dietary Fiber.* Washington, D.C.: National Academies Press, 2001.

Food and Nutrition Information Center. "Dietary Reference Intakes (DRI) and Recommended Dietary Allowances." http://nal.usda.gov/fnic/etext/000105.html.

Gabbe, S. G., J. R. Niebyl, and J. L. Simpson. *Obstetrics: Normal and Problem Pregnancies.* 4th ed. New York: Churchill Livingstone, 2002.

Hershey's Food Corporation. Theobromine. hersheys.com/nutrition_consumer /theobromine.html.

Hinds, T. S., W. L. West, E. M. Knight, and B. F. Harland. 1996. The effect of caffeine on pregnancy outcome variables. *Nutr Rev* 54, no. 7 (July): 203–07.

Kidd, S. A., B. Eskenazi, and A. J. Wyrobek. 2001. Effects of male age on semen quality and fertility: a review of the literature. *Fertil and Steril* 75, no.2 (February 1): 237–48.

Larsen, W. J. *Human Embryology.* 2nd ed. New York: Churchill Livingstone, 1997.

March of Dimes. Caffeine. marchofdimes.com/pnhec/159-816.asp.

Resman, B. H., P. Blumenthal, and W. J. Jusko. 1977. Breast milk distribution of theobromine from chocolate. *J Pediatr* 91, no. 3 (September): 477–80.

Sadler, T. W. *Langman's Medical Embryology.* 7th ed. Baltimore: Williams & Wilkins, 1995.

Sampson, H. A. 1999. Food Allergy. Part 1: Immunopathogenesis and clinical disorders. *J Allergy Clin Immunol* 103, no. 5 Pt. 1 (May): 717–28.

Skopinski P., E. Skopinska-Rozewska, E. Sommer, J. Chorostowska-Wynimko, E. Rogala, I. Cendrowska, D. Chrystowska, M. Filewska, B. Bialas-Chromiec, and J. Bany. 2003. Chocolate feeding of pregnant mice influences length of limbs of their progeny. *Pol J Vet Sci* 6, no. 3 (Suppl): 57–59.

Tsiaras, A., and B. Werth. *From Conception to Birth.* New York: Doubleday, 2002.

Wallock, L. M., T. Tamura, C. A. Mayr, K. E. Johnston, B. N. Ames, and R. A. Jacob. 2001. Low seminal plasma folate concentrations are associated with low sperm density and count in male smokers and nonsmokers. *Fertil Steril* 75, no. 2 (February 1): 252–59.

Chapter 7

Agency for Toxic Substances and Disease Registry. Benzene. atsdr.cdc.gov/tfacts3.html.

———. Formaldehyde. atsdr.cdc.gov/tfacts111.html.

———. Lead. atsdr.cdc.gov/tfacts13.html.

———. Mercury. atsdr.cdc.gov/tfacts46.html.

———. Polychlorinated biphenyls. atsdr.cdc.gov/tfacts17.html.

American Academy of Pediatrics. *2003 Red Book: Report of the Committee on Infectious Diseases.* 26th ed. Elk Grove Village, IL: American Academy of Pediatrics, 2003.

Carson, B. M. *Human Embryology and Developmental Biology.* 2nd ed. St. Louis: Mosby, 1999.

Curl, C. L., R. A. Fenske, and K. Elgethun. 2003. Organophosphorus pesticide exposure of urban and suburban pre-school children with organic and conventional diets. *Environmental Health Perspectives: Journal of the National Institutes of Environmental Health Sciences* 111, no. 3 (March): 377–82. (Available online October 2002. http://ewg.org/pdf/20021122_UWstudy.pdf.)

Environmental Working Group. Mercury in seafood. ewg.org/issues/mercury/index.php
———. EWG tuna calculator. ewg.org/issues/mercury/20031209/calculator.php
———. Toxic fire retardants (PBDEs) in human breast milk. September 23, 2003. ewg.org/reports/mothersmilk/es.php

Food and Drug Administration. Advice for women who are pregnant, or who might become pregnant, and nursing mothers, about avoiding harm to your baby or young child from mercury in fish and shellfish. December 2003. fda.gov/oc/opacom/mehgadvisory1208.html.
———. FDA Talk Paper. FDA advises consumers about fresh produce. cfsan .fda.gov/~lrd/tpproduc.html.

Ikonomidou, C., P. Bittigau, M. J. Ishimaru, D. F. Wozniak, C. Koch, K. Genz, M. T. Price, V. Stefovska, F. Horster, K. Dikranian, and J. W. Olney. 2000. Ethanol-induced apoptotic neurodegeneration and fetal alcohol syndrome. *Science* 287, no. 5455 (February 11): 1056–60.

Jones, K. L. *Smith's Recognizable Patterns of Human Malformation*, 4th ed. Philadelphia, PA: W.B. Saunders Company, 1988.

Jones, K. L., D. W. Smith, C. N. Ulleland, and P. Streissguth. 1973. Pattern of malformation in offspring of chronic alcoholic mothers. *Lancet* 1: 1267–71.

Larsen, W. J. *Human Embryology*. 2nd ed. New York: Churchill Livingstone, 1997.

Lemoine, P., H. Harousseau, J. P. Borteyra, and J. C. Menuet. 1968. Les enfants de parents alcooliques: anomalies observées a propos de 127 cas. *Ovest Med* 21: 476–82.

Li, D., L. Liu, and R. Odouli. 2003. Exposure to non-steroidal anti-inflammatory drugs during pregnancy and risk of miscarriage: Population based cohort study. *Br Med J* 327, no. 7411 (August 16): 368.

Longnecker, M. P., M. A. Klebanoff, H. Zhou, and J. W. Brock. 2001. Association between maternal serum concentration of the DDT metabolite DDE and preterm and small-for-gestational-age babies at birth. *Lancet* 358, no. 9276 (July 14): 110–14.

March of Dimes. Toxoplasmosis. marchofdimes.com/printableArticles/188_667.asp.

Montgomery, S. M., and A. Ekbom. 2002. Smoking during pregnancy and diabetes mellitus in a British longitudinal birth cohort. *Br Med J* 324, no. 7328 (January 5): 26–27.

National Center for Health Statistics. Second national report on human exposure to environmental chemicals. cdc.gov/exposurereport.

Nieburg, P., J. S. Marks, N. M. McLaren, and P. L. Remington. 1985. The fetal tobacco syndrome. *JAMA* 253, no. 20 (May 24): 2998–99.

Sadler, T. W. *Langman's Medical Embryology*. 7th ed. Baltimore: Williams & Wilkins, 1995.

Sood, B., V. Delaney-Black, C. Covington, B. Nordstrom-Klee, J. Ager, T. Templin, J. Janisse, S. Martier, and R. J. Sokol. 2001. Prenatal alcohol exposure and childhood behavior at age 6 to 7 years: dose-response effect. *Pediatrics* 108, no. 2 (August): e34.

State of Massachusetts Department of Public Health. Toxoplasmosis. 2001. state.ma.us/dph/cdc/gsrman/toxopl.pdf.

Surgeon General's Advisory on Alcohol and Pregnancy. 1981. *FDA Drug Bulletin* 11, no. 2 (July): 9–10. http://depts.washington.edu/fadu/surgen.html.

The American Veterinary Medical Association. What you should know about toxoplasmosis. avma.org/communications/brochures/toxoplasmosis /toxoplasmosis_faq.asp.

Tsiaras, A., and B. Werth. *From Conception to Birth*. New York: Doubleday, 2002.

Chapter 8

ACOG Committee Obstetric Practice. 2002. ACOG Committee opinion. Number 267, January 2002: Exercise during pregnancy and the postpartum period. *Obstet Gynecol* 99, no. 1 (January): 171–73.

American College of Obstetricians and Gynecologists. 2003. Exercise during pregnancy and the postpartum period. *Clin Obstet Gynecol* 46, no. 2 (June): 496–99.

Bung, P., R. Artal, N. Khodiguian, and S. Kjos. 1991. Exercise in gestational diabetes: An optional therapeutic approach? *Diabetes* 40, Suppl 2 (December): 182–85.

Carson, B. M. *Human Embryology and Developmental Biology*. 2nd ed. St. Louis: Mosby, 1999.

Cheruku, S. R., H. E. Montgomery-Downs, S. L. Farkas, E. B. Thoman, and C. J. Lammi-Keefe. 2003. Higher maternal plasma docosahexaenoic acid during pregnancy is associated with more mature neonatal sleep-state patterning. *Am J Clin Nutr* 76, no. 3 (September): 608–13.

Clapp, J. F. 2003. The effects of maternal exercise on fetal oxygenation and feto-placental growth. *Eur J Obstet Gynecol Reprod Biol* 110, Suppl (September 22): S80–S85.

Da Costa, D., N. Rippen, M. Dritsa, and A. Ring. 2003. Self-reported leisure-time physical activity during pregnancy and relationship to psychological well-being. *J Psychosom Obstet Gynaecol* 24, no. 2 (June): 111–19.

Davies, G. A., L. A. Wolfe, M. F. Mottola, C. MacKinnon. Society of Obstetricians and Gynecologists of Canada, SOGC Clinical Practice Obstetrics Committee. 2003. Joint SOGC/CSEP clinical practice guideline: Exercise in pregnancy and the postpartum period. *Can J Appl Physiol* 28, no. 3 (June): 330–41.

Farrell, M. 2003. Improving the care of women with gestational diabetes. *Am J Matern Child Nurs* 28, no. 5 (September-October): 301–05.

Gauger V. T., T. Voepel-Lewis, P. Rubin, A. Kostrzewa, and A. R. Tait. 2003. A survey of obstetric complications and pregnancy outcomes in paediatric and nonpaediatric anaesthesiologists. *Paediatr Anaesth* 13, no. 6 (July): 490–95.

Goldstein, I., I. R. Makhoul, D. Nisman, A. Tamir, G. Escalante, and J. Itskovitz-Eldor. 2003. Influence of maternal carbohydrate intake on fetal movements at 14 to 16 weeks of gestation. *Prenat Diagn* 23, no. 2 (February): 95–97.

Hafstrom, O., J. Milerad, and H. W. Sundell. 2002. Altered breathing pattern after prenatal nicotine exposure in the young lamb. *Am J Respir Crit Care Med* 166, no. 1 (July): 92–97.

Katz, V. L. 2003. Exercise in water during pregnancy. *Clin Obstet Gynecol* 46, no. 2 (June): 432–41.

Larsen, W. J. *Human Embryology*. 2nd ed. New York: Churchill Livingstone, 1997.

Mottola, M. F., and M. K. Campbell. 2003. Activity patterns during pregnancy. *Can J Appl Physiol* 28, no. 4 (August): 642–53.

Ning, Y., M. A. Williams, J. C. Dempsey, T. K. Sorensen, I. O. Frederick, D. A. Luthy. 2003. Correlates of recreational physical activity in early pregnancy. *J Matern Fetal Neonatal Med* 13, no. 6 (June): 385–93.

Paterson, J. M., I. M. Neimanis, and E. Bain. 2003. Stopping smoking during pregnancy: are we on the right track? *Can J Public Health* 94, no. 4 (July-August): 297–99.

Pitkin, R., and W. A. Reynolds. 1975. Fetal ingestion and metabolism of amniotic fluid protein. *Am J Obstet Gynecol* 123, no. 4 (October 15): 356–63.

Orskou, J., T. B. Henriksen, U. Kesmodel, and N. J. Secher. 2003. Maternal characteristics and lifestyle factors and the risk of delivering high birth weight infants. *Obstet Gynecol* 102, no. 1 (July): 115–20.

Osorio, R. A., V. L. Silveira, S. Maldjian, A. Morales, J. S. Christofani, A. K. Russo, A. C. Silva, I. C. Picarro. 2003. Swimming of pregnant rats at different water temperatures. *Comp Biochem Physiol A Mol Integr Physiol* 135, no. 4 (August): 605–11.

Sadler, T. W. *Langman's Medical Embryology*. 7th ed. Baltimore: Williams & Wilkins, 1995.

Sorenson, T. K., M. A. Williams, I-M. Lee, E. E. Dashow, M. L. Thompson, and D. A. Luthy. 2003. Recreational physical activity during pregnancy and risk of preeclampsia. *Hypertension* 41, no. 6 (June): 1273–80.

Tsiaras, A., and B. Werth. *From Conception to Birth*. New York: Doubleday, 2002.

Wolfe, L. A., and G. A. Davies. 2003. Canadian guidelines for exercise in pregnancy. *Clin Obstet Gynecol* 46, no. 2 (June): 488–95.

Chapter 9

Carson, B. M. *Human Embryology and Developmental Biology*. 2nd ed. St. Louis: Mosby, 1999.

Facchini, S., and S. M. Aglioti. 2003. Short term light deprivation increases tactile spatial acuity in humans. *Neurology* 60, no. 12 (June 24): 1998–99.

Gabbe, S. G., J. R. Niebyl, and J. L. Simpson. *Obstetrics: Normal and Problem Pregnancies*. 4th ed. New York: Churchill Livingstone, 2002.

Larsen, W. J. *Human Embryology*. 2nd ed. New York: Churchill Livingstone, 1997.

Mennuti, M. T., and D. Driscoll. 2003. A screening for Down's Syndrome—too many choices? *N Engl J Med* 349, no. 15 (October 9): 1471–73.

Nordenberg, T. It's quittin' time: Smokers need not rely on willpower alone. *FDA Consumer*. November–December 1997. Revised 1999.

Reading, A. E., S. Campbell, D. N. Cox, and C. M. Sledmere. 1982. Health beliefs and health care behaviour in pregnancy. *Psychol Med* 12, no. 2 (May): 379–83.

Sadler, T. W. *Langman's Medical Embryology*. 7th ed. Baltimore: Williams & Wilkins, 1995.

Tabor, A., J. Philip, M. Madsen, J. Bang, E. B. Obel, and B. Norgaard-Pedersen. 1986. Randomized controlled trial of genetic amniocentesis in 4,606 low-risk women. *Lancet* 1, no. 8493 (June 7): 1287–93.

Tsiaras, A., and B. Werth. *From Conception to Birth*. New York: Doubleday, 2002.

The Vincent Obstetrics and Gynecology Service at Mass General. Prenatal diagnosis. mgh.harvard.edu/prenataldiagnosis/Vincent_prenataldiagnosisERA.htm.

Waldenstrom, U., O. Axelsson, S. Nilsson, G. Eklund, O. Fall, S. Lindeberg, and Y. Sjodin. 1988. Effects of routine one-stage ultrasound screening in pregnancy: A randomised controlled trial. *Lancet* 2, no. 8611 (September 10): 585–88.

Wapner, R., E. Thom, J. L. Simpson, et al. 2003. First-trimester screening for trisomies 21 and 18. *N Engl Med* 349, no. 15 (October 9): 1405–13.

Chapter 10

American Academy of Pediatrics. 1999. Circumcision policy statement (RE9850). *Pediatrics* 103, no. 3 (March): 686–93.

Carson, B. M. *Human Embryology and Developmental Biology*. 2nd ed. St. Louis: Mosby, 1999.

Dixon, S., J. Snyder, R. Holve, and P. Bromberger. 1984. Behavioral effects of circumcision with and without anesthesia. *J Dev Behav Pediatr* 5, no. 5 (October): 246–50.

Larsen, W. J. *Human Embryology*. 2nd ed. New York: Churchill Livingstone, 1997.

Lerman, S. E., and J. C. Liao. 2001. Neonatal circumcision. *Pediatr Clin North Am* 48, no. 6 (December): 1539–57.

National Center for Health Statistics. Trends in circumcisions among newborns. cdc.gov /nchs/products/pubs/pubd/hestats/circumcisions/circumcisions.htm.

Roe v. Wade, 410 U.S. 113 (1973).

Sadler, T. W. *Langman's Medical Embryology*. 7th ed. Baltimore: Williams & Wilkins, 1995.

Tsiaras, A., and B. Werth. *From Conception to Birth*. New York: Doubleday, 2002.

Chapter 11

Anderson, P., L. W. Doyle, and the Victorian Infant Collaborative Study Group. 2003. Neurobehavioral outcomes of school-age children born extremely low birth weight or very preterm in the 1990s. JAMA 289, no. 24 (June 25): 3264–72.

Auger, J., J. M. Kunstmann, F. Czyglik, and P. Jouannet. 1995. Decline in semen quality among fertile men in Paris during the past 20 years. *N Engl J Med* 332, no. 5 (February 2): 281–85.

Carson, B. M. *Human Embryology and Developmental Biology*. 2nd ed. St. Louis: Mosby, 1999.

Gabbe, S. G., J. R. Niebyl, and J. L. Simpson. *Obstetrics: Normal and Problem Pregnancies*. 4th ed. New York: Churchill Livingstone, 2002.

Greene, A. R. The Millennium Health Oath. March 10, 2000. DrGreene.org /body.cfm?id=21&action=detail&ref=1423.

———. Millennium Health Oath calls doctors to practice medicine in a whole new way. May 1, 2000. DrGreene.org/body.cfm?id=21&action=detail&ref=458.

Hack, M., D. J. Flannery, M. Schluchter, L. Cartar, E. Borawski, and N. Klein. 2002. Outcomes in young adulthood for very-low-birth-weight infants. *N Engl J Med* 346, no. 3 (January 17): 149–57.

Larsen, W. J. *Human Embryology*. 2nd ed. New York: Churchill Livingstone, 1997.

March of Dimes. Prematurity, the answers can't come soon enough. http://209 .73.237.101/prematurity/5415_5808.asp.

Meis, P. J., M. Klebanoff, E. Thom, et al. 2003. Prevention of recurrent preterm delivery by 17 alpha-hydroxyprogesterone caproate. *N Engl J Med* 348, no. 24 (June 12): 2379–85.

Partsch, C. J., M. Aukamp, and W. G. Sippell. 2000. Scrotal temperature is increased in disposable plastic lined nappies. *Arch Dis Child* 83, no. 4 (October): 364–668.

Reuters Health Wire. Man with earache gets vasectomy. August 21, 2003.

Sadler, T. W. *Langman's Medical Embryology.* 7th ed. Baltimore: Williams & Wilkins, 1995.

Strandberg, T. E., A. L. Jarvenpaa, H. Vanhanen, and P. M. McKeigue. 2001. Birth outcome in relation to licorice consumption during pregnancy. *Am J Epidemiol* 153, no. 11 (June): 1085–88.

Tsiaras, A., and B. Werth. *From Conception to Birth.* New York: Doubleday, 2002.

Chapter 12

Brazelton, T. B. *Touchpoints.* Cambridge, MA: Perseus Books, 1992.

Carson, B. M. *Human Embryology and Developmental Biology.* 2nd ed. St. Louis: Mosby, 1999.

Diego, M. A., J. N. Dieter, T. Field, et al. 2002. Fetal activity following stimulation of the mother's abdomen, feet, and hands. *Dev Psychobiol* 41, no. 4 (December): 396–406.

Granier-Deferre, C., J. P. Lecanuet, H. Cohen, and M. C. Busnel. 1985. Feasibility of prenatal hearing test. *Acta Otolaryngol Suppl* 421 (January): 93–101.

Lamont, A. 2003. Toddlers' musical preference and musical memory in the early years. *Ann NY Acad Sci* 999 (November): 518–19.

———. How music heard in the womb is remembered by the child. *Child Of Our Time.* BBC1. July 11, 2001.

Larsen, W. J. *Human Embryology.* 2nd ed. New York: Churchill Livingstone, 1997.

Klaus, M. H., and P. H. Klaus. *Your Amazing Newborn.* Cambridge, MA: Perseus Books, 1998.

Lecanuet, J. P. Fetal sensory competencies. In: *Year Book of Neonatal and Perinatal Medicine.* Edited by A. A. Fanaroff, J. Maisels, and D. K. Stevenson. St. Louis: Mosby, 1997.

Lecanuet, J. P., B. Gautheron, A. Locatelli, B. Schaal, A. Y. Jacquet, and M. C. Busnel. 1998. What sounds reach fetuses: Biological and nonbiological modeling of the transmission of pure tones. *Dev Psychobiol* 33, no. 3 (November): 203–19.

Lecanuet, J. P., C. Granier-Deferre, and M. C. Busnel. 1988. Fetal cardiac and motor responses to octave-band noises as a function of central frequency, intensity and heart rate variability. *Early Hum Dev* 18, no. 2–3 (December): 81–93.

Lecanuet, J. P., C. Granier-Deferre, and M. C. Busnel. 1989. Differential fetal auditory reactiveness as a function of stimulus characteristics and state. *Semin Perinatol* 13, no. 5 (October): 421–29.

Lecanuet, J. P., C. Granier-Deferre, H. Cohen, R. Le Houezec, and M. C. Busnel. 1986. Fetal responses to acoustic stimulation depend on heart rate variability pattern, stimulus intensity and repetition. *Early Hum Dev* 13, no. 3 (June): 269–83.

Lecanuet, J. P., C. Granier-Deferre, A. Y. Jacquet, and M. C. Busnel. 1992. Decelerative cardiac responsiveness to acoustical stimulation in the near term fetus. *Q J Exp Psychol B* 44, no. 3-4 (April): 279–303.

Lecanuet, J. P., C. Granier-Deferre, A. J. DeCasper, R. Maugeais, A. J. Andrieu, and M. C. Busnel. 1987. Fetal perception and discrimination of speech stimuli; demonstration by cardiac reactivity; preliminary results. *C R Acad Sci III* 305, no. 5 (January): 161–64.

Lecanuet, J. P., and A. Y. Jacquet. 2002. Fetal responsiveness to maternal passive swinging in low heart rate variability state: Effects of stimulation direction and duration. *Dev Psychobiol* 40, no. 1 (January): 57–67.

Lecanuet, J. P., C. Granier-Deferre, A. Y. Jacquet, and A. J. DeCasper. 2000. Fetal discrimination of low-pitched musical notes. *Dev Psychobiol* 36, no. 1 (January): 29–39.

Lieberman, E., J. Lang, D. K. Richardson, F. D. Frigoletto, L. J. Heffner, and A. Cohen. 2000. Intrapartum maternal fever and neonatal outcome. *Pediatrics* 105, no. 1 (January): 8–13.

Sadler, T. W. *Langman's Medical Embryology*. 7th ed. Baltimore: Williams & Wilkins, 1995.

Tsiaras, A., and B. Werth. *From Conception to Birth*. New York: Doubleday, 2002.

Chapter 13

Carson, B. M. *Human Embryology and Developmental Biology*. 2nd ed. St. Louis: Mosby, 1999.

Ferber, R. and M. Kryger. *Principles and Practice of Sleep Medicine in the Child*. Philadelphia, PA: W. B. Saunders, 1995.

Kain, Z. N., S. M. Wang, L. C. Mayes, L. A. Caramico, and M. B. Hofstadter. 1999. Distress during the induction of anesthesia and postoperative behavioral outcomes. *Anesth Analg* 88, no. 5 (May): 1042–47.

Klaus, M. H., J. H. Kennell, and P. H. Klaus. *The Doula Book*. Cambridge, MA: Perseus Publishing, 2002.

Kryger M., T. Roth, and W. C. Dement. *Principles and Practice of Sleep Medicine*. Philadelphia, PA: W. B. Saunders, 1994.

Larsen, W. J. *Human Embryology*. 2nd ed. New York: Churchill Livingstone, 1997.

Mulder, E. J., L. P. Morssink, T. van der Schee, and G. H. Visser. 1998. Acute maternal alcohol consumption disrupts behavioral state organization in the near-term fetus. *Pediatr Res* 44, no. 5 (November): 774–79.

Roffwarg, H., J. Muzio, and W. Dement. 1966. Ontogenetic development of the human sleep-dream cycle. *Science* 152: 604.

Sadler, T. W. *Langman's Medical Embryology*. 7th ed. Baltimore: Williams & Wilkins, 1995.

Seron-Ferre, M., R. Riffo, G. J. Valenzuela, and A. M. Germain. 2001. Twenty-four-hour pattern of cortisol in the human fetus at term. *Am J Obstet Gynecol* 184, no. 6 (May): 1278–83.

Tanguay, P., E. M. Ornitz, A. Kaplan, and E. S. Bozzo. 1975. Evolution of sleep spindles in childhood. *Electroencephalogr Clin Neurophysiol* 38, no. 2 (February): 175–81.

Tsiaras, A., and B. Werth. *From Conception to Birth*. New York: Doubleday, 2002.

van Woerden, E. E., H. P. van Geijn, J. M. Swartjes, F. J. Caron, J. T. Brons, and N. F. Arts. 1988. Fetal heart rhythms during behavioural state 1F. *Eur J Obstet Gynecol Reprod Biol* 28, no. 1 (May): 29–38.

Chapter 14

American Academy of Pediatrics. Work Group on Cord Blood Banking. 1999. Cord blood banking for potential future transplantation: subject review. *Pediatrics* 104, no.1 (July):116–18.

American Academy of Pediatrics. 2000. Changing concepts of sudden infant death syndrome: Implications for infant sleeping environment and sleep position (RE9946). *Pediatrics* 105, no. 3 (March): 650–56.

Carson, B. M. *Human Embryology and Developmental Biology.* 2nd ed. St. Louis: Mosby, 1999.

Cord blood registry. http://cordblood.com/index.asp.

Devoe, L. D., C. Murray, A. Youssif, and M. Arnaud. 1993. Maternal caffeine consumption and fetal behavior in normal third-trimester pregnancy. *Am J Obstet Gynecol* 168, no. 4 (April): 1105–11.

Dieter, J. N., T. Field, M. Hernandez-Reif, E. K. Emory, and M. Redzepi. 2003. Stable preterm infants gain more weight and sleep less after five days of massage therapy. *J Pediatr Psychol* 28, no. 6 (September): 403–11.

Gessner, B. D., G. C. Ives, and K. A. Perham-Hester. 2001. Association between sudden infant death syndrome and prone sleep position, bed sharing, and sleeping outside an infant crib in Alaska. *Pediatrics* 108, no. 4 (October): 923–27.

Griffin, R. L., F. J. Caron, and H. P. van Geijn. 1985. Behavioral states in the human fetus during labor. *Am J Obstet Gynecol* 152, no. 7 Pt. 1 (August): 828–33.

Gingras, J. L., and K. J. O'Donnell. 1998. State control in the substance-exposed fetus. I. The fetal neurobehavioral profile: An assessment of fetal state, arousal, and regulation competency. *Ann N Y Acad Sci* 846 (June 21): 262–76.

Johnson, F. L. 1997. Placental blood transplantation and autologous banking: caveat emptor. *J Pediatr Hematol Oncol* 19, no. 3 (May/June):183–86.

Kiuchi, M., N. Nagata, S. Ikeno, and N. Terakawa. 2000. The relationship between the response to external light stimulation and behavioral states in the human fetus: How it differs from vibroacoustic stimulation. *Early Hum Dev* 58, no. 2 (May): 153–65.

Klaus, M. H., and P. H. Klaus. *Your Amazing Newborn.* Cambridge, MA: Perseus Books, 1998.

Larsen, W. J. *Human Embryology.* 2nd ed. New York: Churchill Livingstone, 1997.

Laughlin, M. J., J. Barker, B. Bambach, O. N. Koc, D. A. Rizzieri, J. E. Wagner, S. L. Gerson, H. M. Lazarus, M. Cairo, C. E. Stevens, P. Rubinstein, J. Kurtzberg, 2001. Hematopoietic engraftment and survival in adult recipients of umbilical-cord blood from unrelated donors. *N Engl J Med* 344, no. 24 (June 14): 1815-22. Merchant, J. R., C. Worwa, S. Porter, J. M. Coleman, and R-A O. deRegnier. 2001. Respiratory instability of term and near-term healthy newborn infants in car safety seats. *Pediatrics* 108, no. 3 (September): 647–52.

Mulder, E. J., M. Boersma, M. Meeuse, M. van der Wal, E. van de Weerd, and G. H. Visser. 1994. Patterns of breathing movements in the near-term human fetus: relationship to behavioural states. *Early Hum Dev* 36, no. 2 (February): 127–35.

Mulder, E. J., A. Kamstra, M. J. O'Brien, G. H. Visser, and H. F. Prechtl. 1986. Abnormal fetal behavioural state regulation in a case of high maternal alcohol intake during pregnancy. *Early Hum Dev* 14, no. 3–4 (December): 321–26.

Nijhuis, J. G., J. ten Hof, J. G. Nijhuis, E. J. Mulder, H. Narayan, D. J. Taylor, and G. H. Visser. 1999. Temporal organization of fetal behavior from 24-weeks gestation onwards in normal and complicated pregnancies. *Dev Psychobiol* 34, no. 4 (May): 257–68.

Nijhuis, J. G., H. F. Prechtl, C. B. Martin Jr., and R. S. Bots. 1982. Are there behavioural states in the human fetus? *Early Hum Dev* 6, no. 2 (April): 177–95.

Nijhuis, J. G., M. van de Pas, and H. W. Jongsma. 1998. State transitions in uncomplicated pregnancies after term. *Early Hum Dev* 52, no. 2 (September): 125–32.

Pillai, M., and D. James. 1990. Behavioural states in normal mature human fetuses. *Arch Dis Child* 65, no. 1 (January): 39–43.

Robles de Medina, P. G., G. H. Visser, A. C. Huizink, J. K. Buitelaar, and E. J. Mulder. 2003. Fetal behaviour does not differ between boys and girls. *Early Hum Dev* 73, no. 1–2 (August): 17–26.

Sadler, T. W. *Langman's Medical Embryology.* 7th ed. Baltimore: Williams & Wilkins, 1995.

Scheers, N. J., G. W. Rutherford, and J. S. Kemp. 2003. Where should infants sleep? A comparison of risk for suffocation of infants sleeping in cribs, adult beds, and other sleeping locations. *Pediatrics* 112, no. 4 (October): 883–89.

Stigter, R. H., E. J. Mulder, and G. H. Visser. 1998. Hourly fetal urine production rate in the near-term fetus: Is it really increased during fetal quiet sleep? *Early Hum Dev* 50, no. 3 (February 27): 263–72.

Tsiaras, A., and B. Werth. *From Conception to Birth.* New York: Doubleday, 2002.

van Vliet, M. A., C. B. Martin Jr., J. G. Nijhuis, and H. F. Prechtl. 1985. Behavioural states in the fetuses of nulliparous women. *Early Hum Dev* 12, no. 2 (November): 121–35.

Visser, G. H., H. H. Mulder, H. P. Wit, E. J. Mulder, and H. F. Prechtl. 1989. Vibro-acoustic stimulation of the human fetus: Effect on behavioural state organization. *Early Hum Dev* 19, no. 4 (July): 285–96.

Chapter 15

Albani, A., P. Addamo, A. Renghi, G. Voltolin, L. Peano, and G. Ivani. 1999. The effect on breastfeeding rate of regional anesthesia technique for cesarean and vaginal childbirth. *Minerva Anestesiol* 65, no. 9 (September): 625–30.

Bricker, L., and T. Lavender. 2002. Parenteral opioids for labor pain relief: A systematic review. *Am J Obstet Gynecol* 186, no. 5 (May): S94–109.

Crowell, M. K. 1994. Relationship between obstetric analgesia and time of effective breast feeding. *J Nurse Midwifery* 39, no. 3 (May): 150–56.

Gabbe, S. G., J. R. Niebyl, and J. L. Simpson. *Obstetrics: Normal and Problem Pregnancies.* 4th ed. New York: Churchill Livingstone, 2002.

Hodgkinson, R. 1978. Double-blind comparison of the neurobehaviour of neonates following the administration of different doses of meperidine to the mother. *Can Anaesth Soc J* 25, no. 5 (September): 405–11.

Hodgkinson, R. 1978. Neonatal neurobehavior in the first 48 hours of life: effect of the administration of meperidine with and without naloxone in the mother. *Pediatrics* 62, no. 3 (September): 294–98.

Jacobson, B. 1987. Perinatal origin of adult self-destructive behavior. *Acta Psychiatr Scand* 76, no. 4 (October): 364–71.

Jacobson, B. 1990. Opiate addiction in adult offspring through possible imprinting after obstetric treatment *Br Med J* 301, no. 6760 (November 10): 1067–70.

Kennell, J., M. Klaus, S. McGrath, S. Robertson, and C. Hinckley. 1991. Continuous emotional support during labor in a US hospital. A randomized controlled trial. *JAMA* 265, no. 17 (May 1): 2197–201.

Klaus, M. H., J. H. Kennell, and P. H. Klaus. *The Doula Book*. Cambridge, MA: Perseus Publishing, 2002.

Klaus, M. H., and P. H. Klaus. *Your Amazing Newborn*. Cambridge, MA: Perseus Books, 1998.

Leiberman, E., and C. O'Donoghue. 2002. Unintended effects of epidural analgesia during labor: A systematic review. *J Obstet Gynecol* 186, no. 5 Suppl Nature (May): S31–68.

Leighton, B. L., and S. H. Halpern. 2002. The effects of epidural analgesia on labor, maternal, and neonatal outcomes: A systematic review. *Am J Obstet Gynecol* 186, no. 5 (May): S69–77.

Nissen, E., A. M. Widstrom, G. Lilja, A. S. Matthiesen, K. Uvnas-Moberg, G. Jacobsson, and L. O. Boreus. 1997. Effects of routinely given pethidine during labour on infants' developing breast-feeding behavior. Effects of dose-delivery time interval and various concentrations of pethidine/norpethidine in cord plasma. *Acta Paediatr* 86, no. 2 (February): 201–08.

Nyberg, K. 2000. Perinatal medication as a potential risk factor for adult drug abuse in a North American cohort. *Epidemiology* 11, no. 6 (May): 715–16.

Wolman W. L., B. Chalmers, G. J. Hofmeyr, and V. C. Nikoderm. 1993. Postpartum depression and companionship in the clinical birth environment: a randomized controlled study. *Am J Obstet Gynecol* 168, no. 5 (May): 1388–93.

Chapter 16

American Academy of Pediatrics. *Pediatric Nutrition Handbook*. 5th ed. Elk Grove Village, IL: American Academy of Pediatrics, 2003.

Bader, A. P., and R. D. Phillips. 1999. Fathers' proficiency at recognizing their newborns by tactile cues. *Infant Behav Dev* 22, no. 3: 405–09.

Batki, A., S. Baron-Cohen, S. Wheelwright, J. Connellan, and J. Ahluwalia. 2000. Is there an innate gaze module? Evidence from human neonates. *Infant Behav Dev* 23, no. 2 (February): 223–29.

Behrman, R. E., R. M. Kliegman, H. B. Jenson. *Nelson Textbook of Pediatrics*. 17th ed. Philadelphia: Saunders, 2004.

Berlin, C. M. 1981. Excretion of methylxanthines in human milk. *Semin Perinatol* 5, no. 4 (October): 389–94.

Brazelton, T. B. 1961. Psychobiologic reactions in the neonate: the value of observations in the neonate. *J Pediatr* 58: 308–12.

Brazelton, T. B. *Touchpoints*. Cambridge, MA: Perseus Books, 1992.

Connellan, J. 2000. Sex differences in human neonatal social perception. *Infant Behav Dev* 23, no. 1 (January): 113–18 .

Food and Nutrition Board. *Dietary Reference Intakes for Calcium, Phosphorus, Magnesium, Vitamin D, and Fluoride*. Washington, D.C.: National Academies Press, 1999.

———. *Dietary Reference Intakes for Energy, Carbohydrate, Fiber, Fat, Fatty Acids, Cholesterol, Protein, and Amino Acids (Macronutrients)*. Washington, D.C.: National Academies Press, 2002.

———. *Dietary Reference Intakes for Thiamin, Riboflavin, Niacin, Vitamin B₆, Folate, Vitamin B₁₂, Pantothenic Acid, Biotin, and Choline*. Washington, D.C.: National Academies Press, 1999.

———. *Dietary Reference Intakes for Vitamin A, Vitamin K, Arsenic, Boron, Chromium, Copper, Iodine, Iron, Manganese, Molybdenum, Nickel, Silicon, Vanadium, and Zinc*. Washington, D.C.: National Academies Press, 2001.

———. *Dietary Reference Intakes for Vitamin C, Vitamin E, Selenium, and Carotenoids*. Washington, D.C.: National Academies Press, 2000.

———. *Dietary Reference Intakes: Proposed Definition of Dietary Fiber*. Washington, D.C.: National Academies Press, 2001.

Food and Nutrition Information Center. Dietary Reference Intakes (DRI) and Recommended Dietary Allowances. http://nal.usda.gov/fnic/etext/000105.html.

Fox, N. A., and H. A. Henderson. 1999. Does infancy matter? Predicting social behavior from infant temperament. *Infant Behav Dev* 22, no. 4: 445–55.

Hibbeln, J. R. 2002. Seafood consumption, the DHA content of mothers' milk and prevalence rates of postpartum depression: a cross-national, ecological analysis. *J Affect Disord* 69, no. 1–3 (May): 15–29.

Klaus, M. H., and P. H. Klaus. *Your Amazing Newborn*. Cambridge, MA: Perseus Books, 1998.

Lavelli, M., and M. Poli. 1998. Early mother-infant interaction during breast- and bottle-feeding. *Infant Behav Dev* 21, no. 4: 667–83.

Molina, M., and F. Jouen. 1998. Modulation of the palmar grasp behavior in neonates according to texture property. *Infant Behav Dev* 21, no. 4: 659–66.

Morrongiello, B. A., K. D. Fenwick, and G. Chance. 1998. Crossmodal learning in newborn infants: Inferences about properties of auditory-visual events. *Infant Behav Dev* 21, no. 4: 543–53.

Onozawa, K., V. Glover, D. Adams, N. Modi, R. C. Kumar. 2001. Infant massage improves mother-infant interaction for mothers with postnatal depression. *J Affect Disord* 63, no. 1–3 (March): 201–07.

Prechtl, H. and M. J. O'Brien. Behavioral states of the full-term newborn: the emergence of a concept. In *Psychobiology of the Human Newborn*, edited by P. Stratton. New York, NY: Wiley & Sons, 1982.

Resman, B. H., P. Blumenthal, and W. J. Jusko. 1977. Breast milk distribution of theobromine from chocolate. *J Pediatr* 91, no. 3 (September): 477–80.

Roberts, S. B., and M. B. Heyman. *Feeding Your Child for Lifelong Health*. New York: Bantam, 1999.

Slater, A., C. Von der Schulenburg, E. Brown, M. Badenoch, G. Butterworth, S. Parsons, and C. Samuels. 1998. Newborn infants prefer attractive faces. *Infant Behav Dev* 21, no. 2: 345–54.

The Slow Food Movement. Slow food USA: taste, tradition, and the honest pleasures of food. slowfoodusa.org.

Walkowiak, J., J. A. Wiener, A. Fastabend, B. Heinzow, U. Kramer, E. Schmidt, H. J. Steingruber, S. Wundram, and G. Winneke. 2001. Environmental exposure to polychlorinated biphenyls and quality of the home environment: effects on psychodevelopment in early childhood. *Lancet* 358, no. 9293 (November 10): 1602–07.

Wolff, P. H. 1959. Observation on newborn infants. *Psychosomatic Medicine*. 21: 110–18.

Wolff, P. H. The development of behavioral states and the expressions of emotions in early infancy. In *A New Proposal for Investigation*. Chicago, IL: University of Chicago Press, 1987.

Chapter 17

Behrman, R. E., R. M. Kliegman, H. B. Jenson. *Nelson Textbook of Pediatrics*. 17th ed. Philadelphia: Saunders, 2004.

Groome, L. J., P. C. Loizou, S. B. Holland, D. J. Law, D. M. Mooney, and R. A. Dykman. 2000. Fetuses and neonates have different heart rate responses to low-intensity stimulation in quiet sleep. *Infant Behav Dev* 23, no. 1 (January): 61–77.

Jones, N. A., T. Field, and M. Davalos. 1998. Massage therapy attenuates right frontal EEG asymmetry in one-month-old infants of depressed mothers. *Infant Behav Dev* 21, no. 3: 527–30.

Lucassen, P. L. B. J., W. J. J. Assendelft, J. W. Gubbels, J. van Eijk, and A. C. Douwes. 2000. Infantile colic: crying time reduction with a whey hydrolysate: a double-blind, randomized, placebo-controlled trial. *Pediatrics* 106, no. 6 (December): 1349–54.

Shelov, S. P., ed. *Caring for Your Baby and Young Child: Birth to Age 5*. Rev. ed. New York: Bantam, 1998.

Chapter 18

American Academy of Pediatrics. *Pediatric Nutrition Handbook*. 5th ed. Elk Grove Village, IL: American Academy of Pediatrics, 2003.

Anglo-Kinzler, R. M., and C. L. Horn. 2001. Selection and memory of a lower limb motor-perceptual task in 3-month-old infants. *Infant Behav Dev* 24, no. 3 (March): 239–57.

Behrman, R. E., R. M. Kliegman, H. B. Jenson. *Nelson Textbook of Pediatrics*. 17th ed. Philadelphia: Saunders, 2004.

Durand, K., R. Lécuyer, and M. Frichtel. 2003. Representation of the third dimension: The use of perspective cues by 3- and 4-month-old infants. *Infant Behav Dev* 26, no. 2 (April): 151–66.

Fagard, J. 2000. Linked proximal and distal changes in the reaching behavior of 5- to 12-month-old human infants grasping objects of different sizes. *Infant Behav Dev* 23, nos. 3-4 (March 4): 317–29.

Gamé, F., I. Carchon, and F. Vital-Durand. 2003. The effect of stimulus attractiveness on visual tracking in 2- to 6-month-old infants. *Infant Behav Dev* 26, no. 2 (April): 135–50.

Hsu, H. C., et al. 2001. Infant non-distress vocalization during mother-infant face-to-face interaction: Factors associated with quantitative and qualitative differences. *Infant Behav Dev* 24, no. 1 (January): 107–28.

Kaufman, J., D. Mareschal, and M. H. Johnson. 2003. Graspability and object processing in infants. *Infant Behav Dev* 26, no. 4 (December): 516–28.

Needham, A. 1999. The role of shape in 4-month-old infants' object segregation. *Infant Behav Dev* 22, no. 2: 161–78.

Needham, A., T. Barrett, and K. Peterman. 2002. A pick-me-up for infants' exploratory skills: Early simulated experiences reaching for objects using 'sticky mittens' enhances young infants' object exploration skills. *Infant Behav Dev* 25, no. 3: 279–95.

Patterson, M. L., and J. F. Werkera. 1999. Matching phonetic information in lips and voice is robust in 4.5-month-old infants. *Infant Behav Dev* 22, no. 2: 237–47.

Petitto, L. A., S. Holowka, L. E. Sergio, and D. Ostry. 2001. Language rhythm in baby hand movements. *Nature* 35, no. 6851 (September 6): 35.

Rader, N., and L. A. Vaughn. 2000. Infant reaching to a hidden affordance: Evidence for intentionality. *Infant Behav Dev* 23, no. 3–4 (March 4): 531–41.

Rubin, G. B., J. W. Fagen, and M. H. Caroll. 1998. Olfactory context and memory retrieval in 3-month-old infants. *Infant Behav Dev* 21, no. 4: 641–58.

Shelov, S. P., ed. *Caring for Your Baby and Young Child: Birth to Age 5*. Rev. ed. New York: Bantam, 1998.

Symons, L. A., S. M. J. Hains, and D. W. Muir. 1998. Look at me: Five-month-old infants' sensitivity to very small deviations in eye-gaze during social interactions. *Infant Behav Dev* 21, no. 3: 531–36.

Woodward, A. L. 1999. Infants' ability to distinguish between purposeful and non-purposeful behaviors. *Infant Behav Dev* 22, no. 2: 145–60.

Chapter 19

Ballew, C., M. S. Kuester, and C. Gillespie. 2000. Beverage choices affect adequacy of children's nutritional intakes. *Arch Pediatr Adolesc Med* 154: 1148–52.

Bigelow, A. E., and S. A. Birch. 1999. The effects of contingency in previous interactions on infants' preference for social partners. *Infant Behav Dev* 22, no. 3: 367–82.

Centers for Disease Control and Prevention (CDC). National Center for Health Statistics. Obesity still on the rise, new data show. October 8, 2002. cdc.gov/nchs/releases/02news/obesityonrise.htm

Committee on Nutrition. 2001. The use and misuse of fruit juices in pediatrics (RE0047). *Pediatrics* 107: 1210–13.

Environmental Working Group. Shopper's guide to pesticide in produce. stony fieldfarm.com/Organic/EWGShoppersGuide.pdf.

Fisher, J. O., D. C. Mitchell, H. Smiciklas-Wright, and L. L. Birch. 2001. Maternal milk consumption predicts the tradeoff between milk and soft drinks in young girls' diets. *J Nutr* 131, no. 2 (February): 246–50.

Fox, M. K., S. Pac, B. Devaney, and L. Jankowski. 2004. Feeding infants and toddlers study: what foods are infants and toddlers eating? *J Am Diet Assoc* 104, no. 1 Suppl 1 (January): S22–30.

Fresh Baby. http://myfreshbaby.com.

Gartner, L. M., F. R. Greer; Section on Breastfeeding, Committee on Nutrition. 2003. Prevention of rickets and vitamin D deficiency: New guidelines for vitamin D intake. *Pediatrics* 111, no. 4 Pt. 1 (April): 908–10.

Home-made Baby Recipes. names2be.com/babymeal2.html.

Kayed, N. S., and A. van der Meer. 2000. Timing strategies used in defensive blinking to optical collisions in 5- to 7-month-old infants. *Infant Behav Dev* 23, no. 3-4 (March 4): 253–70.

Makrides, M., M. A. Neumann, R. W. Byard, K. Simmer, and R. A. Gibson. 1994. Fatty acid composition of brain, retina, and erythrocytes in breast- and formula-fed infants. *Am J Clin Nutr* 60, no. 2 (August): 189–94.

Ogden, C. L., K. M. Flegal, M. D. Carroll, and C. L. Johnson. 2002. Prevalence and trends in overweight among US children and adolescents, 1999-2000. *JAMA* 288, no. 14 (October 9): 1728–32.

Pierroutsakos, S. L., and G. L. Troseth. 2003. Video Verité: Infants' manual investigation of objects on video. *Infant Behav Dev* 26, no. 2 (April): 183–99.

Chapter 20

American Academy of Pediatrics, American Academy of Family Physicians. Clinical practice guideline: diagnosis and management of acute otitis media. March 2004. aap.org/policy/aomfinal.pdf

Brenner, R. A., A. C. Trumble, G. S. Smith, E. P. Kessler, and M. D. Overpeck. 2001. Where children drown, United States, 1995. *Pediatrics* 108, no. 1 (July): 85–89.

Crowther, H. L., A. R. Lew, and C. J. Whitaker. 2000. The development of beacon use for spatial orientation in 6–8.5-month-old infants. *Infant Behav Dev* 23, no. 1 (January): 41–59.

Illi, S., E. von Mutius, S. Lau, R. Bergmann, B. Niggemann, C. Sommerfeld, U. Wahn; MAS Group. 2001. Early childhood infectious diseases and the development of asthma up to school age: A birth cohort study. *Br Med J* 322, no. 7283 (February 17): 390–95.

Fresh Baby. http://myfreshbaby.com.

Greene, A. R. *The Parent's Complete Guide to Ear Infections.* New York, NY: Avon Books 1999.

Morales, M., P. Mundy, C. E. F. Delgado, M. Yale, R. Neal, and H. K. Schwartz. 2000. Gaze following, temperament, and language development in 6-month-olds: A replication and extension. *Infant Behav Dev* 23, no. 2 (February): 231–36.

McCall, D. D., and R. K. Clifton. 1999. Infants' means-end search for hidden objects in the absence of visual feedback. *Infant Behav Dev* 22, no. 3: 297–302.

Morrongiello, B. A., and K. D. Fenwick. 1998. Spatial co-location and infants' learning of auditory-visual associations. *Infant Behav Dev* 21, no. 4: 745–60.

Pediatric Synopsis Book. 2003. Best articles relevant to pediatric allergy and immunology. *Pediatrics* 112, no. 2 Suppl (August): 453–94.

Roberts, S. B., and M. B. Heyman. *Feeding Your Child for Lifelong Health.* New York: Bantam, 1999.

Sampson, H. A. 1999. Food Allergy. Part 1: Immunopathogenesis and clinical disorders. *J Allergy Clin Immunol* 103, no. 5 Pt. 1 (May): 717–28.

Shelov, S. P., ed. *Caring for Your Baby and Young Child: Birth to Age 5.* Rev. ed. New York: Bantam, 1998.

Siegel, R. M., M. Kiely, J. P. Bien, E. C. Joseph, J. B. Davis, S. G. Mendel, J. P. Pestian, and T. G. DeWitt. 2003. Treatment of otitis media with observation and a safety-net antibiotic prescription. *Pediatrics* 112, no. 3 Pt. 1 (September): 527–31.

Taylor, J. A., W. Weber, L. Standish, H. Quinn, J. Goesling, M. McGann, and C. Calabrese. 2003. Efficacy and safety of echinacea in treating upper respiratory tract infections in children: A randomized controlled trial. *JAMA* 290, no. 21 (December 3): 2824–30.

Chapter 21

Bayley, N. *Bayley Scales of Infant Development*. New York: Psychological Corp., 1969.

Dixon, S. D., and M. T. Stein. *Encounters with Children*. 2nd ed. St. Louis: Mosby, 1992.

Fraiberg, S. H. *The Magic Years*. New York: Charles Scribner's Sons, 1959.

Wang, S. H., L. Kaufman, and R. Baillargeon. 2003. Should all stationary objects move when hit? Developments in infants' causal and statistical expectations about collision events. *Infant Behav Dev* 26, no. 3 (August): 529–67.

Index

Alan Greene, M.D., FAAP

On his quest to educate and inspire parents about their children, Dr. Alan Greene has become one of the world's most trusted and beloved pediatricians. It's no wonder that Intel named him the Children's Health Hero of the Internet. A practicing pediatrician and father of four, Dr. Greene has devoted himself to freely giving real answers to parents' real questions. His answers combine cutting-edge science, practical wisdom, warm empathy, and a deep respect for parents, children, and the environment. He is an electrifying public speaker and has become a go-to expert in children's health. He has personally reached many families during his talks in North America, Europe, Asia, and the Middle East.

Dr. Greene entered primary care pediatrics in January 1993. In 1995, he launched DrGreene.com, cited by the AMA as the first physician website on the Internet. In addition to being the founder of DrGreene.com, he is the chief medical officer of A.D.A.M., a leading publisher of interactive health information. He is a graduate of Princeton University and the University of California at San Francisco. Upon completion of his pediatric residency program at Children's Hospital Medical Center of Northern California, he served as chief resident. He is a Fellow of the American Academy of Pediatrics and passed the Pediatric Boards in the top 5 percent of the nation.

Dr. Greene currently teaches medical students and pediatric residents at the Stanford University School of Medicine, and is an attending pediatrician at Stanford's Lucile Packard Children's Hospital. He is a senior Fellow at the University of California San Francisco's Center for the Health Professions and the president of Hi-Ethics (Health Internet Ethics). In addition to his work on DrGreene.com, Dr. Greene is the pediatric expert for Yahoo! Health and Iamyourchild.org.

Dr. Greene is a sought-after public speaker and appears frequently on TV, radio, websites, and in newspapers and magazines around the world.

Dr. Greene was named a "Community Hero" for his heroism during the 1989 Loma Prieta earthquake and was selected to carry the Olympic Torch in the 1996 Centennial Olympic Torch Relay. He loves to think about challenging ideas, collect encyclopedias, and wear green socks.